**Riots
in Urban
America**

BOOKMARKS

Violence and Riots in Urban America

edited by

Rodney F. Allen and Charles H. Adair
Florida State University

Charles A. Jones Publishing Company
Worthington, Ohio

The cover of this book is adapted from a design by Charles H. Adair, Sr., Alhambra, California.

Support for Rodney F. Allen's work on this project was provided by the Thomas McKean High School, Wilmington, Delaware.

1 2 3 4 5 6 7 8 9 10 / 74 73 72 71 70 69

L. C. Cat. Card No.: 79-84014

Printed in the United States of America

Foreword

When future generations of students read the history of twentieth century America, they will learn to identify this as a period when the United States was torn by domestic violence in its cities while its troops were fighting in Vietnam. The records which the historians will use in their research will show that these two conflicts, one at home and one abroad, were the problems which loomed largest in the minds of both government officials and the public. The future may show that this period was a turning point in American history as significant as the American Revolution, the War between the States, or the Great Depression. We can only speculate, however, as to the outcome of this time of crisis. Whatever the outcome, the long hot summers when people took to the streets to burn, loot, and otherwise demonstrate their dissatisfaction with their lot in society will provide material for one of the most memorable chapters in American history.

The violence in the cities will seem to tomorrow's students as far away in time and space as the conflict in the little country of Vietnam, halfway around the world. Millions of today's students read of the riots in the daily newspapers, not in history books, yet this violence is just as remote to them as is the war in Vietnam. Some of them, it is true, are witnessing the violence firsthand or even participating in it. Far more know of it only indirectly, through bold newspaper headlines, through vivid pictures on television screens, or through the discussions of their parents and teachers. Their knowledge is fragmented and poorly organized, put together from bits and pieces of information left behind as the tide of mass communication flows over them.

Years later, as adults, they may read scholarly, coherent books which attempt to describe and explain what was going on. Their children will come home from school with the then current theories of the history of the period. They may challenge their parents' knowledge and understanding of what was going on at the time they were in school. How well will they be able to meet this challenge? Unfortunately, the study of current events, of history in the making, is rarely as thorough and systematic as the study of history already made.

Some current events are of such a controversial nature that their very nearness in time and significance makes a contemporary, objective analysis extremely difficult. Much of what is currently written about them cannot be objective reporting nor historical analysis. The school itself, buffeted by the winds of political controversy, may become a storm shelter in which the pupils are shielded from the harsh impact of social reality. But of what avail is it for students to dig deeply into the past if they do not, at the same time, look squarely at the harsh realities of the present?

In *Violence and Riots in Urban America,* a generation of students will find an opportunity to examine the history that is being made in their time from many viewpoints. While the full story of this crisis is yet to be written, social scientists, government agencies, and the popular press have already produced a vast body of literature documenting and analyzing the urban violence of the twentieth century. Those fortunate Americans who have never lived in the slums can nevertheless read graphic descriptions of both the physical conditions and the psychological mood of the new-style ghetto. Students who have never met one of the angry young rioters may read the bitter words which these men have uttered when asked to describe their reasons for rioting and the feelings which their violent actions evoked. They can weigh in their own minds the findings of social scientists who have sought to describe and explain the various uprisings of the last few years with the aid of techniques and theories of their disciplines.

In a sense, students are asked to participate in the research process themselves, for Allen and Adair recognize that neat and definitive explanations of these momentous events do not yet exist. Readers are exposed to much of what is known so far about violence and riots, and to many of the theories which have been tentatively advanced to explain them. They are given no doctrinal theories, nor any pat solutions, however. Instead they are challenged to think deeply for themselves on the meaning of these events and the existing knowledge about them.

There is no disagreement as to the importance of contemporary urban violence to the future of American society, but there is a wide range of opinion as to what the disorders signify. What name to attach to them is even a matter of some controversy — are they riots, insurrections, or battles in an emerging revolution? To some observers, the disorders simply constitute instances of collective lawlessness signifying a breakdown of law and order. The rioters are viewed as hoodlums who would be unwilling to conform to the laws of any society. From this standpoint quick and harsh punishment for these and other lawbreakers seems the logical measure to restore domestic harmony.

Other analysts see the perpetrators of violence as lawbreakers, but as lawbreakers who are seeking to create a better society for themselves and people like them. According to this view it is not just the rioter's lack of respect for law but his loss of confidence in a social order which has not accorded him full human dignity that leads to his rebellion. Harsher law enforcement unaccompanied by a fuller measure of justice would lead only to more determined, more widespread insurrections. In the most extreme view, the American social system has reached a stage of inflexibility in which the Negro underclass will attempt a desperate, violent revolution against all odds.

It is such questions as these that students will be encouraged to ponder as they use this volume. At the same time, they will be enabled to put the crisis of their own time into historical perspective. Despite the high drama and the ominous portents of the urban riots of the 1960's, it is not the first time that violence has erupted in American cities. The students who will use this volume have the opportunity to compare the current outburst of violence to other outbursts involving Americans of a different race, different religions, different national origins, and living at different times in the nation's history. The Whiskey Insurrection of 1794, the draft riots of the Civil War, the labor wars of the late nineteenth century, and the race riots of the early twentieth century are oft-neglected chapters of the United States history which assume new significance and deserve careful reexamination in light of the most recent upsurge of violence. The report of the Commission on Race Relations in Chicago, published following the Chicago race riot of 1919, was a significant forerunner of the *Report of the National Advisory Commission on Civil Disorders,* released nearly fifty years later. Analysis of the similarities of the recommendations of the two reports, and awareness of how little was done in American cities to correct the conditions which the first report identified, should deepen the students' understanding of the desperation which so many Negro Americans feel today.

Violence is an unpleasant and painful topic for peaceful, law-abiding men to contemplate. The conflict which has arisen from so many of America's problems and accompanied so much of its progress has often been treated as a shameful secret to be passed over lightly in the social studies. This comprehensive collection of readings on violence in America, past and present, provides an opportunity for students to explore in depth this significant but neglected facet of American life. Hopefully, it may help them make informed and constructive contributions to the solutions of the problems which they must face as citizens.

Lewis M. Killian
Chairman, Department of Sociology
The University of Connecticut

Preface

The editors of this volume are deeply committed to the premise that social studies instruction which loses sight of the present has missed the point, for the present is the prime experience for students and teachers. The conditions of our own time and the problems and dilemmas of today's world are the most relevant topics for inquiry in a social studies classroom. The legacy of the past, our history, may be focused to provide insights. Concepts and generalizations of the social sciences may be used to generate hypotheses and explanations, to guide analysis and verification. Learning to wrestle with today's problems in terms of inquiry skills, value conflicts, and public policy decisions is a critical preparation for the students' future—a future not within the classroom, but rather, within the larger community with its problems, conflicts, and accomplishments. As John W. Gardner stresses with his conception of a "self-renewing society,"

> Instead of giving young people the impression that their task is to stand in dreary watch over the ancient values, we should be telling them the grim but bracing truth that it is their task to re-create those values continuously in their own behavior, facing the dilemmas and catastrophies of their own time.

There is no more crucial domestic problem, no more searching dilemma, than that of violence in urban areas. The nation's main domestic issue centers upon poverty, frustration, and racial conflict. While rioting and violence are the lowest forms of political participation to achieve goals, a few Americans feel the need to participate at this level. The promise of American life has not been realized if some element of the populace goes into the streets in violent protest, if it sees riots as providing an outlet for grievances, an opportunity for the fulfillment of unrealized ambitions, or as an extra-legal means of obtaining a solution to their problems

Many writers attempt to explain why some Americans have resorted to violence and civil unrest to achieve goals. Newspapers and television newscasts keep a constant barrage of data and opinion before the public, while the library shelves and booksellers' stalls feel the increased burden of books upon the subject. Much of the reporting in the mass media (television, radio, magazines, and newspapers) is an emotional response or draws upon conventional explanations of such behavior without serious analysis. While on the other hand, the product of scholars' pens uses such an abstract theoretical basis that students are likely to find it difficult and dull.

The editors' design is not to add to the sheer bulk of the literature, but to provide a concise book drawing upon the social sciences for concepts to guide inquiry and to structure evidence about riots and unrest and for powerful theories to generate some stark, challenging hypotheses. Scholarly and popular writings provide data for students to read. The problem and the readings will sufficiently motivate those who want to put the hypotheses to the data to gain insights on urban riots. Generalizations will be derived which will serve as the basis for understanding the causation and participation in such social phenomenon.

But to understand is not sufficient. To seek pat answers and nostrums is futile. To be able to state explanations for urban unrest does not conclude the labor. If social studies is to grapple with the real world's problems, it must move even beyond social science analysis to decision-making upon public policy issues and upon individual behavior. While exploring causation and participation in riots, the readings will be found to be disturbing as well as provocative. The language of the readings is frank; the opinions expressed are often brutal. They were selected with this in mind, for students need the "disturbing" and not comfortable explanations from conventional wisdom. They should see men grappling with hard problems without answers awaiting "discovery."

John Dewey suggested that students had to get into more than an intellectual bind to test their own beliefs. This is the essence of pragmatism in American life. Public policy decisions are made in the arena of value-conflict; decisions concerning individual action are made by struggling with value-conflict. Sets of public policy proposals are included in the final section of this volume. The editors hope that students will be provoked by the earlier readings to seek ameliorative measures through both public policy and individual behavior. Classroom dialogue upon such policies and behavior, stressing the implications of value positions, can clarify conflicts for evaluation and personal commitment by each student and his teacher.

The editors wish to thank the authors and publishers who have graciously granted permissions to reprint the articles included in this volume.

Rodney F. Allen
Charles H. Adair
Editors

*At what point shall we expect the approach of danger? By
what means shall we fortify against it? Shall we expect some
trans-Atlantic military giant to step the ocean and crush us
at a blow? Never! All of the armies of Europe, Asia, and
Africa combined with all the treasure of the earth in their
military chest with a Bonaparte for a commander, could not
by force take a drink from the Ohio or make a track on the
Blue Ridge in a trial of a thousand years.*

*At what point, then, is the approach of danger to be
expected? I answer, if it ever reach us, it must spring up
amongst us; it cannot come from abroad. If destruction be
our lot, we must ourselves be its author and finisher. As
a nation of free men, we must live through all time, or
die by suicide.*

—Abraham Lincoln, 1838—

Contents

**Violence
and
Riots
in Urban
America**

Chapter **1**

The Contemporary Crisis: An Introduction

It was a warm June 2nd, the beginning of a "long, hot summer." It was one of the largest cities in the world. In the streets there began, quietly enough, a demonstration on civil liberties. As the demonstration gathered momentum, it turned into a riot. For six days and nights, 60,000 persons raged through the streets – and through the central part of the city. More than 800 persons were killed or injured. There was an orgy of senseless destruction, plundering, and looting. Jails were opened, and prisoners let out by the hundreds. The city's largest bank was invaded and pillaged. Government offices were raided. Tens of thousands of people wandered the streets in gangs, and even the military was powerless to restrain them. Nearly a week later, the riot subsided out of sheer exhaustion. Only 21 rioters were executed, and only a tiny fraction of the plunderers and burners were ever punished at all.

The dates of this disaster were June 2nd to June 8th, 1780. The city was London, England. The demonstration was by Protestants against Catholics in England; they felt that if the Catholics were allowed civil rights, they would soon take over the country. They felt that Catholics must forever be treated like second-class citizens. And when the British government began to relax the severity of the laws discriminating against Catholics, they went amok. . . .[1]

On Monday morning, July 13th, groups of workingmen began to gather in the streets. During the morning their numbers grew. Some carried signs protesting the draft. By ten-thirty mobs crashed the draft office doors and destroyed the interior with its lists of potential draftees. The police rushed to the scene with federal troops; several rioters were

[1] Quoted from a newspaper column by Sydney J. Harris. Reprinted by permission by Sydney J. Harris and Publishers-Hall Syndicate.

killed. The mob reacted by setting fires. Then, it moved in swarms toward the Negro districts, pillaging, looting, and lynching. After two days, federal troops moved heavy guns into the city and fired into the crowds. The streets were raked. After two more days, the city was an armed camp, but quiet. Over two million dollars damage was inflicted. Some •sources say two thousand persons were killed, but more conservative estimators say about 400 persons lost their lives.

The city was New York. The dates were July 13th to 17th, 1863, during the Civil War. The crowds gathered to protest the passage of America's first draft law of March, 1863, and the initial drawing of names in the city on July 11th. New York had to fulfill a draft quota of 33,000 men. Wealthy men could employ substitutes to take their place in the Union armies, and the city's poorer workingmen resented the war and their forced participation. An insurrection against federal law during the Civil War turned into a race riot against Negroes — after all, the Negroes were responsible, wasn't the war fought to free Negro slaves? . . .

Today there is violence and rioting in the streets of American cities. Former President Johnson in an address to the American Bar Association noted that these "are very extraordinary times, they are times of danger and yet are full of promise for our society. Our old social institutions are under serious challenge. There is tension between the generations, between the 'haves' and the 'have nots,' between the schooled and the unschooled." The President also observed that "The line between freedom and license has become unclear to many people. Threats and counterthreats fill the air every day. There is a degree of intolerance and almost totalitarian vehemence that says 'Either see it my way or you will be sorry.' "

These words from an American president and the recent riots force us to ask why such civil unrest occurs. What has happened in America? What has taken place within our society that draws men into the streets, behind barricades, and into urban stores with open arms and fire-bombs? We are also forced to ask what can be done to prevent future violence and rioting. What can I do? What can our government do?

The vehement demands and the unrest force us to recall the 1780 riots in London between religious factions and the 1863 draft riots in New York. We are made to understand that urban violence and riots do not happen only in "foreign countries," but can happen, did happen, and are happening in American cities. We are compelled to discover why riots occurred in the past and what this suggests.

Civil unrest does not happen in perfect societies, for if all men's needs and desires were fulfilled there would be no riots. Men might live in peace with their neighbors, their government, and other nations. Men only seek happiness. Individuals form goals which they want to attain including a good environment in which to live and rear their children. Some individuals succeed in attaining their goals, some fail. Some men obtain power and wealth; other men hunger for enough to eat. Some men are satisfied; some are dissatisfied with their lot.

Because societies cannot fulfill all men's needs and desires they must establish a system to allocate available resources. For example, the production of goods and services is limited, but people's demands are unlimited. Men compete for jobs and higher salaries which, when converted into cash incomes, permit them to go into the marketplace and command goods and services. The available goods are unevenly allocated by this economic competition. Some workers achieve their economic goals, but others do not. Some get large flashy cars and split-level suburban homes, while others walk and eat government-surplus foodstuffs, and dissatisfaction prevails.

Individuals and groups within the society compete for a better share of wealth, power, or social status, as well as goods and services. To control this competition and rivalry, the society maintains rules which participants are expected to follow en route to strive for rewards. The society, for example, allocates power and status to persons who achieve leadership positions in government by popular election. A man who develops his skills and works diligently may be promoted within his firm and obtain a higher salary and social status. A student who practices daily on the basketball court may make the team — winning the esteem of his classmates.

But not all boys can make the basketball team; not all politicians win elections; not all diligent workers are promoted. The rewards are limited. Because persons find a conflict between what they have and what they want or see others having, the society must maintain ways of handling grievances. If people want a higher status, increased wealth, or a greater voice in government, some action must be taken to satisfy them.

There are acceptable, legal ways to permit the expression of discontent. The voter may speak at the polls on election day. The union member may stand up at the local meeting. The son may have a friendly chat with his dad about car privileges. The student might speak to the principal or school board about dress regulations. The veteran may petition the governor, while the shopper might go to the Better Business Bureau. A member of a minority might march on Washington, D. C., join a protest organization, or stage a sit-in.

These are legal, orderly ways to handle grievances, but what if changes do not occur? What happens if the grievances are not removed and the affected persons are not satisfied? Obviously the affected *may* elect to follow illegal action. Such illegal action may take one of the following forms, somewhat in this order:

1. *individual violence:* attacks by individuals upon persons and property;
2. *riots:* mob attacks upon persons and property;
3. *insurrection* or *rebellion:* organized uprising against a law, government policy, or government official; or
4. *revolution:* organized uprising against a government with the goal of establishing a new government or social system.

Recently, social protest has led with greater fervor and frequency to a riot, for riots can serve the group in achieving its goals. Civil unrest may be useful in accelerating peaceful reforms within the social system such as fair trade practices, equal treatment by police, and fair use of recreational facilities. It may force a new or improved system for allocating goods, status, or power. The society may fear a more widescale rebellion, and thus, grant concessions to the rioters. The violence may compel the government to accept a specific policy which it might not have found acceptable before. Certainly, the threat of violence is useful for a minority group without power to improve conditions. The act of rioting may serve to dramatize the conflict within the society, the frustration of a minority, or the pressure of a specific grievance.

The society can react in many ways. It can accommodate the rioting minority group by granting concessions, passing new legislation, or by more general social change. It can react in turn – with violence – using "monster" forces to fight the "monster." In any event, the society cannot ignore the unrest. As Lyndon Johnson said, these are extraordinary times. The danger is obvious, but the President also noted that these times are "full of promise for our society." The great concern about social problems in America may now permit us to make further progress toward the high goals our society set for itself in 1776 and 1789 with the Declaration of Independence and the Constitution.

As you read this chapter, keep the following general questions in mind:

1. Why do American students need to know the causes, processes, and results of urban riots? Why do adults need to know? Why did former President Johnson and why does President Nixon need to know?
2. Why are urban riots occurring now? Why did they occur in the past? How accurate are the popular explanations for civil unrest in America?
3. Why did former President Johnson think that these are times full of promise for our society, as well as danger? Do you agree? What can we do to prevent further unrest?

A. The Need to Know

"Remarks of the President upon Issuing an Executive Order Establishing A National Advisory Commission on Civil Disorders, July 29, 1967," *Report of the National Advisory Commission on Civil Disorders.* Washington, D. C.: Government Printing Office, 1968, pp. 296-97.

The National Advisory Commission was chaired by Governor Otto Kerner of Illinois with Mayor John Lindsay of New York as Vice-Chairman. The other members were: Senator Fred R. Harris, Oklahoma; Senator Edward B. Brooke, Massachusetts; Congressman James C. Corman, California; Congressman William M. McCulloch, Ohio; I. W. Abel, President, United Steel Workers; Charles B. Thornton, President, Litton Industries; Roy Wilkins, Executive Director, NAACP; Katherine Graham Peden, Commissioner of Commerce, Kentucky; and Herbert Jenkins, Chief of Police, Atlanta, Georgia.

1. Why did former President Johnson appoint a special advisory commission on civil unrest? What did he hope to achieve? What questions did he want the Commission to answer?

2. Can you accurately answer the former President's questions? How do you know if your answers are valid or inaccurate?

3. Would accurate answers to the former President's questions help to design public policies (laws) to improve the situation? Why? How?

The civil peace has been shattered in a number of cities. The American people are deeply disturbed. They are baffled and dismayed by the wholesale looting and violence that has occurred both in small towns and great metropolitan centers.

No society can tolerate massive violence, any more than a body can tolerate massive disease. And we in America shall not tolerate it.

But just saying that does not solve the problem. We need to know the answers, I think, to three basic questions about these riots:

—What happened?

—Why did it happen?

—What can be done to prevent it from happening again and again?

Beyond these basic questions there are others — the answers to which can help our Governors and our mayors, our chiefs of police and our citizens all over the country to cope with their immediate and their long-range problems of maintaining order:

—Why riots occur in some cities and do not occur in others?

—Why one man breaks the law, while another, living in the same circumstances, does not?

—To what extent, if any, there has been planning and organization in any of the riots?

—Why have some riots been contained before they got out of hand and others have not?

—How well equipped and trained are the local and State police, and the State guard units, to handle riots?

—How do police-community relationships affect the likelihood of a riot — or the ability to keep one from spreading once it has started?

—Who took part in the riots? What about their age, their level of education, their job history, their origins, and their roots in the community?

—Who suffered most at the hands of the rioters?

—What can be done to help innocent people and vital institutions escape serious injury?

—How can groups of lawful citizens be encouraged, groups that can help to cool the situations?

—What is the relative impact of the depressed conditions in ghetto — joblessness, family instability, poor education, lack of motivation, poor health care — in stimulating people to riot?

—What Federal, State and local programs have been most helpful in relieving those depressed conditions?

—What is the proper public role in helping cities repair the damage that has been done?

—What effect do the mass media have on the riots?

What we are really asking for is a profile of the riots — of the rioters, of their environment, of their victims, of their causes and effects.

We are asking for advice on

—short-term measures that can prevent riots,

—better measures to contain riots once they begin,

—and long-term measures that will make them only a sordid page in our history.

I know this is a tall order . . .

So, Mr. Chairman and Mr. Vice Chairman, let your search be free. . . . As best you can, find the truth, the whole truth, and express it in your report.

I hope you will be inspired by a sense of urgency, but also conscious of the danger that lies always in hasty conclusions.

The work that you do ought to help guide us not just this summer, but for many summers to come and for many years to come.

B. The 1960's

"The 1960's," *Report of the National Advisory Commission on Civil Disorders,* Washington, D.C.: Government Printing Office, 1968, pp. 19-22.

1. Since this report was written, the riots in American cities have continued. Recall the events following the assassination of the Reverend Martin Luther King, Jr., and the "happenings" during the 1968 Democratic National Convention in Chicago. Can you explain why riots occur?

2. According to this reading, what happened to cause the riots? Why did they occur? Were they planned? Were they part of a foreign conspiracy? Or were they spontaneous outbursts?

1963-64

In 1963, serious disorders, involving both whites and Negroes, broke out in Birmingham, Savannah, Cambridge, Md., Chicago, and Philadelphia. Sometimes the mobs battled each other; more often they fought the police.

The most violent encounters took place in Birmingham. Police used dogs, firehoses, and cattle prods against marchers, many of whom were children. White racists shot at Negroes and bombed Negro residences. Negroes retaliated by burning white-owned businesses in Negro areas. On a quiet Sunday morning, a bomb exploded beneath a Negro church. Four young girls in a Sunday school class were killed.

In the spring of 1964, the arrest and conviction of civil rights demonstrators provoked violence in Jacksonville. A shot fired from a passing car killed a Negro woman. When a bomb threat forced evacuation of an all-Negro high school, the students stoned policemen and firemen and burned the cars of newsmen. For the first time, Negroes used Molotov cocktails in setting fires.

Two weeks later, at a demonstration protesting school segregation in Cleveland, a bulldozer accidentally killed a young white minister. When police moved in to disperse a crowd composed primarily of Negroes, violence erupted.

In late June, white segregationists broke through police lines and attacked civil rights demonstrators in St. Augustine, Florida. In Philadelphia, Mississippi, law enforcement officers were implicated in the lynch murders of three civil rights workers. On July 10, Ku Klux Klansmen shot and killed a Negro U.S. Army lieutenant colonel, Lemuel Penn, as he was driving through Georgia.

On July 16, in New York City, several young Negroes walking to summer school classes became involved in a dispute with a white building superintendent. When an off-duty police lieutenant intervened, a 15-year-old boy attacked him with a knife. The officer shot and killed the boy.

A crowd of teenagers gathered and smashed store windows. Police arrived in force and dispersed the group.

On the following day, the Progressive Labor Movement, a Marxist-Leninist organization, printed and passed out inflammatory leaflets charging the police with brutality.

On the second day after the shooting, a rally called by the Congress of Racial Equality [CORE] to protest the Mississippi lynch murders developed into a march on a precinct police station. The crowd clashed with the police; one person was killed, and 12 police officers and 19 citizens were injured.

For several days thereafter, the pattern was repeated: despite exhortations of Negro community leaders against violence, protest rallies became uncontrollable. Police battled mobs in Harlem and in the Bedford-Stuyvesant section of Brooklyn. Firemen fought fires started with Molotov cocktails. When bricks and bottles were thrown, police responded with gunfire. Widespread looting followed and many persons were injured.

A week later, a riot broke out in Rochester when police tried to arrest an intoxicated Negro youth at a street dance. After two days of violence, the National Guard restored order.

During the first two weeks of August disorders took place in three New Jersey communities: Jersey City, Elizabeth, and Paterson.

On August 15, when a white liquor store owner in the Chicago suburb of Dixmoor had a Negro woman arrested for stealing a bottle of whiskey, he was accused of having manhandled her. A crowd gathered in front of the store, broke the store window, and threw rocks at passing cars. The police restored order. The next day, when the disturbance was renewed, a Molotov cocktail set the liquor store afire. Several persons were injured.

The final violence of the summer occurred in Philadelphia. A Negro couple's car stalled at an intersection in an area known as "The Jungle" – where, with almost 2,000 persons living in each block, there is the greatest incidence of crime, disease, unemployment, and poverty in the city. When two police officers, one white and one black, attempted to move the car, the wife of the owner became abusive, and the officers arrested her. Police officers and Negro spectators gathered at the scene. Two nights of rioting, resulting in extensive damage, followed.

1965

In the spring of 1965, the Nation's attention shifted back to the South. When civil rights workers staged a nonviolent demonstration in Selma, Alabama, police and state troopers forcibly interrupted their march. Within the next few weeks racists murdered a white clergyman and a white housewife active in civil rights.

In the small Louisiana town of Bogalusa, when Negro demonstrators attacked by whites received inadequate police protection, the Negroes formed a self-defense group called the "Deacons for Defense and Justice."

As late as the second week of August, there had been few distrubances outside the South. But, on the evening of August 11, as Los Angeles sweltered in a heat wave, a highway patrolman halted a young Negro driver for speeding. The young man appeared intoxicated, and the patrolman arrested him. As a crowd gathered, law enforcement officers were called to the scene. A highway patrolman mistakenly struck by a bystander used his billy club. A young Negro woman, who was accused of spitting on the police, was dragged into the middle of the street.

When the police departed, members of the crowd began hurling rocks at passing cars, beating white motorists, and overturning cars and setting them on fire. The police reacted hesitantly. Actions they did take further inflamed the people on the streets.

The following day, the area was calm. Community leaders attempting to mediate between Negro residents and the police received little cooperation from municipal authorities. That evening the previous night's pattern of violence was repeated.

Not until almost 30 hours after the initial flareup did window smashing, looting, and arson begin. Yet the police utilized only a small part of their forces.

Few police were on hand the next morning when huge crowds gathered in the business district of Watts, two miles from the location of the original disturbance, and began looting. In the absence of police response, the looting became bolder and spread into other areas. Hundreds of women and children from five housing projects clustered in or near Watts took part. Around noon, extensive firebombing began. Few white persons were attacked; the principal intent of the rioters now seemed to be to destroy property owned by whites in order to drive white "exploiters" out of the ghetto.

The chief of police asked for National Guard help, but the arrival of the military units was delayed for several hours. When the Guardsmen arrived, they, together with police, made heavy use of firearms. Reports of "sniper fire" increased. Several persons were killed by mistake. Many more were injured.

Thirty-six hours after the first Guard units arrived, the main force of the riot had been blunted. Almost 4,000 persons were arrested. Thirty-four were killed and hundreds injured. Approximately $35 million in damage had been inflicted.

The Los Angeles riot, the worst in the United States since the Detroit riot of 1943, shocked all who had been confident that race relations were improving in the North, and evoked a new mood in Negro ghettos across the country.

1966

The events of 1966 made it appear that domestic turmoil had become part of the American scene.

In March, a fight between several Negroes and Mexican-Americans resulted in a new flareup in Watts. In May, after a police officer accidentally shot and killed a Negro, demonstrations by Negro militants again increased tension in Los Angeles.

Evidence was accumulating that a major proportion of riot participants were youths. Increasing race pride, skepticism about their job prospects, and dissatisfaction with the inadequacy of their education, caused unrest among students in Negro colleges and high schools throughout the country. Students and youths were the principal participants in at least six of the 13 spring and early summer disorders of 1966.

July 12, 1966, was a hot day in Chicago. Negro youngsters were playing in water gushing from an illegally opened fire hydrant. Two police officers, arriving on the scene, closed the hydrant. A Negro youth turned it on again, and the police officers arrested him. A crowd gathered. Police reinforcements arrived. As the crowd became unruly, seven Negro youth were arrested.

Rumors spread that the arrested youths had been beaten and that police were turning off fire hydrants in Negro neighborhoods but leaving them on in white areas. Sporadic window breaking, rock throwing, and firebombing lasted for several hours. Most of the participants were teenagers.

In Chicago, as in other cities, the long-standing grievances of the Negro community needed only minor incidents to trigger violence.

In 1961 when Negroes, after being evacuated from a burning tenement, had been sheltered in a church in an all-white area, a crowd of residents had gathered and threatened to attack the church unless the Negroes were removed.

Segregated schools and housing had led to repeated picketing and marches by civil rights organizations. When marchers had gone into white neighborhoods, they had been met on several occasions by KKK [Ku Klux Klan] signs and crowds throwing eggs and tomatoes. In 1965, when a Chicago firetruck had killed a Negro woman in an accident, Negroes had congregated to protest against the fire station's all-white complement. Rock throwing and looting had broken out. More than 170 persons were arrested in two days.

On the evening of July 13, 1966, the day after the fire hydrant incident, rock throwing, looting and firebombing began again. For several days thereafter, the pattern of violence was repeated. Police responding to calls were subjected to random gunfire. Rumors spread. The press talked in highly exaggerated terms of "guerilla warfare" and "sniper fire."

Before the police and 4,200 National Guardsmen managed to restore order, scores of civilians and police had been injured. There were 533 arrests, including 155 juveniles. Three

Negroes were killed by stray bullets, among them a 13-year-old boy and a 14-year-old pregnant girl.

Less than a week later, Ohio National Guardsmen were mobilized to deal with an outbreak of rioting that continued for 4 nights in the Hough section of Cleveland. It is probable that Negro extremists, although they neither instigated nor organized the disorder, exploited and enlarged it. Amidst widespread reports of "sniper fire," four Negroes, including one young woman, were killed; many others, several children among them, were injured. Law enforcement officers were responsible for two of the deaths, a white man firing from a car for a third, and a group of young white vigilantes for the fourth.

Some news media keeping "tally sheets" of the distrubances began to apply the term "riot" to acts of vandalism and relatively minor disorders.

At the end of July, the National States Rights Party, a white extremist organization that advocates deporting Negroes and other minorities, preached racial hatred at a series of rallies in Baltimore. Bands of white youths were incited into chasing and beating Negroes. A court order halted the rallies.

Forty-three disorders and riots were reported during 1966. Although there were considerable variations in circumstances, intensity, and length, they were usually ignited by a minor incident fueled by antagonism between the Negro population and the police.

Spring, 1967

In the spring of 1967, disorders broke out at three Southern Negro universities at which SNCC [Student Nonviolent Coordinating Committee], a militant anti-white organization, had been attempting to organize the students.

On Friday, April 7, learning that Stokely Carmichael was speaking at two primarily Negro universities, Fisk and Tennessee A&I, in Nashville, and receiving information that some persons were preparing to riot, the police adopted an emergency riot plan. On the following day, Carmichael and others, including South Carolina Senator Strom Thurmond, spoke at a symposium at Vanderbilt University.

That evening, the Negro operator of a restaurant located near Fisk University summoned police to arrest an allegedly intoxicated Negro soldier.

Within a few minutes, students, many of them members of SNCC, began to picket the restaurant. A squad of riot police arrived and soon became the focus of attention. Spectators gathered. When a city bus was halted and attacked by members of the crowd, a Negro police lieutenant fired five shots into the air.

Rocks and bottles were thrown and additional police were called into the area. Officers fired a number of shots over the heads of the crowd. The students and spectators gradually dispersed.

On the following evening, after negotiations between students and police broke down, crowds again began forming. Police fired over their heads, and shots were fired back at the police. On the fringes of the campus, several white youths aimed shots at a police patrol wagon.

A few days later, when police raided the home of several young Negro militants, they confiscated a half-dozen bottles prepared as Molotov cocktails.

About a month later, students at Jackson State College, in Jackson, Mississippi, were standing around after a political rally when two Negro police officers pursued a speeding car, driven by a Negro student, onto the campus. When the officers tried to arrest the driver, the students interfered. The police called for reinforcements. A crowd of several hundred persons quickly gathered, and a few rocks were thrown.

On the following evening, an even larger crowd assembled. When police attempted to disperse it by gunfire, three persons were hit. One of them, a young Negro, died the next day. The National Guard restored order.

Six days later, on May 16, two separate Negro protests were taking place in Houston. One group was picketing a garbage dump in a Negro residential neighborhood, where a Negro child had drowned. Another was demonstrating at a junior high school on the grounds that Negro students were disciplined more harshly than white.

That evening college students who had participated in the protests returned to the campus of Texas Southern University. About 50 of them were grouped around a 21-year-old student, D. W., a Vietnam veteran, who was seeking to stimulate further protest action. A dispute broke out, and D. W. reportedly slapped another student. When the student threatened D. W., he left, armed himself with a pistol, and returned.

In response to the report of a disturbance, two unmarked police cars with four officers arrived. Two of the officers questioned D. W., discovered he was armed with a pistol, and arrested him.

A short time later, when one of the police cars returned to the campus, it was met by rocks and bottles thrown by students. As police called for reinforcements, sporadic gunshots reportedly came from the men's dormitory. The police returned the fire.

For several hours, gunfire punctuated unsuccessful attempts by community leaders to negotiate a truce between the students and the police.

When several tar barrels were set afire in the street and shooting broke out again, police decided to enter the dormitory. A patrolman, struck by a ricocheting bullet, was killed. After clearing all 480 occupants from the building, police searched it and found one shotgun and two .22 caliber pistols. The origin of the shot that killed the officer was not determined.

As the summer of 1967 approached, Americans, conditioned by three years of reports of riots, expected violence. But they had no answers to hard questions: What was causing the turmoil? Was it organized and, if so, by whom? Was there a pattern to the disorders?

C. The Attitudes of the Man on the Street

"After the Riots: A Survey," *Newsweek,* August 21, 1967, pp. 18-19. Reprinted with permission of the publishers.

1. According to the survey taken by Louis Harris and his associates, what is the dominant attitude toward riots and rioters? What are the differences between Negro and white opinions? Are these differences important? Why? Why not?

2. What are the popular "explanations" for riots in America? Which do you think are most accurate?

3. How do opinions about riots and popular "explanations" of causation affect the search for the means to improve the situation?

From the vantage point of a Negro rioter, it might almost appear that the war of the slums has achieved its undeclared goals: the white American is frightened, and he is ready to approve even the most drastic Federal programs to attack the root causes of violence in the ghettos. But if this is a victory, there is also a ... [great] cost, measurable not only in the damage and injury within the ghettos themselves but in the decline of support and understanding for the Negro cause.

The white's concern about the black man has been quickened — but it seems vitally lacking in affection. Fear and resentment have apparently displaced their weight in sympathy, and the white man's endorsement of massive aid to the ghettos may seem to him an imperative more pragmatic than moral. These are the implications in a Louis Harris survey of Negro and white reaction to the summer's racial upheavals.

The Harris survey [made in 1967] shows both blacks and whites largely in agreement on a number of points:

—The riots have hurt the Negro cause.

—Most Negroes do not support the ghetto violence.

—Looting and fire-bombing are criminal acts.

—Large-scale Federal programs to set up summer camps for youngsters and work programs for the unemployed, to eradicate rats and tear down urban ghettos, would be effective measures against future racial disorders.

But beyond that, a curious ambiguity [confusion] develops in the attitudes of a majority of whites. They profess to be less disturbed than ever about Negroes sharing public places - restaurants, movie theaters, rest rooms — with them, and at the same time they are more inclined than at any time in recent years to admit to sterotyped views reflecting anti-Negro prejudice, e.g., that Negroes are lazier, more slovenly, more immoral and less intelligent than whites — and more prone to violence. They acknowledge that the ghetto Negro needs help, yet they seem largely unaware or unbelieving of some of the conditions the Negro considers most responsible for rioting: price gouging by white store owners, brutality by white police and an over-all lack of significant progress for Negroes in white America.

The Harris survey elicited speculations on the riot causes in two ways: by an "open-ended" question that asked whites and Negroes to volunteer their own views, and by asking them to choose likely items from a list of reasons given by others in the past. The result was that as many as 45 per cent of whites attributed the disorders to "outside agitators," and, despite the statement of J. Edgar Hoover that he found no discernible pattern of conspiracy in the riots, 71 per cent of whites felt the riots were "mainly organized."

'Commies': A typical array of white comments came from a young Oswego, N. Y., farmer: "Agitation by Commies, civil-rights Carmichaels and Browns . . ."; a Phoenix, Ariz., pensioner: "I think it's outside aggression . . . some hothead Communism-coached leaders egging them on," and James Evans, a Cranston, R.I., college student: "The Black Muslims are finally putting through the plan they threatened years ago."

A MAJORITY FOR GHETTO AID

Whites and Negroes were asked whether they thought each of several recent proposals to prevent future racial outbreaks would be effective.

Those in favor:	White %	Negro %
Setting up large-scale government work projects to give jobs to all the unemployed	66	91
Federal program to tear down ghettos in cities	63	84
Setting up massive summer camps	55	78
Federal program to exterminate rats	59	72

In contrast, Negroes tend to say the riots were spontaneous and by more than 2 to 1, they feel police brutality is a major cause — a proposition whites reject by 8 to 1. (Only 16 per cent of whites believe there is any police brutality to Negroes.) The more educated whites recognize such sources of ghetto unrest as decrepit [worn out] housing, lack of job opportunities and unfulfilled promises by the white leadership. A total of 40 per cent answering the open-ended question attributed the ghetto unrest to continuing maltreatment of the Negro. But another 37 per cent of the whites cited such riot causes as "Negroes are too lazy to work for their rights"; "Uneducated people — don't know what they're doing"; "Law has been too lax"; "Gotten too much too fast." From the list of causes cited in the past, only 8 per cent of the whites indicated "Police brutality against Negroes" as a factor, while 23 per cent credited, "Desire of Negroes for violence."

Among the white majority, even the more moderate comments are tainted with bitterness. "The colored people asked for a better chance, but when they got it, it went to their heads," said a 54-year-old Morris, Okla., oil-field worker. "They want the whole hog or none." And an elderly Californian observed: "They need food, work and education, but . . . they just use these as excuses to riot." Far fewer whites tended to echo the sentiment of Father Clifford Brier, a white Catholic priest in Oswego: "So much time has gone by and so little has been accomplished [for the Negro]. The whites just think they are superior." Or of a Negro farmer in Utica, Miss.: "The Negro has been down and mistreated all his life, and the Federal government has opened doors for him and he is determined to keep them open."

Rosy View: In fact, though a diminishing majority of whites continue to believe Negroes are discriminated against (55 per cent in 1967 as against 61 per cent in 1966 and 71 per cent in 1963), whites on the whole prefer to think the Negro is getting a "better break," particularly in jobs (87 per cent against 74 per cent in 1963) and education (63 per cent against 41 per cent four years ago). And while the majority acknowledges Negroes live in inferior housing, 35 per cent of the whites, mainly in the South and Midwest, say the Negro is not discriminated against at all. A typical comment (from a Madison Heights, Mich., housewife): "They have everything I have, and some have even more."

All of this seems eerily [strangely] out of register with the firmly held view of 93 per cent of Negroes that an essential lack of progress in jobs, education and housing contributed critically to the riot atmosphere. Seven in every ten Negroes identify deficient housing as a fundamental grievance, and within riot-torn ghettos, the majority of Negroes say they know someone who lives in a home or apartment where rats, roaches, overcrowding, faulty plumbing and crumbling ceilings are inescapable conditions.

Stereotypes: Perhaps the most interesting – and most disturbing – aspect of the Harris survey is the indicated shift back to discredited myths about the Negro. On the one hand, substantial majorities of whites – larger than in the past – insisted they were "not concerned" about such practical, everyday examples of integration as having a Negro sitting next to them in a restaurant or movie theater, a Negro using the same public rest room or trying on clothes in a store before a white customer. (The majority dwindles sharply on the old barrier of a white child bringing a Negro home to supper, and all but vanishes, to a 7 per cent minority who would be unconcerned if their teen-age child dated a Negro.) Yet in a list of standard indexes of white prejudice toward non-whites, nearly every familiar sterotype of the Negro finds greater acceptance by white majorities than it did last year. Thus 70 per cent of the whites agree that "Negroes have less ambition than white people," against 65 per cent who thought this way in 1966; 47 per cent agree "Negroes keep untidy homes," against 39 per cent a year ago, and 58 per cent accept a flat statement that "Negroes have looser morals," compared with 50 per cent last year. The trend was the same on assertions that Negroes "laugh a lot," "have less native intelligence," "want to live off the handout."

In almost every instance, the responses sharply reversed a downward trend in the acceptance of stereotypes that past surveys had shown to be developing between 1963 and 1966.

Any easy conclusion drawn from these seemingly contra-dictory moods in the white majority would be suspect and debatable. But clearly, most whites in the Harris survey were angry about the latest ghetto rioting, and evidently, in the more permissive national climate of resentment, they felt freer to express their basic mistrust of the Negro. On one hand, they showed somewhat greater readiness to accept closer personal association with the Negro, and on the other, they seemed to say, "The closer he gets, the more threatening he looks."

Fear: Unmistakably, white fears were increasing. In 1966, only 49 per cent admitted they were "personally more worried about race riots" than the year before. This summer, 76 per cent said they were more worried, and 51 per cent said they are "personally more uneasy on the streets," against

43 per cent a year ago. As a Michigan mother typically expressed it: "You just never know what's going to happen. I'm afraid to go downtown any more."

But responses among Negroes paint something other than a picture of blacks relishing the discomfiture of whites. Negroes, in even greater numbers than whites — 65 per cent — feel unsafe on the streets: "Because you can get killed so easy on the street now without doing anything to be killed for," as one Mississippi Negro put it. "On Friday and Saturday I don't walk the streets . . . That's all they look for is bustin' in your head," said a 25-year-old Philadelphia Negro. "Rocks and bullets have no names on them," grimly commented a Negro laborer in riot-scarred Dayton, Ohio.

But common ground for whites and Negroes in the wake of the riots is scarce. There is agreement that looters and fire-bombers are committing criminal acts. There is even a measure of agreement (68 per cent whites, 47 per cent . . . Negroes) that fire-bombers in riots should be shot. But only 27 per cent of Negroes feel looters should be shot down, while 62 per cent of whites say they want looters shot.

Even in the strong white and Negro concurrence on the need for dramatic measures to aid the ghettos, there is a possible note of discordant motives — the Negro supporting the idea of tearing down the ghettos and setting up large-scale summer camps and public-works projects out of a firsthand experience with a ghetto he knows and hates, and the white endorsing the same urgent measures, possibly from fear of a ghetto he scarcely cares to know.

Only in the answers to the survey's final question does there begin to be a strong suggestion that whites can accept the Negro viewpoint. They were asked: "As an individaul, what do you think it feels like to be discriminated against as a Negro? What do you feel it does to Negroes as individuals?" The largest number of whites, 26 per cent, felt it might incite them to fight back, even to riot.

"It hurts them real bad. I'd probably be rioting right with them," said a 49-year-old Texas salesman. Mitchell Miller, a Ridgecrest, Calif., truck driver, commented: "It degrades him [the Negro], which no one likes. Therefore it is a natural instinct to fight back. The more educated ones will fight by improving themselves. The less educated will fight back with violence inspired by misguided leaders." And Mrs. Margaret Lamb, an Owensboro, Ky., widow, replied: "It makes you wonder that they do as good as they do the way people treat them sometimes. You see things that make you wonder why they put up with it."

THE BASIC CAUSES OF THE NEGRO RIOTING

White and Negro adults were first asked to suggest in their own words what they thought might be "the two or three main reasons" for the recent Negro riots. These were the most frequent replies:

	White %	Negro %
Outside agitation	45	10
Prejudice—promises not kept, bad treatment	16	36
Poverty—slums, ghetto conditions	14	28
Lack of jobs—unfair employment	10	29
Negroes are too lazy to work for their rights	13	5
Uneducated people—don't know what they are doing	11	9
Teen-agers looking for trouble	7	7
Law has been too lax	7	½

Then they were given a list of some commonly cited causes of rioting and asked to specify which they considered major ones. The results:

	White %	Negro %
Lack of jobs for young Negroes	34	67
Lack of firmness by local mayors and governors	37	24
Hatred of whites by Negroes	33	20
Desire of Negroes for violence	23	13
Lack of decent housing for Negroes	39	68
Desire of Negroes to loot stores	26	9
Lack of good education for Negroes	46	61
Police brutality against Negroes	8	49
Lack of progress in giving Negroes equality	30	72

D. Predicting More Conflict and Aggression

George A. Chauncey, "Violence and the Judgment of God," Richmond, Virginia: Board of Christian Education, Presbyterian Church in the United States, 1968, mimeographed, pp. 1-4. Reprinted with permission of the Board of Christian Education and the author.

George A. Chauncey is Director of Studies, Division of Church and Society, Presbyterian Church in the U.S., Richmond, Virginia. His paper was prepared for an adult study packet entitled CRISIS IN THE NATION.

1. According to the author, what caused the recent urban riots in America?

2. Why does the author predict more violence and riots in American cities?

3. Do you agree with the author's conclusions about the attitudes of white Americans? Why? Why not?

[In 1967]. . . our nation experienced its third summer of wide-spread civil disorder. In 1965, it was Harlem, and the disaster of Watts. In 1966, it was Cleveland, Omaha, Atlanta, Dayton, San Francisco, and twenty-four other cities. In 1967, Newark and Detroit were only the most tragic of 67 explosions of violence in the streets. An Associated Press survey reports that 85 persons were killed, more than 3,200 were injured, over 16,000 were arrested, and more than $100 million in property was stolen, damaged, or destroyed.

We Can Expect More Violence

Four elements in our explosive situation lead me to believe that we can only expect more − much more − of the same in the months ahead.

The *first* is the fact that our nation has made promises which it has simply not fulfilled. We have made these promises through our Constitution, court decisions, civil rights legislation, and TV commercials. We have reaffirmed them with preachments, proclamations, pronouncements, and political pledges. Day in and day out — through the media of radio and TV — we have told every man, woman, and child in America that he lives in a great big wonderful world. To be an American, we have said, is to enjoy — not as a gift but as a right — freedom and justice and equality, a good education, a decent place to live, and full opportunity to earn one's fair share of bread.

These are the promises our society has made. And we simply haven't fulfilled them. We have reneged. Despite all our promises and pledges, and despite the many judicial and legislative victories which have been achieved in the past few years, our common life is still marred by cruel oppression of the Negro.

A joint study of the Bureau of the Census and the Bureau of Labor Statistics published October 1967 reveals, for example, that:

Unemployment rates for nonwhites have been twice those for whites for the past dozen years.

More than a third of the nation's nonwhite families are officially classified as poor.

Of the 9.6 million nonwhites classified as poor, only a third receive welfare assistance of any kind.

Negro family income is only 58 percent of white family income nationwide, and only 51 percent in the South.

Nearly 1.7 million nonwhite families, 29 percent of the total, live in substandard housing. In the South, the figure is 46 percent.

The life expectancy of nonwhites in 1965 was lower than for whites in all age groups in prime working years.

The likelihood that a nonwhite mother will die in giving birth to her child is four times greater than for a white mother.

Nonwhite infant mortality rates are also much higher than for whites, and the difference increases each year.

Bayard Rustin observes in a recent article that "if a society is interested in stability, it should either not make promises or it should keep them." He goes on to say:

> Economic and social deprivation, if accepted by its victims as their lot in life, breeds passivity, even docility. The miserable yield to their fate as divinely ordained or as their own fault. And indeed, many Negroes of earlier generations felt that way.
>
> Today young Negroes aren't having any. They don't share the feeling that something must be wrong with them, that they are responsible for their own exclusion from this affluent society. The civil-rights movement — in fact, the whole liberal trend beginning with John Kennedy's election — has told them otherwise.
>
> Conservatives will undoubtedly seize the occasion [of this summer's violence] for an attack on the Great Society, liberalism, the welfare state and Lyndon Johnson. But the young Negroes are right: the promises made to them were good and necessary and long, long overdue. The youth were right to believe in them. The only trouble is that they were not fulfilled. Prominent Republicans and Dixiecrats are demanding not that the promises be fulfilled, but that they be revoked.
>
> What they and the American people absolutely must understand now is that the promises cannot be revoked.[2]

A *second* factor which makes our situation so critical is that an increasing number of Negroes have come to believe that violence is the only way they can secure their rights. This is by no means the feeling of the majority of Negroes. But an increasingly vocal minority is asserting that violence is the answer.

They assert this, on the one hand, because they believe that non-violence as a strategy or tactic, simply hasn't produced the goods. That the so-called civil rights movement was — on the part of Negroes — non-violent for so long, and is as non-violent

[2] Bayard Rustin, "A Way Out of the Exploding Ghetto," *The New York Times Magazine,* August 13, 1967, pp. 62 ff. © 1967 by The New York Times Company. Reprinted by permission.

as it is today, is a cause for both amazement and gratitude, but it is increasingly clear that this tactic is losing its appeal. On the other hand, violence as a means of getting things done is becoming increasingly appealing. Violence, as Harvey Cox has recently reminded us, has "worked" in American history. As Cox says:

> Every fourth grader knows that America won its independence through a violent revolution, wrenched the West from the Indians by brute force, preserved the Union in a bloody Civil War, became a world power through two destructive world wars and is now protecting the luckless people of Vietnam by incinerating their tiny country with napalm and high explosives. After all this, to scold the inmates of our black ghettos for resorting to violence when singing, marching, praying and picketing have failed seems at best a trifle hypocritical.[3]

Moreover, there are a number of black Americans who, even if convinced that violence as a strategy were self-defeating, would strike out violently at our society because they are so alienated from it that they simply don't care what happens.

Last summer's explosion has revealed starkly that members of the present generation of violated, black Americans are unafraid to die. The words of a Detroit sniper as reported in *Newsweek* are haunting: "I don't care if I die, so you know that I don't care if I kill you."

A *third* fact which makes our national situation so extremely dangerous is that violence provokes repression, and repression provokes, if not more violence, at least the will to more violence. We are now caught in a vicious circle which will be extremely difficult for us to break. Thus, a disorder occurs; it is put down by undisciplined military action; and in the very manner of its repression, seeds for future disorders are sown. When one responds to riots simply with military power,

---

[3] Harvey Cox. "The Riots: No Winners — Only Losers." Reprinted from *Christianity and Crisis*, August 7, 1967; copyright by Christianity and Crisis, Inc., 1967.

anti-riot bills and loud expressions of determination "not to reward rioters," one can only expect more riots.

Moreover, the very language which we speak in the face of social disruption is itself provocative of more of the same. Thus, the call for "law and order" only provokes increased anger on the part of those who interpret the call as simply a demand for the preservation of an unjust status quo. Thus, expressions of dismay over looting, burning, and the deliberate destruction of property only provoke disgust on the part of those who note a relative silence in the face of indiscriminate slaughter and arrests. And thus, the very sense of urgency which we feel now in the light of this summer's potential violence only provokes cynical questions about why we were so indifferent so long to the revolting conditions from which this revolution has sprung.

The viciousness of this circle and its terrible horror were poignantly expressed by Pat Watters in these agonizing words about the element of joy in this summer's action and reaction:

> The riots have been for all of us most of all a dramatic display of a society in real disorder, the thing just not working any more. Here were people come to full expression of all the rage of life cheated of all good, and here were the cities and states and finally the United States Government saying that the only answer they could give was brutal force. Not the least of the terrible elements was a feel of joy in it — the rioters laughing in the release of all the years of resentment, the forces of "law and order" bearing the grim grin of the righteous, licensed to kill.[4]

The *final* reason I believe that we are probably in for unprecedented (since the Civil War) national anguish is my fear that as the viciousness of the circle grows the white man in America will be increasingly tempted to repress the Negro rather than reconstruct society, and the black man will be increasingly tempted to destroy the American dream rather than to work for its realization.

[4] Pat Watters, "Summer of 1967," *New South,* Summer 1967, p. 112. Reprinted by permission.

I believe that we still have a moment of grace. . . . There is perhaps still time for us to make the radical changes in our society that are necessary if we are to survive. Perhaps we will seize this moment of grace.

My optimism is inevitably dampened, however, when I reflect on the mood in our nation today, or when I review the actions of the Congress, or when I recall what happened in Plainfield, N. J., where the National Guard, upon orders of the Governor, but without search warrants as required by the Constitution, conducted a house-to-house search of Negro homes to find 46 semiautomatic rifles that had been stolen during the rioting earlier in the week.

Every black man in America knows — and every white man should surely acknowledge — that no white neighborhood anywhere in our nation would have been subjected to the sort of search which that black neighborhood endured this summer. That illegal search demonstrated as did nothing else the danger we are in of becoming a police state.

As we are tempted more and more to do "anything necessary" to maintain order, we would do well to heed the warning issued by James Baldwin five years ago: "The Negroes of this country may never be able to rise to power, but they are very well placed indeed to precipitate chaos and ring down the curtain on the American dream." [5]

[5] James Baldwin, *The Fire Next Time* (New York: The Dial Press, 1964), p. 119.

Chapter **2**

Riots in Historical Perspective

Today many people see urban unrest as a new phenomenon in American history. They are alarmed by riots and violence. They look at current disorder and are shocked, vainly looking for causes for this unhappy situation. Is a foreign conspiracy at work, lurking behind the scene to spread discord and destroy the moral fiber of American society? Are new, young minority group leaders, trained in communist tactics, trying to overthrow the government of our Republic? Are Americans getting soft, expecting too much to come too easily in a nation with creeping socialism? Are persons now refusing to work hard, as other Americans supposedly did, but instead demanding comforts and advantages without putting forth personal endeavor?

A glance backward might offer some answers. Scholars identified thirty-three major interracial disturbances in the United States between 1900 and 1949, so this problem is not really new in our country. Between 1915 and 1919, during the time of World War I, there were eighteen race riots of major proportions. On May 28 and July 2, 1917, East St. Louis, Illinois, experienced serious racial outbursts when Negroes were used as strikebreakers. Thirty-nine Negroes were killed. The intense violence and arson were subdued only by the use of the National Guard and increased police activity. This major riot was followed in 1919 by the Chicago race riot, which lasted for two weeks and tolled thirty-eight dead and hundreds injured. Thousands were left homeless. Between 1940 and 1945, the years of World War II, there were five major disturbances. In 1943 a round of major urban riots occurred: Harlem in New York, anti-Mexican and Negro violence in Los Angeles, and the Detroit riot. The Detroit outburst was an intense explosion of hatred which left twenty-five Negroes and nine whites dead with thousands of dollars worth of property destroyed.

But not all unrest in the American past was linked to interracial strife. The New York draft riots of 1863 did have racial overtones; however, the Philadelphia riots in 1844 were anti-Catholic. The Irish-Catholic population of that city had grown rapidly prior to the 1840's and some Protestant feelings were unleashed in May and on July 4th of that year, with loss of life and property. In the 1870's Chinese immigrants felt the wrath of Los Angeles residents, and later, the anger of other Californians.

Some of the most violent urban conflicts arose between labor and management. As labor began to organize into unions and demand the right to bargain with businessmen to improve working conditions, intense conflicts ensued. In 1892 the Carnegie Steel Company of Pittsburgh was struck by workers. The company, owned by Andrew Carnegie, locked out workers, hired strikebreakers, and used armed guards to protect its property along the Monongahela River. The strikers attacked the steel mills and after some days' time, the National Guard was able to put an end to the strife. In 1894 the workers of the Pullman Palace Car Company (manufacturing railroad sleeping cars) struck factories at Pullman, Illinois, outside of Chicago. Violence broke out and the state militiamen and federal troops were called in to suppress the unrest. Labor relations produced so much violence that a Commission on Industrial Relations was established by President Taft in 1912. The final report of this group noted that (a) American laborers felt they had not received a fair share of their nation's wealth, (b) there was a growing trend of monopoly of land and mineral resources, (c) the workers almost universally felt that they were denied "justice," and (d) labor was denied the right to organize, a necessity since an individual could not bargain with a huge corporation. Labor violence continued into the 1920's and '30's despite the commission's report and recommendations.

For those who still prefer to see the recent riots as un-American or as a new phenomenon in America, it might help to recall two revered symbols of American patriotism — the Boston Massacre and the Boston Tea Party. Both were illegal protests. Also, The Stamp Act Riots during 1765 spread throughout the colonies as violent protest against legislation passed in a parliament 3,000 miles across the Atlantic. These activities meet the Webster's dictionary definition of *riot:* "a wild and loose festivity; disorderly behavior, the tumultuous disturbance of the public peace." Certainly, the protests were attempts to force change by using methods of physical coercion.

The fact of unrest in American history is no justification for violence today. It is no excuse for continued violence, loss of life and property. But in context it does help to focus upon a scholarly search for real causes and real cures, dismissing the "prophets of doom" and the predictions that this *new* discord means the end of everything American!

Every riot is brought about by previously existing factors. The build-up may not be apparent, but the atmosphere which contributes to a riotous situation develops over a period of time and *many factors* are involved. As one scholar noted, "Riots are the products of thousands upon thousands of little events that have affected the habits and emotions of thousands upon thousands of people." Those who identify but one cause of a riot just cannot understand.

Any unjust denial of man's basic rights, needs, or aspirations can give rise to a feeling of frustration and desperation. It makes little difference whether this "unjust denial" is actually true or merely imagined by the persons involved. The fact that men believe that there is unjust denial is often sufficient to prompt them to turn to violence. This is especially true when these men cannot find socially acceptable ways of being successful or removing their discontent. Rioters may not know where they are going, but they always dislike where they have been!

As you read, keep these general questions in mind:

1. Why did riots occur in the past? What does this suggest about the causes for recent urban violence?

2. Why do riots and periods of civil unrest continually crop up in our history?

E. The Chicago Riot, 1919

The Negro in Chicago: A Study of Race Relations and a Race Riot, Chicago: University of Chicago Press, 1922, pp. 595-601. Reprinted with permission of the publisher. Copyright 1922 by The University of Chicago.

1. During the Chicago riots in 1919, what happened? Why did it happen? What were the results?

2. How did this riot differ from the recent civil unrest in American cities? Were there any similarities?

In July, 1919, a race riot involving whites and Negroes occurred in Chicago. For some time thoughtful citizens, white and Negro, had sensed increasing tension, but, having no local precedent of riot and wholesale bloodshed, had neither prepared themselves for it nor taken steps to prevent it. The collecting of arms by members of both races was known to the authorities, and it was evident that this was in preparation for aggression as well as for self-defense.

Several minor clashes preceded the riot. On July 3, 1917, a white saloon-keeper who, according to the coroner's physician, died of heart trouble, was incorrectly reported in the press to have been killed by a Negro. That evening a party of young white men riding in an automobile fired upon a group of Negroes at Fifty-third and Federal streets. In July and August of the same year recruits from the Great Lakes Naval Training Station clashed frequently with Negroes, each side accusing the other of being the aggressor.

Gangs of white "toughs," made up largely of the membership of so-called "athletic clubs" from the neighborhood between Roosevelt Road and Sixty-third Street, Wentworth Avenue and the city limits — a district contiguous to the neighborhood of the largest Negro settlement — were a constant menace to Negroes who traversed sections of the territory going to and returning from work. The activities of these gangs and "athletic clubs" became bolder in the spring of 1919, and on the night of June 21, five weeks before the riot, two wanton murders of Negroes occurred, those of Sanford Harris and Joseph Robinson. Harris, returning to his home on Dearborn Street about 11:30 at night, passed a group of young white men. They threatened him and he ran. He had gone but a short distance when one of the group shot him. He died soon afterward. Policemen who came on the scene made no arrests, even when the assailant was pointed out by a white woman witness of the murder. On the same evening Robinson, a Negro laborer, forty-seven years of age, was attacked while returning from work by a gang of white "roughs" at Fifty-fifth Street and Princeton Avenue, apparently without provocation, and stabbed to death.

Negroes were greatly incensed over these murders, but their leaders, joined by many friendly whites, tried to allay their fears and counseled patience.

After the killing of Harris and Robinson, notices were conspicuously posted on the South side that an effort would be made to "get all the niggers on July 4th." The notices called for help from sympathizers. Negroes in turn whispered around the warning to prepare for a riot; and they did prepare.

Since the riot in East St. Louis, July 4, 1917, there had been others in different parts of the country which evidenced a widespread lack of restraint in mutual antipathies and suggested further resorts to lawlessness. Riots and race clashes occurred in Chester, Pennsylvania; Longview, Texas; Coatesville, Pennsylvania; Washington, D. C.; and Norfolk, Virginia, before the Chicago riot.

Aside from general lawlessness and disastrous riots that preceded the riot here discussed, there were other factors which may be mentioned briefly here. In Chicago considerable unrest had been occasioned in industry by increasing competition between white and Negro laborers following a sudden increase in the Negro population due to the migration of Negroes from the South. This increase developed a housing crisis. The Negroes overran the hitherto recognized area of Negro residence, and when they took houses in adjoining neighborhoods friction ensued. In the two years just preceding the riot, twenty-seven Negro dwellings were wrecked by bombs thrown by unidentified persons.

Story of the Riot

Sunday afternoon, July 27, 1919, hundreds of white and Negro bathers crowded the lake-front beaches at Twenty-sixth and Twenty-ninth streets. This is the eastern boundary of the thickest Negro residence area. At Twenty-sixth Street Negroes were in great majority; at Twenty-ninth Street there were more whites. An imaginary line in the water separating the two beaches had been generally observed by the two races. Under the prevailing relations, aided by wild rumors and reports, this line served virtually as a challenge to either side to cross it. Four Negroes who attempted to enter the water from the "white" side were driven away by the whites. They returned with more Negroes, and there followed a series of attacks with stones, first one side gaining the advantage, then the other.

Eugene Williams, a Negro boy of seventeen, entered the water from the side used by Negroes and drifted across the line supported by a railroad tie. He was observed by the crowd on the beach and promptly became a target for stones. He suddenly released the tie, went down and was drowned. Guilt was immediately placed on Stauber, a young white man, by Negro witnesses who declared that he threw the fatal stone.

White and Negro men dived for the boy without result. Negroes demanded that the policeman present arrest Stauber. He refused, and at this crucial moment arrested a Negro on a white man's complaint. Negroes then attacked the officer.

These two facts, the drowning and the refusal of the policeman to arrest Stauber, together marked the beginning of the riot.

Two hours after the drowning, a Negro, James Crawford, fired into a group of officers summoned by the policeman at the beach and was killed by a Negro policeman. Reports and rumors circulated rapidly, and new crowds began to gather. Five white men were injured in clashes near the beach. As darkness came, Negroes in white districts to the west suffered severely. Between 9:00 P.M. and 3:00 A.M. twenty-seven Negroes were beaten, seven stabbed, and four shot. Monday morning was quiet, and Negroes went to work as usual.

Returning from work in the afternoon many Negroes were attacked by white ruffians. Street-car routes, especially at transfer points, were the centers of lawlessness. Trolleys were pulled from the wires, and Negro passengers were dragged into the street, beaten, stabbed, and shot. The police were powerless to cope with these numerous assaults. During Monday, four Negro men and one white assailant were killed, and thirty Negroes were severely beaten in street-car clashes. Four white men were killed, six stabbed, five shot, and nine severely beaten. It was rumored that the white occupants of the Angelus Building at Thirty-fifth Street and Wabash Avenue had shot a Negro. Negroes gathered about the building. The white tenants sought police protection, and one hundred policemen, mounted and on foot, responded. In a clash with the mob the police killed four Negroes and injured many.

Raids into the Negro residence area then began. Automobiles sped through the streets, the occupants shooting at random. Negroes retaliated by "sniping" from ambush. At midnight, surface and elevated car service was discontinued because of a strike for wage increases, and thousands of employees were cut off from work.

On Tuesday, July 19, Negro men en route on foot to their jobs through hostile territory were killed. White soldiers and sailors in uniform, aided by civilians, raided the "Loop" business section, killing two Negroes and beating and robbing several others. Negroes living among white neighbors in Englewood, far to the south, were driven from their homes, their household goods were stolen, and their houses were burned or wrecked. On the West Side an Italian mob, excited by a false rumor that an Italian girl had been shot by a Negro, killed Joseph Lovings, a Negro.

Wednesday night at 10:30 Mayor Thompson yielded to pressure and asked the help of the three regiments of militia which had been stationed in nearby armories during the most severe rioting, awaiting the call. They immediately took up positions throughout the South Side. A rainfall Wednesday night and Thursday kept many people in their homes, and by Friday the rioting had abated. On Saturday incendiary fires burned forty-nine houses in the immigrant neighborhood west of the Stock Yards. Nine hundred and forty-eight people, mostly Lithuanians, were made homeless, and the property loss was about $250,000. Responsibility for the fires was never fixed.

The total casualties of this reign of terror were thirty-eight deaths – fifteen white, twenty-three Negro – and 537 people injured. Forty-one per cent of the reported clashes occurred in the white neighborhood near the Stock Yards between the south branch of the Chicago River and Fifty-fifth Street, Wentworth Avenue and the city limits, and 34 per cent in the "Black Belt" between Twenty-second and Thirty-ninth streets, Wentworth Avenue and Lake Michigan. Others were scattered.

Responsibility for many attacks was definitely placed by many witnesses upon the "athletic clubs," including " Ragen's Colts," the "Hamburgers," "Aylwards," "Our Flag," the "Standard," the "Sparklers," and several others. The mobs were made up for the most part of boys between fifteen and twenty-two. Older persons participated, but the youth of the rioters was conspicuous in evcy clash. Little children witnessed the brutalities and frequently pointed out the injured when the police arrived.

Rumors and the Riot

Wild rumors were in circulation by word of mouth and in the press throughout the riot and provoked many clashes. These included stories of atrocities committed by one race against the other. Reports of the numbers of white and Negro dead tended to produce a feeling that the score must be kept even. Newspaper reports, for example, showed 6 per cent more whites injured than Negroes. As a matter of fact there were 28 per cent more Negroes injured than whites. The *Chicago Tribune* on July 29 reported twenty persons killed, of whom thirteen were white and seven colored. The true figures were exactly the opposite.

Among the rumors provoking fear were numerous references to the arming of Negroes. In the *Daily News* of July 30, for example, appeared the sub-headline: "Alderman Jos. McDonough tells how he was shot at on South Side visit. Says enough ammunition in section to last for years of guerrilla warfare." In the article following, the reference to ammunition was repeated but not elaborated or explained.

The alderman was quoted as saying that the mayor contemplated opening up Thirty-fifth and Forty-seventh streets in order that colored people might get to their work. He thought this would be most unwise for, he stated, "They are armed and white people are not. We must defend ourselves if the city authorities won't protect us." Continuing his story, he described bombs going off: "I saw white men and women running through the streets dragging children by the hands and carrying babies in their arms. Frightened white men told me the police captains had just rushed through the district crying, For God's sake, arm; they are coming; we cannot hold them.' "

Whether or not the alderman was correctly quoted, the effect of such statements on the public was the same. There is no record in any of the riot testimony in the coroner's office or state's attorney's office of any bombs going off during the riot, nor of police captains warning the white people to arm, nor of any fear by whites of a Negro invasion. In the Berger Odman case before a coroner's jury there was a statement to the effect that a sergeant of police warned the Negroes of Ogden Park to arm and to shoot at the feet of rioters if they attempted to invade the few blocks marked off for Negroes by the police. Negroes were warned, not whites.

Conduct of the Police

Chief of Police John J. Garrity, in explaining the inability of the police to curb the rioters, said that there was not a sufficient force to police one-third of the city. Aside from this, Negroes distrusted the white police officers, and it was implied by the chief and stated by States' Attorney Hoyne, that many of the police were "grossly unfair in making arrests." There were instances of actual police participation in the rioting as well as neglect of duty. Of 229 persons arrested and accused of various criminal activities during the riot, 154 were Negroes and seventy-five were whites. Of those indicted, eighty-one were Negroes and forty-seven were whites. Although this, on its face, would indicate great riot activity on the part of Negroes, further reports of clashes show that of 520 persons injured, 342 were Negroes and 178 were whites. The fact that twice as many Negroes appeared as defendants and twice as many Negroes as whites were injured, leads to the conclusion that whites were not apprehended as readily as Negroes.

Many of the depredations outside the "Black Belt" were encouraged by the absence of policemen. Out of a force of 3,000 police, 2,800 were massed in the " Black Belt" during the height of the rioting. In the "Loop" district, where two Negroes were killed and several others wounded, there were only three policemen and one sergeant. The Stock Yards district, where the greatest number of injuries occurred, was also weakly protected.

The Militia

Although Governor Lowden had ordered the militia into the city promptly and they were on hand on the second day of the rioting, their services were not requested by the mayor and chief of police until the evening of the fourth day. The reason expressed by the chief for this delay was a belief that inexperienced militiamen would add to the deaths and disorder. But the troops, when called, proved to be clearly of high character, and their discipline was good, not a case of breach of discipline being reported during their occupation. They were distributed more proportionately through all the riotous areas than the police, and although they reported some hostility from members of "athletic clubs," the rioting soon ceased.

Restoration of Order

Throughout the rioting, various social organizations and many citizens were at work trying to hold hostilities in check and to restore order. The Chicago Urban League, Wabash Avenue Y.M.C.A., American Red Cross, and various other social organizations and the churches of the Negro community gave attention to caring for stranded Negroes, advising them of dangers, keeping them off the streets and, in such ways as were possible, co-operating with the police. The packing companies took their pay to Negro employees, and various banks made loans. Local newspapers in their editorial columns insistently condemned the disorder and counseled calmness.

The Aftermath

Of the thirty-eight persons killed in the riot:

Fifteen met death at the hands of mobs. Coroner's juries recommended that the members of the unknown mobs be apprehended. They were never found.

Six were killed in circumstances fixing no criminal responsibility: three white men were killed by Negroes in self-defense, and three Negroes were shot by policemen in the discharge of their duty.

Four Negroes were killed in the Angelus riot. The coroner made on recommendations, and the cases were not carried further.

Four cases, two Negro and two white, resulted in recommendations from coroner's juries for further investigation of certain persons. Sufficient evidence was lacking for indictments against them.

Nine cases led to indictments. Of this number four cases resulted in convictions.

Thus in only four cases of death was criminal responsibility fixed and punishment meted out.

Indictments and convictions, divided according to the race of the persons criminally involved, were as follows:

	NEGRO		WHITE	
	Cases	Persons	Cases	Persons
Indictments	6	17	3	4
Convictions	2	3	2	2

Despite the community's failure to deal firmly with those who disturbed its peace and contributed to the reign of lawlessness that shamed Chicago before the world, there is evidence that the riot aroused many citizens of both races to a quickened sense of the suffering and disgrace which had come and might again come to the city, and developed a determination to prevent a recurrence of so disastrous an outbreak of race hatred. . . .

Outstanding Features of the Riot

This study of the facts of the riot of 1919, the events as they happened hour by hour, the neighborhoods involved, the movements of mobs, the part played by rumors, and the handling of the emergency by the various authorities, shows certain outstanding features which may be listed as follows:

a) The riot violence was not continous hour by hour, but was intermittent.

b) The greatest number of injuries occurred in the district west and inclusive of Wentworth Avenue, and south of the south branch of the Chicago River to Fifty-fifth Street, or in the Stock Yards district. The next greatest number occurred in the so-called " Black Belt": Twenty-second to Thirty-ninth streets, inclusive, and Wentworth Avenue to the lake, exclusive of Wentworth Avenue; Thirty-ninth to Fifty-fifth streets, inclusive, and Clark Street to Michigan Avenue, exclusive of Michigan Avenue.

c) Organized raids occurred only after a period of sporadic clashes and spontaneous mob outbreaks.

d) Main thoroughfares witnessed 76 per cent of the injuries of the South Side. The streets which suffered most severely were State, Halsted, Thirty-first, Thirty-fifth, and Forty-seventh. Transfer corners were always centers of disturbances.

e) Most of the rioting occurred after work hours among idle crowds on the streets. This was particularly true after the street-car strike began.

f) Gangs, particularly of young whites, formed definite nuclei for crowd and mob formation. "Athletic clubs" supplied the leaders of many gangs.

g) Crowds and mobs engaged in rioting were generally composed of a small nucleus of leaders and an acquiescing mass of spectators. The leaders were mostly young men, usually between the ages of sixteen and twenty-one. Dispersal was most effectively accomplished by sudden, unexpected gun fire.

h) Rumor kept the crowds in an excited, potential mob state. The press was responsible for giving wide dissemination to much of the inflammatory matter in spoken rumors, though editorials calculated to allay race hatred and help the forces of order were factors in the restoration of peace.

i) The police lacked sufficient forces for handling the riot;

they were hampered by the Negroes' distrust of them; routing orders and records were not handled with proper care; certain officers were undoubtedly unsuited to police or riot duty.

j) The militiamen employed in this riot were of an unusually high type. This unquestionably accounts for the confidence placed in them by both races. Riot training, definite orders, and good staff work contributed to their efficiency.

k) There was a lack of energetic co-operation between the police department and the state's attorney's office in the discovery and conviction of rioters.

The riot was merely a symptom of serious and profound disorders lying beneath the surface of race relations in Chicago. The study of the riot, therefore, as to its interlocking provocations and causes, required a study of general race relations that made possible so serious and sudden an outbreak. Thus to understand the riot and guard against another, the Commission probed systematically into the principal phases of race contact and sought accurate information on matters which in the past have been influenced by dangerous speculation; and on the basis of its discoveries certain suggestions to the community are made.

F. Is America a Violent Society?

Richard Hofstadter, "Spontaneous, Sporadic, and Disorganized," *The New York Times Magazine,* April 28, 1968, p. 112. © 1967/1968 by The New York Times Company. Reprinted by permission of the author and the publisher.

Richard Hofstadter is Professor of American History at Columbia University, New York. He is the author of *The American Political Tradition* and numerous other books and articles, including materials for students.

1. Is America a nation with a violent past? What is the author's attitude? Would you characterize American history as a history of violence?

2. Have men often turned to violence and riots to release frustrations or to achieve goals which were beyond their reach by legal means? Have people turned to violence often enough in America for it to merit the label "a violent society?"

There is a small semantic trap in asking whether America is "by nature" a violent society. "By nature" suggests the possibility of an unchangeable national character. In this I do not believe. But I do think that America, by history and by habit, has been a violent society.

Americans seem to me to show surprising tolerance of violence and a remarkably passive acceptance of the probability that it will recur. The feebleness of our efforts at gun control, even in the face of the grave crisis that is upon us, is an illustration of this passivity. But the distinctive thing about American violence is that it has been spontaneous, sporadic and disorganized. Traditionally, Americans were always strongly antimilitarist. What this meant was not that they had a penchant for pacifism but simply that they did not like standing armies — that is, they were against *institutional* militarism.

Again, it has long seemed to me that the case of the American labor movement is quite pertinent to this theme. As the laboring classes of the industrial world go, ours has been relatively lacking in class-conscious militancy, but no national labor history is so heavily marked by violent struggles in which lives and property were destroyed.

Race has always provided a background for violent conflict, whether in Indian wars, slave insurrections, lynchings or race riots. The race riots of 1919 were as formidable, though not as numerous, as the ghetto riots we have experienced in the last few years. The week-long Chicago riot of 1919, one of a number in the postwar period, left 15 whites and 23 Negroes dead, and 537 injured. The hiatus in major riots that occurred between the Detroit, Harlem, and Los Angeles riots of 1943 and the riots of 1964 may have caused us to forget the frequency of this kind of violence in our history. But we are unlikely to forget it so readily again.

The historical catalogue of American violence is a formidable one. Mob action was already a force of some importance in the political life of colonial America. It goes on from there: a number of fitful rebellions, the long, ruthless struggle with the Indians, our slave insurrections, our filibustering expeditions, our burned convents and mobbed abolitionists and lynched Wobblies, our Homesteads, Pullmans, and Patersons, our race lynchings, race riots, and ghetto riots, our organized gangsterism, our needless wars.

There seems to be more truth than we care to admit in the famous dictum of D. H. Lawrence that (I am quoting from memory) "the essential American soul is hard, isolate, stoic and a killer." It exists, oddly enough, along with a remarkable tenderness about life under certain circumstances. It also exists along with a great readiness to declare ourselves for law and order, to admonish against violence, so long as we are not expected to do anything about it. We have, now, a mountain of fresh sermons against violence, but any zealot, any maniac, can still buy a gun if he has the price. This is one of the sacred rights of American manhood, and it will be hard to give it up, even after we have suffered within the span of a few years the murders of two cherished public men, and even after the black nationalists, in *their* quest of manhood, have started to take their cue from the whites.

G. Is Violence an American Tradition?

St. Clair Drake, "What Is 'Natural' Today Need Not be Natural Tomorrow," *The New York Times Magazine,* April 28, 1968, pp. 24-25. © 1967/1968 by The New York Times Company. Reprinted with permission of the author and the publisher.

St. Clair Drake is Professor of Sociology, Roosevelt University, Chicago. His most famous work is *Black*

Metropolis, a study of Chicago, and he is a popular speaker and prolific author.

1. Is violence expected in America? Is violence traditional? Is it "as American as cherry pie?" How does St. Clair Drake's opinion compare to Richard Hofstadter's argument?

2. Is violence a "natural" outlet for a man's frustration? Or is violence "learned" by Americans as they grow up in our society?

However repulsive and shocking H. Rap Brown's quip may seem — "Violence is as American as cherry pie" — his motive in saying it must not obscure the fact that he was telling it like it is.

The American white-collar set have so little direct experience with violence that it is difficult for them to conceive of it as an ever-present reality — or possibility — in a person's daily life, although they know that the Indians were herded onto the reservations by force, that violence was used both to keep Negroes in slavery and to free them, and that assault and battery, rape and murder occur every now and then. The older people in the labor movement know something of the historic confrontations between trade unionists and the forces of law and order, though younger workers know almost nothing of the great labor struggles of the past. Negroes understand the reality of violence better than most Americans, for most of them have witnessed it in varied forms, even if they have not experienced it. But all Americans need to face the fact that American society — as compared with some others in the world — is a *very* violent society. Self-delusion is self-defeating. We can never lower the level of violence unless we admit that it is omnipresent and understand the forces that generate it.

To admit that "American society is by nature a violent society" is not to succumb to any kind of defeatist determinism, for the intensity of violence has been reduced in some areas of the national life over the past century and its patterning has undergone constant change. The episodes so vividly described in Louis Adamic's "Dynamite, The Story of Class Violence in America," could not possibly occur today. And the barbaric ritual of lynching that used to claim the lives of more than a hundred black men a year disappeared before World War II. The crucial centers of violence shift their locus [place], and more covert and sophisticated forms replace the cruder types of torture and murder. But violence has always functioned in America as a direct or indirect force for changing the status quo [present conditions] as well as for preserving it — and its practitioners seem never to feel guilty or apologetic.

The only interest groups in America which do not have a tradition of using violence to protect themselves from aggressors or to achieve group goals are the Afro-Americans. Yet the segregated Negro communities in America have been characterized by a high rate of *interpersonal* violence for the past hundred years — fighting among family members, brawls incident to drinking and gambling, mayhem and occasional homicide.

These are traits associated with the culture of poverty everywhere, induced by insecurity, frustration, overcrowding and inadequate incomes. Since twice as many families are below the poverty line among Negroes as among whites, a higher level of such violence is to be expected. It was characteristic of Irish, Italian, and Polish communities in the United States before World War I, but for Negroes in the South during the same period the incidence of such violence was higher, because of the additional pressures placed upon them by an oppressive white society and the tendency of courts to be less concerned about the violence of Negroes toward one another than about aggression against white people.

From the end of World War II till 1964, the Northern ghettos were relatively quiet except for this interior violence. Meanwhile, the black people of the South were dismantling the entire caste structure in an amazing exhibition of well-organized nonviolent social action, undeterred by police dogs, water hoses, and cattle prods. The white die-hard segregationists eventually turned to terrorism and assassination, ultimately taking the life of Martin Luther King himself.

In 1964, the "Harlem pattern" of rioting that had emerged more than two decades before was repeated in several cities, as some of the ghetto dwellers began to focus their aggression outward, venting their fury upon " Whitey's" property though not his person. The incidents were usually set off as unplanned, spontaneous protests against a specifically vicious form of American violence that has rubbed the sores raw among ghetto dwellers — police brutality. But it is the stores of white men who do business in the black community that suffer the consequences of black wrath.

This type of violence has escalated, culminating in the arson and looting in more than 100 cities when Dr. King was assassinated [1968]. There is an ominous movement within the black masses away from the nonviolent Afro-American tradition and into the mainstream of the *American* tradition – of Shays's Rebellion and barn-burners; of the Molly Maguires and Ku Klux Klan; of the draft riots of 1863 and John Brown's raid at Harpers Ferry. The black militants who have repudiated non-violence and are making a bid for mass leadership will inevitably draw upon this tradition – as well as upon Frantz Fanon's "Wretched of the Earth," which is now their Bible.

Counterescalation will not eliminate these newly emergent patterns of ghetto violence. However, the transformation of life in the ghetto can — or, alternatively, the dissolution of the ghetto. An answer to labor's needs, not the use of the Army, ended labor violence in America. What is "natural" today need not be natural tomorrow.

Chapter **3**

Toward Explanations for Recent Urban Violence

Turn where you will to listen to differing explanations of riots and urban violence. It would seem that commentators on television and in the newspapers give us little more information than the barber cutting our hair or the mechanic fixing our car. A threatened world is filled with notions about the causes and effects of a riot when it is a recent event. We need common sense, and more, in these days.

This introduction to readings exposing some of the causes of riots attempts to spell out many fundamental ideas of social science. You may judge the value of these ideas in light of the facts in the readings which follow.

The most convenient explanation of the riots is the conspiracy claim. This assumes that groups, either foreign or domestic, have planned and carried out some strategy to incite mob violence and urban turmoil within a given city. The conspirators are thought to attempt radical changes or even a violent overthrow of the existing government. The use of violence and riots may, of course, serve as a strategy to achieve revolutionary goals. Even the threat of violence may serve to get the government to accept certain demands and make reforms. Yet former President Johnson's 1967 commission on civil disorders, often called the Kerner Commission after its chairman, found little evidence of foreign or domestic conspiracy. Other scholarly studies found little evidence of national plotting. Militant statements by radical leaders have tended to arouse officials and the general public — yet these radical leaders have not caused riots within the ghettos, if we believe research reports.

Another convenient theory notes that man is instinctively aggressive. According to this theory, aggression is a basic drive of all humans, as sex or hunger. When man is denied some goal, a general tendency to draw upon his aggressive urges, his deepest, hidden, violent tendencies, become evident. Violence is viewed as a normal way to behave when one is frustrated or provoked.[1] This "human nature" theory is a strongly-held belief of some psychiatrists and many popular authors.

David Potter, an eminent historian of American life, has examined the influence of material abundance on the formation of the American character. He attempts to explain in a rational manner and to avoid mysticism and sentiment. According to his theory, we have benefitted not only by a great wealth of natural resources within the nation, but also, by an exceptional ability to use raw materials to produce vast quantities of finished goods. For most Americans, Potter's explanations would appear to be as follows:[2]

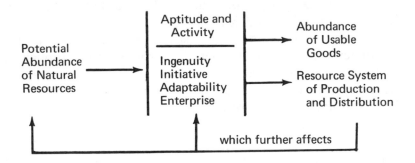

This model reveals inputs and outputs that one associates with American society. Inside the society dynamic activity and aptitude are at work. The outputs of usable goods and an improving system for distributing the goods to people may be thought of as rewards which return to constantly stimulate the discovery and development of more resources and the best

[1] Konrad Lorenz, *On Aggression* (New York: Harcourt, Brace & World, Inc., 1966).
[2] David Potter, *People of Plenty: Economic Abundance and the American Character* (Chicago: University of Chicago Press, Phoenix Books, 1954).

use of our energies. Americans know that they are affluent and they can see how Potter's theory explains their abundance. As one reflects on the reality — the poverty and hopelessness — of ghetto life, however, we can see how Potter's theory is inversely terrible for the "Other America." Urban, Black Americans have had little wealth or credit to capitalize on the natural resources. They have had little chance to change their lot — for the rewards to stimulate further "aptitude and activity" have not come to *them* as return on *their* endeavors. Furthermore, their poverty surrounded by affluence is startling!

Psychological Reasoning

Journalists and psychologists generally agree on a convenient explanation of violence called "scapegoating," or more precisely, "displacement." A frustrated person may find it easier to release his frustration on a weaker party as the immediate target of aggression than on the true source of his difficulty. The true source may be powerful or difficult to reach. For example, the white worker, thrown out of his job by a business depression, cannot attack economic statistics or the causes of the depression to vent his frustrations. But he may attack Negroes migrating from the South into "his" city. The Negroes serve as a weak target, a scapegoat.

More often, psychologists have viewed aggression as one of three possible results of successive, negative experience which frustrates the attainment of a goal.[3] Each repeated effort to attain the goal becomes greater and more intense and frustration gets correspondingly greater. when, finally, the limit of one's tolerance for frustration is reached, the actor will give up the goal (change goals), sink into an imaginary world to pretend that he is succeeding (withdrawal), or lash out in fury at the obstacle in his way (aggression).

---

[3] James Sawrey, "Frustration and Conflict," *Introduction to Psychology* (Dubuque, Iowa: William C. Brown Company, Publishers, 1969).

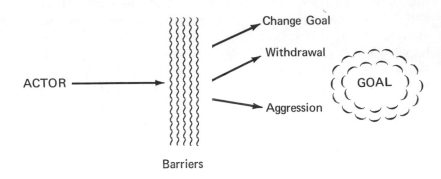

Barriers

This process may be seen in a student who repeatedly fails in school. He may drop out, quietly give up study and pretend to be succeeding, or attack the school windows or teacher in some aggressive way. The notion that whole groups of people, even nations, behave in these ways is easy to believe in light of history. The very least one can say for this frustration-aggression theory is that it suggests a state of readiness for violent behavior when individuals or groups are under stress. On a hot steamy evening when teenagers who can't pay admission into the cool theater are told by the police not to stand on the street corner, they well may act differently from kids awaiting their mother after a morning's swim at the suburban country club.

Life in the ghetto is destructive to the young and old. From early childhood the ghetto dweller experiences treatment from society's agents (the police, garbagemen, shop owners, court officials, etc.) which is most often negative. A small boy learns in school that policemen are his friends, yet cops do not always act toward him in a friendly manner. As his negative experiences with police add up over the years, the boy's "cognitive dissonance" grows. According to the theory of "cognitive dissonance,"[4] the boy filters what he sees through the prejudices he has learned. He begins to see only what is consistent with his prejudices and preconceived

[4] L. Festinger, *A Theory of Cognitive Dissonance* (New York: Harper & Row, Publishers, 1957).

notions. He interprets others' behaviors with set, preestablished notions about how people and society operate. Black Americans in the ghettos are quite understandably frustrated, prone to aggression, and estranged. One would be surprised if cognitive dissonance did not aggravate their hurts as they contact white men, leading them to perceive white men as "enemies" and white society as "oppressive."

Another psychological explanation of behavior is "operant conditioning." When a person has repeated experiences and he reacts to these experiences in a certain manner, this manner is learned and becomes part of his behavior. As similar experiences arise in the future, he draws upon his set pattern of behavior to act.[5] For example, a young male slum dweller learns that a small act of violence helps him achieve his goal (say, a pair of shoes or a theater admission) and the act does not bring any punishment from his fellows or from his society. If this violence, when repeatedly experienced, consistently aids in goal attainment, it tends to support the use of further violence. Violence and the threat of violence become a "normal" pattern.

When we consider *frustration, cognitive dissonance,* and *operant conditioning,* it is amazing to recall that most ghetto aggression is directed toward the ghetto dwellers!

Social Psychological Reasoning

Men do not perceive problems unless they have some goals. First come the goals, then come the obstacles which interfere with the achievement of the goals. Kurt Lewin, a professor of social psychology, illustrated the frustration arising from conflicts over goals by describing a donkey frustrated in three ways.[6] A donkey smells two sweet bales of hay which are widely separated. The double attraction pulls him apart,

[5]The term "operant conditioning" was coined by B. F. Skinner of Harvard University. See R. M. Gagne, *The Conditions of Learning* (New York: Holt, Rinehart & Winston, Inc., 1965), p. 71.
[6]Kurt Lewin, *Field Theory in Social Science,* edited by Darwin Cartwright (New York: Harper & Row, Publishers, 1951). pp. 260-72.

"breaks him up!" He is attracted to both — but he can't approach both at once. He must decide.

The second situation is that of being between two skunks. In this dilemma, the donkey is repelled by both objects but frustrated because getting away from one means getting closer to the other! He must make a move, but which way?

The final situation is called "approach-avoidance" and is the most frustrating of all because the donkey can see and smell both objects so much better — the skunk is sitting on the bale of hay! The donkey is both attracted and repelled by the skunk-hay combo. This is truly distressing.

Life in the ghetto community calls for distressing decisions. To be evicted from a tenement or steal to gain the rent money is a tough problem for an unemployed and "unemployable" man. To drop out of school and get that job at $1.25 per hour or to stick-it-out and hope to get a better job with a diploma is a constant issue for kids. You can recall other conflicts in decision-making situations from earlier readings.

Another theory concerns man's needs and what society expects of him. Man in his happiest state is integrated, that is, he understands what his role is (what is expected of him) and he feels that his personal needs are fulfilled by carrying out that role. Mr. Brown knows what society expects of him as a father, a husband, a worker, a citizen, and a brother. He feels that what society and his family expect him to do is what he personally wants to do. But an observation of ghetto life reveals the conditions of life's failures. What if Mr. Brown's society expects him to provide for his kids, but he can't fulfill this role the way he thinks he should? He wants Johnny to go to college, but he can't muster the required tuition funds. Johnny takes a car wash job. He wants a better house, but can't save enough with five mouths to feed. Mr. Jones wants to be a skilled and industrious worker, as his society expects, but he cannot afford night school classes. If Mr. Jones were to attend night classes, how could he adequately play the father role, expected in our society? These are mild cases. When need disposition and social role expectations are very different, men are unable to satisfy themselves or others.[7]

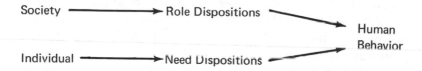

People living in such a manner become highly confused, disorganized, or frustrated. They are confused about what to do or about what is "right." This confusion and feeling of disorganization is called "anomie" by social scientists.

The confused individual or group, feeling this anomie, becomes alienated or estranged from the society. The ghetto

[7] Jacob Getzels, "Administration as a Social System," *Administrative Theory In Education,* ed. Andrew Kaplan (Chicago: Midwest Education Center, 1968), p. 156.

dweller in such a circumstance becomes goalless, apathetic, and defensive. He comes to believe that he cannot control his own destiny, *his* future, or *his* present. An air of futility and hostility toward the organized and otherwise respected ways of society hangs over him in all that he tries and all that he does.

If we accept these theories as explaining behavior in the ghetto and if we see conditions of "social disorganization" and "anomie" in the slums, we can say that the old habits and forms of social control no longer function efficiently. The psychological and social forces that normally mediate for and against violence tend to become unbalanced easily. Belief in the "Golden Rule" and in the rule of law are values which become loosened due to either social pressures to be "successful" in a ghetto where one cannot get the education to obtain a decent job or by examples of persons ignoring the law. Others, forced by environment into petty illegal acts, are dealt with severly by society's defenders of law and order. The confusion over "right" and "wrong" and over other basic values means that there is confusion about the use of rioting, looting, and violence.

Too often one may observe people in authority making decisions without regard for the environment with its many figures affecting the life of each individual. Gordon Allport, a professor at Harvard, has suggested that personal relationships are mediated by the behavior of many apparently disinterested parties. Social welfare professionals as well as police, employers, shop owners, and others take a simple view of their relationship with ghetto dwellers. Welfare policies and school programs to aid ghetto dwellers are restricted when the library checks out books for two days to "slum kids" and for three weeks to their affluent neighbors. The merchants' meat prices and qualities are psychological cues. Police behavior signals to teenagers their status more than talk about Job Corps. Likewise, a gas station owner's decision to lend tools to his "hired hand" for fixing his car at home may have a very positive impact upon the "hand's" thought about night school. Pawn-shop owners, slum neighbors, and the entire ghetto social environment have their impact upon each person's behavior.[8]

Some students of urban social problems have developed a theory of "social cramp." This theory is used to explain the growth of frustration and hostility by persons who do have high aspirations and who are moving up the social ladder. The basic premise is that "strain" emerges due to a maladjustment in a society, for as people labor to improve their position they are dissatisfied by the slow rate of change in their status or by their failure to get what they thought they were going to achieve. Negroes, who struggled for a college education and find that they get jobs with mediocre white, high school educated workers, feel cramped. Conversely, federal legislation, long sought by the NAACP, removed discrimination in employment opportunities, but did not qualify Negroes for the jobs they wanted in technical, high-paying positions. Being *closer* than before to an unobtainable goal is even *more frustrating,* for it again leads to a hopeless condition from which one wishes to burst forth.

Sociological Reasoning

Our effort to explain some reasons why various groups may behave aggressively suggests the question, "At what point in the development of general disorganization, frustration, and anomie will men revolt?" The social psychologist would immediately say that such social conditions just create a readiness to act aggressively and that persons in "readiness" need visual or verbal cues (police, rumors, bill collectors, agitators) to invoke violent acts. Sociologists, however, would use other theories. We may attempt to use the thoughts of Robert Mertin, Kai Erickson, and James C. Davies. Merton notes that anyone who seeks solutions to the problem of obtaining his goals falls into one of four categories if he is to remain obedient to current social procedures.[9]

[8] Gordon W. Allport, *Personality: A Psychological Interpretation* (New York: Holt, Rinehart & Winston, Inc., 1937), p. 364.

[9] Robert Merton, *Social Theory and Social Structure* (Glencoe, Ill.: The Free Press, 1949), p. 133.

GOALS

		+	−
MEANS	+	Conformist	Ritualist
	−	Innovator	Retreatist

The *conformist* adjusts to the goals set for him by society and to the procedures deemed acceptable for him in pursuing goals. Most middle class Americans may be in this category, seeking the goals agreed upon by society and in the manner established by society. The accountant rushes off to work each morning in white collar and blue suit, hoping for a raise and perhaps some carpeting on the office floor with the next promotion. The teenager emerges from the suburban home each morning to pursue the Good Life by getting "A's" on true/false tests at school. Most inhabitants of the ghetto do not follow this pattern; those who do are held in contempt by the militant leaders. The *innovator* accepts the goals of the society but does not accept the means which are prescribed. Dr. Martin Luther King was an innovator as he advocated civil disobedience. The *ritualist* does not agree with the goals but accept the means which he performs in a mechanical way. The NAACP and the Urban League patiently fought for minority rights in the courts for years, using the means to goals provided by the society, without always accepting the goals dictated by society. The *retreatist* disagrees with both the goals and the means to goal attainment, does nothing about it, and tends to withdraw. Should a retreatist shed his apathy, he is likely to become part of a rebellion. Negroes have traditionally retreated in America, but it seems superfluous to note that fewer are withdrawing now.

The minority of individuals who are not in any of the four categories are those ready to participate in open rebellion against social controls and authority. They are the violent ones who will come forward to riot and destroy the physical characteristics of the despised ghetto with no more provocation than now exists. Others may join them as anomie increases and they lose faith in the goals and means provided by society.

Kai Erickson suggests that the ghetto dweller is incited to riot when anomie is greatest. This is the point when the distance between the values of people (their goals) and their actual conditons of life (reality) is greatest. Erickson refers to this distance between goals and reality as "The Anomic Gap." Logically, it follows that the probability of a riot occurring is reduced after the point of maximum distance has passed. [10]

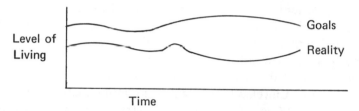

Professor Davies believes that revolutions are most likely to occur when a different, yet related, set of factors are present. When a prolonged period of economic and social advancement is followed by a short, sharp reversal, the chance of rebellion is greatest. People in this situation have been getting a higher standard of living or greater freedom and have increased their expectations of future improvements. They have received more and expect still more in the future. The sharp reversal (an economic depression, a war, an adverse government policy) thwarts their anticipated advances and may threaten the improvements obtained in the past. The thwarting is the creator of frustration and aggression. [11]

[10] Kai Erickson, *Wayward Puritans: A Study In The Sociology of Deviance* (New York: John Wiley & Sons, Inc., 1966).

[11] James C. Davies, "Toward A Theory of Revolution," *The American Sociological Review,* Volume 27 (1962), 5-19.

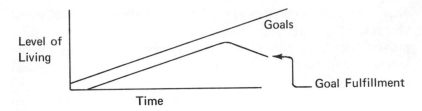

Davies' and Erickson's theories have several common features: the comparison of goals and aspirations over time, the comparison of reality as seen by people over time, and the critical distance between goals and perceived reality. Davies stresses that rebellion comes after people have experienced some successful movement toward their goals, which suddenly become threatened. Erickson notes that anomie is a gradual build-up, with persons gradually deserting the goals and means established and approved by the society. These persons join a rebellious, alienated "camp."

As you read about the violence of Kansas City, Detroit, Los Angeles, and Cleveland, you will find some analysis and many facts. The profile of a rioter will strengthen your intuition and sharpen your knowledge. This effort to view the causes in psychological and sociological ways is to give some structure to the facts. It is your task to explain the causes and it is the scholars' task to help in this effort. Refer back to their theories as you read.

H.   The Turn to Violence

James E. Alsbrook, "The Turn to Violence," *The New Republic*, February 17, 1968, pp. 15-16. Copyright 1968 by Harrison-Blaine of New Jersey, Inc. Reprinted with permission of the publisher.

1. Why did the boys throw rocks? What was their objective? What did they hope to gain by this behavior?

2. Why did the author stress the middle class background of the rock-throwers?

3. Why do people turn to violence and rioting? What does the author think rioters hope to gain by their behavior? Do you agree? Why? Why not? Can you tie his thoughts to one or more of the social science theories in the introduction to this chapter?

At almost midnight, three Negro boys walked silently through an alley near a furniture store. Bricks in hand, they looked up and down the well-lighted street, threw the bricks through two large plate-glass windows and ran like scared rabbits.

"I feel better now," one said when they slowed to a trot several blocks away. "We got even with that peckerwood," another said.

The place was Kansas City, Kansas. The time was before World War II, and I was one of the boys.

Our neighborhood was not a slum or ghetto. It was quiet, with grassy lawns and single-family homes. Strong father-figures and male breadwinners were in each of our homes. We played with neighborhood white boys nearly every day. Our grandparents had been in the North since the 1880's. My mother was a public schoolteacher and church organist.

Why did we strictly reared boys of the so-called middle class suddenly and deliberately violate firm rules that had been pounded into us at home, at school and at church?

We didn't really know. We told ourselves we were "getting even." That white merchant was advertising mattresses by showing life-size paintings of plantation "niggers" happily picking cotton and eating watermelon. We had asked him to remove them and he laughed, calling us a word we never heard before — "pickaninnies."

We couldn't explain to ourselves why on Halloween night we felt relieved after we had ruined the merchant's front door, painted insults on his windows and dumped more paint on new lumber piled behind his store. We were proud of ourselves when later we saw his white truck driver try to deliver a load of furniture we had ordered to an address in the middle of Big Eleven Lake. "Stupid . . . stupid," one of us said, as the driver stared into the deep water.

If these were the tumultuous feelings of three middle-class, carefully disciplined, Northern-bred Negro boys, what extremes are possible when the Negro is poverty-plagued, ghetto-bound, educationally handicapped, self-hating, racially humiliated, frustrated?

After the riots in Negro ghettos during the last three summers, I visited Harlem, Brooklyn, Philadelphia, Cincinnati, Chicago, and East St. Louis, talking with people. Listening to their explanations and justifications for the violence, I could see that they – like we three teen-agers in Kansas City – had experienced a badly needed sort of therapy. The rioter *does* gain self-esteem by publicly playing the role of a bold, uncompromising fellow whom others fear. (Example from Philadelphia: "I felt free – 'born again' – after I saw what I had done.")

They were rejecting too . . . white men's values. Unable to achieve "manhood" and equality in a racially biased value system, the rioter rejects the system as a whole and adopts rules consonant with *his* aspirations. (Chicago: "The white man made the rules and then dealt himself all the aces. To hell with him.")

Symbols of that white power – the police and the exploiting merchants – have to be dishonored, and in the presence of one's peers. (Example from Harlem: "Hell yes, and I'm glad I did it. . . I cleaned him good. Blue eyes has been robbing and killing us with the law on his side. Got to get rid of him before we can get ourselves straight." Listeners agreed.)

In looting, rioters were taking "part payment" for nearly 250 years of slave labor and 100 years of discriminatory jobs and wages. (Brooklyn: "I was just taking what belongs to one of my great-grandparents.") (From Philadelphia: "They owe us a hell of a lot more than we took.") Society got the message – and was meant to. (Chicago: "I'm sick of all this crap about violence in the streets. Where I come from a black son-of-a-bitch ain't safe from the white bastards even at home or in church, let alone the damned streets.") (Harlem: "Yes we're mad and we want them to know it. We need to burn the whole damned thing down – or blow it up – and get a new start!")

The knowledge that frustration breeds aggression is old and worldwide. The Matsushita Electrical Company of Osaka, Japan, has set up a "human control room" into which an angry or frustrated employee is urged to go, grab a bamboo stick and beat effigies [images] of his bosses until his anger has subsided. The smiling effigies are labeled with the names of supervisors.

We've seen this frustration-aggression pattern again and again in America. When Nat Turner, a half-literate Negro preacher, led 75 freedom-seeking slaves into revolt [1831], killing 55 whites, he and 16 of his followers were executed – following which mobs of whites took revenge by killing more than 100 innocent slaves and free Negroes.

In 1863, after President Lincoln had drafted more New York City men for the Union Army, hundreds of white men raged through town, robbing stores and sacking and burning buildings. Many Negroes, including women and children, were beaten to death or hanged to lamp posts. Deaths were estimated at from 400 to 2,000. Eight years later, 33 persons were killed during riots of the Irish in New York.

But my concern here is the black man, whose whole American experience has been dominated by violence. He was enslaved, emancipated, disfranchised, segregated and suppressed – all by violence or the threat of it. For years the lynchings (nearly 4,000 since 1889 – principally of Negroes), church bombings, street murders, Klan floggings and burnings generally went unpunished. No loud outcry welled up over the nation! Not then!

Now some people have the effrontery to wonder why the black man turns to violence!

I. The Hard-Core Ghetto Mood

"The Hard-Core Ghetto Mood," *Newsweek,* August 21, 1967, pp. 20-26. Reprinted with permission of the publisher.

1. Does the riot fervor stem from the *emotional state* of ghetto dwellers? Are they seeking thrills and excitement? Expressing repressed emotions?

2. Does the riot fervor stem from the hostile, aggressive *habits* of ghetto dwellers? Are they acting out learned hostility toward whites? Is violence a usual type of behavior?

3. Which theory of causation does this article support? Why? Does it support more than one theory? How?

He is a child of Detroit's ravaged ghetto, a lanky, spidery-legged kid whose hand-me-down pants stop at shin's length short of his narrow, pointy shoes. He sat with some of his pals on the railing outside an apartment house, gazing dully across Dexter Avenue at a block of charred ruins. It had been two weeks, but the acrid scent of smoke still hung in the air.

"Those buildings goin' up was a pretty sight," the long-legged kid said. "I sat right here and watched them go. And there wasn't nothin' them honkies could do but sweat and strain to put it out."

"Yeah, man," a pal chimed in, "it's about time those honkies started earnin' their money in this neighborhood."

"You know," said Long Legs, "we made big news. They called this the country's worst race riot in history."

"Yeah," said another gangly kid, straddling the railing. "My

*kids goin' to study about that in school and they'll know
their old man was part of it."*

"We got the record, man," exulted another youth, the
beefiest of the lot. *"They can forget all about Watts and
Newark and Harlem. This is where the riot to end all riots
was held."*

"That little girl that got shot, man," Long Legs said. *"She
shouldn't have been shot."*

"That's the breaks, brother," Beefy replied, absently patting
at the deep waves in his processed hair. *"We in a war. Or
hasn't anybody told you that?"*

Everybody laughed.

They are another country, a land behind the looking-glass, a
people as tragically distant from the ken of most white and
many Negro Americans as the dark side of the moon. For
decades, their world was invisible; now, in this fourth long,
hot summer, it stands silhouetted in the light of a thousand
fires — and as remote from understanding as ever. "First — let
there be no mistake about it — the looting, arson, plunder
and pillage which have occurred are not part of a civil-rights
protest," Lyndon Johnson said in his post-Detroit television
report [1967] to the nation. "That is crime — and crime
must be dealt with forcefully, swiftly, certainly . . ." It was an
accurate statement of the American law and the American
will. But the hard-core ghetto — and particularly the ghetto
young — speak quite another language.

And their tongue, in an hour of national peril, is well worth
understanding. It is not the common tongue of Negro
Americans. It tends at once to excite and chill those Negroes
who have struggled somehow into a growing black middle
class. It troubles many of the ghetto poor themselves —
particularly the older poor whose lives are centered on the
day-to-day issues of survival. It is instead the lingua franca
[common language] of a minority within a minority: the
angry young men consigned from broken homes through
inadequate schools to a future of work at poverty wages — or,
for more than one ghetto youth in four, the dole and the

streets. It is the language of the people who make riots — and its use is spreading fast.

It is also the language of a garrison state. In the view from the street corners of Harlem or Watts or Detroit's West Side, the riots are rebellions, the rioters not criminals at all but the freedom fighters of an oppressed, beleaguered, powerless colony of the white world downtown. Words of bitterness suppressed for generations become the common currency. Stokely Carmichael and Rap Brown are the heroes because they say aloud, on national TV, what older Negroes had hardly dared think. "I hope you don't expect me to rap Rap," says a pert Harlem girl of 18 who wears her close-cropped "natural" coif almost like a flag of liberation. "He's kinda crazy — but it's a feel-good crazy."

There is now an air of desperation in the ghettos. Some say Whitey may listen; others actually believe he might even contemplate a Final Solution of concentration camps and gas chambers; but many of the ghetto young think the risk is worth all — even a man's life. Ed Bowen is a high-school dropout of 26; he fled from one failure to another, in the Army in Georgia, where he stole a jeep, wrecked it, and was cashiered just thirteen days before his honorable discharge was due. Now he is back scuffling in Harlem and he says: "People have been begging for years for a decent place to live, a job, some food, but they ain't got nothing, so they burn things down and maybe they'll get it," Bowen is, relatively speaking, an optimist. Others simply expect to die fighting — and are beyond caring. "I don't mind gettin' killed," says Donald, a jobless, 19-year-old corner boy in Chicago. "When I'm dead, they'll tell my kid, 'He died for a good cause'."

The cause, as the street corner sees it, is to seize the white man's attention by force, since a decade of nonviolent protest seems not to have altered the ghetto's life materially, and to make him look at what he has wrought. The riots are blind, deadly, destructive, criminal, yes — but to say they have nothing to do with "civil rights" is quite to miss the point. The rioters range, says Dr. Alvin Poussaint, a Negro psychiatrist at Tufts University, "from the plain damn angry to those with fantasies of taking over, to those who want a TV set, to those angry at their father and mother, to those caught up in hysteria, to those who will act only when they see the cops shoot someone." But he adds: "Rage is common to all of them." The rage is directed at the cheated hopes, the despondence and finally the suffocating emptiness of the ghetto. "The chronic riot of their day-to-day lives," says Negro psychologist Kenneth Clark, "is, as far as they're concerned, no better than the acute riots. . . . They don't have anything to lose, including their lives. It's not just desperation — it's what-the-hell."

Nor can the riots be written off as merely the holiday of the chronic criminal. In the benchmark insurrections of four summers — Watts, Newark, Detroit — roughly half the Negroes arrested on miscellaneous riot charges had no police records at all. " There is a growing body of myths emerging about the riots," said a UCLA task force reporting on a newly completed two-year study of Watts [1965]. "They center around the effort to distinguish between the 'good Negro' and the 'bad Negro'. . . .This leads to the numbers game of guessing the percentage of 'bad Negroes' (2 to 5 per cent seems to be popular) and to a rationalization of better use of police power to deal with them." The task force's findings were quite to the contrary: its study indicated that 15 per cent of adult Watts Negroes actually joined the riot and 35 to 40 per cent were "active" — and approving — spectators. And afterward, one Watts Negro in three approved of the riot; the majority who disapproved often expressed sympathy with the rioters or a sort of community pride that they had made the invisible man visible around the world.

Pride, indeed, is the first stunning fact discovered by the alien — and most whites today are alien — who crosses the line into that other country. "There's some sort of emancipation in it," says Poussaint. "It's like a festival, a sudden release of tensions, a feeling that they have freed themselves." Frederick J. Hacker, a white University of

Southern California psychiatrist who crossed the line into postwar Watts, came back with similar findings. As Watts saw it, Hacker wrote, the riot "was the metamorphosis [changing point] of the Negroes . . . from victims — historical objects — to masters . . . The people of Watts felt that for those four days they represented all Negroes; the historic plight of the Negroes; all the rebellions against all injustice. . . . What must be understood by the rest of America is that, for the lower-class Negro, riots are not criminal, but a legitimate weapon in a morally justified Civil War."

The sense of accomplishment is, of course, misplaced. The Watts riot did evoke successive visitations of the National Guard, the governor of California and whole platoons of social scientists, social workers and social engineers, all with precious little impact on the day-to-day facts of life in poverty. Yet the anniversary of the riot is still memorialized in a weeklong summer festival, and not even Mayor Sam Yorty — a man little noted for his pre-riot attentions to Watts — feels he can afford to stay away. "Watts is not a rat-infested slum like you find in the East," Yorty beamed at the opening of Watts's second birthday party last week [1967], "and the true face of Watts is represented here today."

Maybe. But one very real face of Watts today is the face of victory — the face of the invisible man made visible. Efelka Brown, 29, is the assistant manager of a newly opened service station where Watts's equivalent of the Veterans of Foreign Wars, the "Sons of Watts," will train the idle young in a tradeable skill. "We rioted in Watts," says Brown. "The Man put up the doctors' building down the street, they going to build us up a clinic and the way I heard, people don't have to pay but a dollar a year and that's for paper work. They have did this for us after the riot. What are these people riotin' about in other cities? They want recognition . . . and the only way they goin' get it is to riot. The only way . . . We don't want to overthrow the country — we just want what we ain't got."

And there is the equally real face of defeat. On the burnt-out block called Charcoal Alley No. 1, Henry Leonard

Johnson Jr. lay flat in the grass, slugged at a 50-cent bottle of Applejack wine and delivered a soliloquy to a relentlessly sunny and utterly indifferent sky. He had, he announced, spent twelve of his 28 years in jail; as a consequence he could not find work; there is a car-wash job in Torrance, but Torrance is 20 miles away and Johnson has no car. So he lay in the grass and sipped his wine and told the sky, "F—— Whitey. I don't believe in nothin'. I feel like they ought to burn down the whole world. Just let it burn down, baby."

Henry Leonard Johnson Jr. is an authentic American monument — a ruin of the Negro's passage from slavery through the serfdom of cropping shares in the South and the northward flight to what the late Negro sociologist E. Franklin Frazier aptly predicted would prove "the city of destruction." The South, which preens itself today on having escaped the most savage of the slum rioting, prepared the Negro for that passage by bringing him up a segregated, semiliterate field hand. And the North, which often fancies that is has been laboring toward full equality since Emancipation, tends to forget that segregation was tacitly accepted national policy at least into the 1940's and 1950's (when Harry Truman abolished it in the armed forces and the Supreme Court outlawed it in the schools). The invisible man is quite painfully aware that he has been visible mostly when he made himself so. "The riots," says Berkeley sociologist Robert Blauner, "are the culmination of ten years of organized protest . . . [The school decision in] 1954 was the last time a basic change in race relations was brought about by a white institution. Now the Negroes themselves have become the prime historic factors, not just the objects of history."

Yet the Negro remains, in the city of destruction, a prisoner of his history. He is the last of the immigrants. A black population that was three-fourths Southern rural in 1910 is three-fourths urban today, and the northward exodus has spilled 5.3 million black newcomers into the ghettos since 1950. The Negro arrived with few more marketable assets than a strong back at precisely a period of history when strong backs were becoming obsolescent. The new technology swallowed up unskilled and semiskilled jobs; now machines dig ditches, wash dishes, run elevators. The new suburbia drained off middle-class whites; two big cities (Washington and Newark) have black majorities today and 23 others may have by 1982 at the ghetto's present explosive rates of birth and migration.

Nor has the spate [increased amount] of civil-rights and poverty legislation of the 1960's substantially changed anything. The ghetto's core problems are as staggeringly bad as ever. Some are getting worse.

Unemployment in the black slums runs at depression levels by the conventional measures: the latest Bureau of Labor Statistics reading, issued last week, placed unemployment rates at 7.2 per cent for Negroes generally, 24.8 per cent for Negro youth. Both figures are roughly double the rates for whites – a gap that has persisted for thirteen years. And those figures are almost comforting against the realities of the black slums. They do not count people who have given up looking for work, or who cannot draw subsistence wages, or who are working part-time when they need full-time jobs. And they miss those literally invisible souls – perhaps a fifth to a third of the ghetto's adult Negro men – who simply vanish when the census-taker comes calling.

So the U. S. Labor Department went back to the drawing boards last fall, ran a ten-ghetto survey that counted in the hidden unemployed and underemployed, and concluded: "Unemployment – or sub-employment – in the city slums is so much worse than it is in the country as a whole that the national measurements of unemployment are irrelevant . . . The situation there is that more than a third are unable to earn a living, and between 10 and 20 per cent of those who ought to be working aren't working at all." The economic boom was equally irrelevant. "No conceivable increase in the gross national product would stir these backwaters," the Labor report said. ". . . Unemployment in these areas is primarily a story of inferior education, no skills, police and garnishment records, discrimination, fatherless children, dope addiction, hopelessness."

Ghetto housing is a disaster; 43 per cent of it is substandard and overcrowded. Government slum-clearance programs have leveled 700,000 dwellings since 1937, replaced them with only 600,000 public-housing units (plus a good many middle-income towers) and thus accelerated the squeeze on the slum's moldering, rat-ridden tenements. Ghetto schools are a failure, more segregated now than they were in 1954 and tragically ill-equipped to deal with the children of the city of destruction. A three-year-old Harlem study shows that pupil performance — and even IQ's — actually declined between the third and sixth grades. Preschoolers respond to Head Start classes, then backslide when they reach the ghetto's regular classrooms. Children are bucked along from grade to grade till they graduate — or drop out, as nearly half do.

"Our average applicant," says Gary Robinson, director of an employment center in Boston's Roxbury ghetto, "has an eleventh-grade education and a third-grade reading level." Sociologist Philip Morris Hauser, chairman of the University of Chicago's Center for Urban Studies, ponders the dreary record and concludes: "We're making sure the next generation of Negro children will be as unprepared as this generation."

Everything conspires against the Negro. He has no resources and therefore no power; even Harlem's numbers racket, as psychologist Clark once dourly noted, is run by white men downtown. The welfare system at once sustains him (six of ten Negro children subsist at one time or another on the dole) and humiliates him in the process. "Our society," says Mary Piven of Columbia University's school of social work, "always punishes people before it helps them." The ghetto's mental state, says psychiatrist Hacker, amounts to a "form of chronic mild depression." Only death doesn't short-change the Negro; his disease rates run high — one Harlem block is so TB-ridden that residents call it "Lung Street" — and he dies, on the average, seven years younger than whites.

The whole brutal cycle ends in what academicians call the "culture of poverty" — a sort of permanent anomie in which crime rates spiral, liquor and drugs beckon the desperate, families crumble, and failure becomes an accepted condition of life. Urbanist Daniel (Pat) Moynihan catalogued all the ugly statistics of destruction two years ago in the much-publicized, much-misunderstood "Moynihan Report": the numbingly high rates of family breakup, welfare dependency, illegitmate births. Those figures have been getting worse, too. "Probably not more than a third of the children of low-income Negro families now reach 18 having lived all their life with both their parents," Moynihan wrote in a follow-up piece for Long Island's Newsday. ". . . Breakdown in family relations among poor persons is a pretty good clue that a *lumpenproletariat* is forming" — a depressed, alienated and finally destructive urban underclass.

They roared on two wheels into "Burma Road" — Harlem's name for Lenox Avenue — and braked for beers at the Royal Flush Bar. The car belongs to Joe-Joe, a chunky, dark 20-year-old who stuck through high school and now works at the Post Office. But the bierklatsch [party] is on J. B., a young man of flash and dash in his crisp yellow sport shirt, his hip-hugging black gabardines, and his rakish, stingy-brim straw hat. J.B., at 20, is a numbers runner; he has a hustle, and he has it made.

"The Man, he worried now," say J.B., " 'cause he know we ain't takin' no more his s———. Anybody come rollin' into a city with tanks got to be afraid of somethin'. Anyplace you see a tank, you know there got to be a war goin' on, right? And that's what this is, baby — war!"

No one disagrees. Someone mentions Rap Brown.

"That's my man!" J.B. exclaims. "Ain't nobody in the world gonna get nothin' if he don't fight for it. The black man's been takin' low too long."

'That's right, that's right," says Skeeter. He is 19 and nowhere, a dropout (at 14) living with a sister and an aunt, and whatever J.B. says, Skeeter echoes, "That's right."

But Joe-Joe half disagrees. "I used to watch ole Stokely up there on TV tellin' off the white people. I thought he was crazy, 'cause I thought he was gonna get hisself killed like Malcolm. But you know, when a man says what all the time you been thinkin', you wonder if maybe you ain't crazy. I mean like if you feel inside knotted all the time, maybe it's better if you make some noise." He sips at his beer. "Like when I broke my big toe cuttin' the fool [roughhousing] out at Coney Island. I went on limpin' around grinnin', not lettin' on to nobody I was hurt. But I had to tell 'em 'cause I couldn't stand it no more. And like, you know, these two cats crossed their arms and made like a seat and carried me to the beach clinic. Now supposin' I hadn't said nothin'?"

So Joe-Joe figures that, if there is another Harlem riot, he will join in. "Man," he says, "you know my sister wouldn't let me in the street that last time. But I bet you I'm gonna get me somethin' next time . . . I just might break me some windows, grab me some rags and throw me some bottles."

J.B. isn't sure. He "wouldn't mind knockin' me some cracker heads together," but, like any budding entrepreneur, ["businessman"] he thinks rioting might be bad for business. Yet he too will be there if a new riot comes. "I mean," he says, "that's where it's at."

And so the riots are, at least in part, a declaration of dependence on white America; they are as well, in a curious way, an act not of utter despair but of flickering hope that white America may at last listen. But a riot is, of course, the most primitive form of protest, and some of the public dialogue the riots have produced — notably in the U.S. Congress — has been a response in kind. There is the widespread superstition that to attempt to understand the roots of rioting is to condone the riots, that to act would be to reward the rioters. It was in just such a spirit that the House laughed down a $40 million slum rat-control program Snorted sociologist Hauser afterward: "The Marie Antoinette Congress 'Let them have rats'."

Even among those disposed to listen, the riots have produced a wave of confusion — and a sense not of defeat but of the failure of all that has been done so far. "The riots themselves are the best evaluations of what's been done," says Kenneth Clark, and even some of the Great Society's own architects agree. Civil-rights legislation has been largely directed at Southern-style Jim Crow, not the ills of the Northern ghetto. Urban renewal has tightened the white noose around the black slums. An undernourished poverty program has reached no more than 10 per cent of the 2 million adult poor and the 1 million jobless young who need training or experience to get work. Some of the idle have been trained for nonexistent jobs. There is a recognition at once that vast sums of money are needed and that money alone will not do the trick. "Administratively," says Ralph Gakenheimer, a University of North Carolina city planner, "the easiest thing to do is spend money." But few cities spent as much as Detroit, and now a sobered Washington topsider says glumly: "There will be more Detroits."

For no one imagines any longer that there will be any quick solutions. The talk now, among urban-affairs experts in and out of government is that only a massive public commitment and at least a generation of effort will be required to repair and thus pacify the ghettos. Some feel a generation has been lost already — the disaffected down-and-outers among today's ghetto young. "There are a number of Negroes already who can't be won back," says a Negro government civil-rights man. "From here on there will be revolutionaries, and offering them a job, a TV, or a car will no longer bring them back." . . .

And the clock is running.
Percy Wiggins went into the Army with a police record, served a year in Vietnam, came home to Chicago three

months ago confident that his service record would help him land a job. It hasn't, and now Wiggins is bitter. "I couldn't even get a job driving a cab," he said. "The lowest job in the world and I couldn't even get that. You know, now I feel I made a great mistake goin' to Vietnam. Over there I fought with the white guys and I was considered a man. Now I'm nothin' but a lousy dog."

So now he runs with the old crowd, the hard ghetto kids he thought he had outgrown in the Army, and he is beginning to speak their language. "I'm not sayin' it's good to burn down another man's home," he says. "But if that's what it takes to do it, I say burn it down."

J. The Profile of a Rioter

Report of the National Advisory Commission on Civil Disorders, Washington, D. C.: Government Printing Office, 1968, pp. 73-77.

1. What characteristics of rioters did the 1967 Commission find through its study? How does its "profile of a rioter" compare to your image of the "typical rioter?"

2. How do the characteristics of the rioters relate to the theories in the introduction to this chapter?

The Profile of a Rioter

The typical rioter in the summer of 1967 was a Negro, unmarried male between the ages of 15 and 24. He was in many ways very different from the stereotype. He was not a migrant. He was born in the state and was a lifelong resident of the city in which the riot took place. Economically his position was about the same as his Negro neighbors who did not actively participate in the riot.

Although he had not, usually, graduated from high school, he was somewhat better educated than the average inner-city Negro, having at least attended high school for a time.

Nevertheless, he was more likely to be working in a menial or low status job as an unskilled laborer. If he was employed, he was not working full time and his employment was frequently interrupted by periods of unemployment.

He feels strongly that he deserves a better job and that he is barred from achieving it, not because of lack of training, ability, or ambition, but because of discrimination by employers.

He rejects the white bigot's stereotype of the Negro as ignorant and shiftless. He takes great pride in his race and believes that in some respects Negroes are superior to whites. He is extremely hostile to whites, but his hostility is more apt to be a product of social and economic class than of race; he is almost equally hostile toward middle class Negroes.

He is substantially better informed about politics than Negroes who were not involved in the riots. He is more likely to be actively engaged in civil rights efforts, but is extremely distrustful of the political system and of political leaders.

Race

Of the arrestees 83 percent were Negroes; 15 percent were whites. Our interviews in 20 cities indicate that almost all rioters were Negroes.

Ages

The survey data from Detroit, the arrest records, and our interviews in 20 cities all indicate that the rioters were late teenagers or young adults. In the Detroit survey, 61.3 percent of the self-reported rioters were between the ages or 15 and 24, and 86.3 percent were between 15 and 35. The arrest data indicate that 52.5 percent of the arrestees were between 15 and 24, and 80.8 percent were between 15 and 35.

Of the noninvolved, by contrast, only 22.6 percent in the Detroit survey were between 15 and 24, and 38.3 percent were between 15 and 35.

Sex

In the Detroit survey, 61.4 percent of the self-reported rioters were male. Arrestees, however, were almost all male — 89.3 percent. Our interviews in 20 cities indicate that the majority of rioters were male. The large difference in proportion between the Detroit survey data and the arrestee figures probably reflects either selectivity in the arrest process or less dramatic, less provocative riot behavior by women.

Family Structure

Three sources of available information — the Newark survey, the Detroit arrest study, and arrest records from four cities — indicate a tendency for rioters to be single. The Newark survey indicated that rioters were single — 56.2 percent — more than the noninvolved — 49.6 percent.

The Newark survey also indicates that rioters were more likely to have been divorced or separated — 14.2 percent — than the noninvolved — 6.4 percent. However, the arrest records from four cities indicate that only a very small percentage of those arrested fall into this category.

In regard to the structure of the family in which he was raised, the self-reported rioter, according to the Newark survey, was not significantly different from many of his Negro neighbors who did not actively participate in the riot. Twenty-five and five-tenths percent of the self-reported rioters and 23 percent of the noninvolved were brought up in homes where no adult male lived.

Region of Upbringing

Both survey data and arrest records demonstrate unequivocally that those brought up in the region in which the riot occurred are much more likely to have participated in the riots. The percentage of self-reported rioters brought up in the North is almost identical for the Detroit survey — 74.4 percent — and the Newark survey — 74 percent. By contrast, of the noninvolved, 36 percent in Detroit and 52.4 percent in

Newark were brought up in the region in which the disorder occurred.

Data available from five cities on the birthplace of arrestees indicate that 63 percent of the arrestees were born in the North. Although birthplace is not necessarily identical with place of upbringing, the data are sufficiently similar to provide strong support for the conclusion.

Of the self-reported counterrioters, however, 47.5 percent were born in the North, according to the Detroit survey, a figure which places them between self-reported rioters and the noninvolved. Apparently, a significant consequence of growing up in the South is the tendency toward noninvolvement in a riot situation, while involvement in a riot, either in support of or against existing social institutions, was more common among those born in the North.

Residence

Rioters are not only more likely than the noninvolved to have been born in the region in which the riot occurred, but they are also more likely to have been long-term residents of the city in which the disturbance took place. The Detroit survey data indicate that 59.4 percent of the self-reported rioters, but only 34.6 percent of the noninvolved, were born in Detroit. The comparable figures in the Newark survey are 53.5 percent and 22.5 percent.

Outsiders who temporarily entered the city during the riot might have left before the surveys were conducted and therefore may be underestimated in the survey data. However, the arrest data, which is contemporaneous with the riot, suggest that few outsiders were involved: 90 percent of those arrested resided in the riot city, 7 percent lived in the same state, and only 1 percent were from outside the state. Our interviews in 20 cities corroborate these conclusions.

Income

In the Detroit and Newark survey data, income level alone does not seem to correlate with self-reported riot participation. The figures from the two cities are not directly comparable since respondents were asked for individual income in Detroit and family income in Newark. More Detroit self-reported rioters (38.6 percent) had annual incomes under $5,000 per year than the noninvolved (30.3 percent), but even this small difference disappears when the factor of age is taken into account.

In the Newark data, in which the age distributions of self-reported rioters and the noninvolved are more similar, there is almost no difference between the rioters, 32.6 percent of whom had annual incomes under $5,000, and the noninvolved, 29.4 percent of whom had annual incomes under $5,000.

The similarity in income distribution should not, however, lead to the conclusion that more affluent Negroes are as likely to riot as poor Negroes. But surveys were conducted in disturbance areas where incomes are considerably lower than in the city as a whole and the surrounding metropolitan area. Nevertheless, the data show that rioters are not necessarily the poorest of the poor.

While income fails to distinguish self-reported rioters from those who were not involved, it does distinguish counterrioters from rioters and the noninvolved. Less than 9 percent of both those who rioted and those not involved earned more than $10,000 annually. Yet almost 20 percent of the counterrioters earned this amount or more. In fact, there were no male self-reported counterrioters in the Detroit survey who earned less than $5,000 annually. In the Newark sample there were seven respondents who owned their own homes; none of them participated in the riot. While extreme poverty does not necessarily move a man to riot, relative affluence seems at least to inhibit him from attacking the existing social order and may motivate him to take considerable risks to protect it.

Education

Level of schooling is strongly related to participation. Those with some high school education were more likely to riot than those who had only finished grade school. In the Detroit survey, 93 percent of the self-reported rioters had gone beyond grade school, compared with 72.1 percent of the noninvolved. In the Newark survey the comparable figures are 98.1 and 85.7 percent. The majority of self-reported rioters were not, however, high school graduates.

The counterrioters were clearly the best educated of the three groups. Approximately twice as many counterrioters had attended college as had the noninvolved, and half again as many counterrioters had attended college as rioters. Considered with the information on income, the data suggest that counterrioters were probably well on their way into the middle class.

Education and income are the only factors which distinguish the counterrioter from the noninvolved. Apparently, a high level of education and income not only prevents rioting but is more likely to lead to active, responsible opposition to rioting.

Employment

The Detroit and Newark surveys, the arrest records from four cities, and the Detroit arrest study all indicate that there are no substantial differences in unemployment between the rioters and the noninvolved.

Unemployment levels among both groups were extremely high. In the Detroit survey, 29.6 percent of the self-reported rioters were unemployed; in the Newark survey, 29.7 percent; in the four-city arrest data, 33.2 percent; and in the Detroit arrest study, 21.8 percent. The unemployment rates for the noninvolved in the Detroit and Newark surveys were 31.5 and 19.0 percent.

Self-reported rioters were more likely to be only intermittently employed, however, than the noninvolved. Respondents in Newark were asked whether they had been unemployed for as long as a month or more during the last year. Sixty-one percent of the self-reported rioters, but only 43.4 percent of the noninvolved, answered, "yes."

Despite generally higher levels of education, rioters were more likely than the noninvolved to be employed in unskilled jobs. In the Newark survey, 50 percent of the self-reported rioters, but only 39.6 percent of the noninvolved, had unskilled jobs.

Attitudes About Employment

The Newark survey data indicate that self-reported rioters were more likely to feel dissatisfied with their present jobs than were the noninvolved.

Only 29.3 percent of the rioters, compared with 44.4 percent of the noninvolved, thought their present jobs appropriate for them in responsibility and pay. Of the self-reported rioters, 67.6 percent, compared with 56.1 percent of the noninvolved, felt that it was impossible to obtain the kind of job they wanted. Of the self-reported rioters, 69 percent, as compared with 50 percent of the noninvolved, felt that racial discrimination was the major obstacle to finding better employment. Despite this feeling, surprising numbers of rioters (76.9 percent) responded that "getting what you want out of life is a matter of ability, not being in the right place at the right time."

Racial Attitudes

The Detroit and Newark surveys indicate that rioters have strong feelings of racial pride, if not racial superiority. In the Detroit survey, 48.6 percent of the self-reported rioters said that they felt Negroes were more dependable than whites. Only 22.4 percent of the noninvolved stated this. In Newark, the comparable figures were 45 and 27.8 percent. The Newark survey data indicate that rioters wanted to be called "black" rather than "Negro" or "colored" and were somewhat more likely than the noninvolved to feel that all Negroes should study African history and languages.

To what extent this racial pride antedated the riot or was produced by the riot is impossible to determine from the survey data. Certainly the riot experience seems to have been associated with increased pride in the minds of many participants. This was vividly illustrated by the statement of a Detroit rioter:

> Interviewer: You said you were feeling good when you followed the crowds?
>
> Respondent: I was feeling proud, man, at the fact that I was a Negro. I felt like I was a first-class citizen. I didn't feel ashamed of my race because of what they did.

Similar feelings were expressed by an 18-year-old Detroit girl who reported that she had been a looter:

> Interviewer: What is the Negro then if he's not American?
>
> Respondent: A Negro, he's considered a slave to the white folks. But half of them know that they're slaves and feel they can't do nothing about it because they're just going along with it. But most of them they seem to get it in their heads now how the white folks treat them and how they've been treating them and how they've been slaves for the white folks.

Along with increased racial pride there appears to be intense hostility toward whites. Self-reported rioters in both Detroit and Newark surveys were more likely to feel that civil rights groups with white and Negro leaders would do better without the whites. In Detroit, 36.1 percent of the self-reported rioters thought that this statement was true, while 21.1 percent of the noninvolved thought so. In the Newark survey, 51.4 percent of the self-reported rioters agreed; 33.1 percent of the noninvolved shared this opinion.

Self-reported rioters in Newark were also more likely to agree with the statement, "Sometimes I hate white people." Of the self-reported rioters, 72.4 percent agreed; of the noninvolved, 50 percent agreed.

The intensity of the self-reported rioters' racial feelings may suggest that the recent riots represented traditional interracial hostilities. Two sources of data suggest that this interpretation is probably incorrect.

First, the Newark survey data indicate that rioters were almost as hostile to middle-class Negroes as they were to whites. Seventy-one and four-tenths percent of the self-reported rioters, but only 59.5 percent of the noninvolved, agreed with the statement, "Negroes who make a lot of money like to think they are better than other Negroes." Perhaps even more significant, particularly in light of the rioters' strong feelings of racial pride, is that 50.5 percent of the self-reported rioters agreed that "Negroes who make a lot of money are just as bad as white people." Only 35.2 percent of the noninvolved shared this opinion.

Second, the arrest data show that the great majority of those arrested during the disorders were generally charged with a crime relating to looting or curfew violations. Only 2.4 percent of the arrests were for assault and 0.1 percent were for homicide, but 31.3 percent of the arrests were for breaking and entering — crimes directed against white property rather than against individual whites.

Political Attitudes and Involvement

Respondents in the Newark survey were asked about relatively simple items of political information, such as the race of prominent local and national political figures. In general, the self-reported rioters were much better informed than the noninvolved. For example, self-reported rioters were more likely to know that one of the 1966 Newark mayoral candidates was a Negro. Of the rioters, 77.1 percent — but only 61.6 percent of the noninvolved — identified him correctly. The overall scores on a series of similar questions also reflect the self-reported rioters' higher levels of information.

Self-reported rioters were also more likely to be involved in activities associated with Negro rights. At the most basic level of political participation, they were more likely than the noninvolved to talk frequently about Negro rights. In the

Newark survey, 53.8 percent of the self-reported rioters, but only 34.9 percent of the noninvolved, said that they talked about Negro rights nearly every day.

The self-reported rioters also were more likely to have attended a meeting or participated in civil rights activity. Of the rioters, 39.3 percent — but only 25.7 percent of the noninvolved — reported that they had engaged in such activity.

In the Newark survey, respondents were asked how much they thought they could trust the local government. Only 4.8 percent of the noninvolved, said that they felt they could trust it most of the time; 44.2 percent of the self-reported rioters and 33.9 percent of the noninvolved reported that they could almost never trust the government.

In the Detroit survey, self-reported rioters were much more likely to attribute the riot to anger about politicians and police than were the noninvolved. Of the self-reported rioters, 43.2 percent — but only 19.6 percent of the noninvolved — said anger against politicians had a great deal to do with causing the riot. Of the self-reported rioters, 70.5 percent, compared with 48.8 percent of the noninvolved, believed that anger against the police had a great deal to do with causing the riot.

Perhaps the most revealing and disturbing measure of the rioters' anger at the social and political system was their response to a question asking whether they thought "the country was worth fighting for in the event of a major world war." Of the self-reported rioters, 39.4 percent in Detroit and 52.8 percent in Newark shared a negative view. In contrast, 15.5 percent of the noninvolved in Detroit and 27.8 percent of the noninvolved in Newark shared this sentiment. Almost none of the self-reported counterrioters in Detroit — 3.3 percent — agreed with the self-reported rioters.

Some comments of interviewees are worthy of note:

> Not worth fighting for — if Negroes had an equal chance it would be worth fighting for.

Not worth fighting for — I am not a true citizen so why should I?

Not worth fighting for — because my husband came back from Vietnam and nothing had changed.

K. Why Did It Happen? Some Theories

Harvey Wheeler, "A Moral Equivalent for Riots," *The Saturday Review,* May 11, 1968, pp. 19-22, 51. Reprinted with permission of the author and publisher. Copyright 1968, Saturday Review, Inc.

Harvey Wheeler is a Fellow at the Center for the Study of Democratic Institutions in Santa Barbara, California. Students and their teachers will remember him as the co-author of *Fail-Safe.*

1. What were the ten theories or "propositions" about violence and riots identified by Mr. Wheeler and his interviewees?

2. Can you relate the ten theories to those theories presented in the introduction of this chapter? Any new, powerful ideas in the Wheeler article to help explain aggressive behavior? Which ones? Why?

About a year ago Malcolm Moos, who is president of the University of Minnesota but who was then an executive at the Ford Foundation, asked me to make a general investigation into the topic of violence. I had not previously engaged in any special studies qualifying me as an expert in this field, but perhaps Dr. Moos felt that this was in my favor. At least I had no preconceptions or predispositions toward one or another of the various contending schools of thought.

I did not want to look solely into the subject of ghetto riots — though obviously this would be one of the chief problems. Initially, I wanted to find out about all forms of violence: sporadic acts by assassins or snipers, such as that of the berserk student who mounted a tower at the University of Texas and shot down at people; the violence of the student demonstrators, both when directed against their universities and when directed against our nation's war; the hippies, who in one sense are waging a violent attack on the conventional morality of the established culture. Finally, I wanted to study the various national liberation movements among the peoples of the third world.

I was given complete freedom to decide where to go, whom to seek out, and how to prepare the study. I visited Los Angeles, Stanford, Berkeley, Harvard, North Carolina, New York, London, Paris, Geneva, and many other places. I talked to famous leaders of the civil rights movement and to infamous leaders of street gangs; to philosophers, psychologists, sociologists, political scientists, reporters, public officials, and others. I taped more than 400 hours of interviews; my wife, who sat in on most of them, is only now completing the transcriptions.

First, a summary of the theories about violence held by respondents:

1) Most respondents agreed that violence itself is not the thing to look at if one wants to understand it. That is, violence is a symptom rather than a cause, and if one wishes to reduce violence it will be of little avail to attack it directly as if it were something that could be cured or eliminated head on. Rather, one must try to get at the underlying causes or roots of what elicits violence.

2) Most respondents, in one way or another, believed violence to be an indelible part of human nature in some fundamental way. (This opinion was held by such otherwise diverse respondents as Hans J. Morgenthau and Martin Luther King, Jr.) So it is not possible, or even desirable, for us to achieve the complete elimination of violence. Rather, we may eliminate some of its most destructive manifestations, and

perhaps divert it into more harmless, or even constructive, channels.

3) There was a tendency to point out that, while all societies are violent, and the United States is especially so, societies draw lines between what they consider "good" violence and "bad" violence. Many Southern whites, for example, consider violence against Negroes to be a good thing. Many of those interviewed recently about Martin Luther King's assassination clearly betrayed the feeling that it was probably a good thing that he was shot. (I must relate that a close relative of mine, in a phone call the day after the assassination, mentioned that he thought the assassination a "blessing.") Such thoughts, though really quite horrifying, are harbored in the breasts of a large number of Americans, and we must face that fact.

The National Advisory Commission on Civil Disorders referred to the root of the problem as lying in a deepseated racism that permeates American society. Most of my respondents assented to this theory. It is very difficult, therefore, to distinguish between acts of violence that differ only in that some have our approval. We officially approve of search-and-destroy violence in the Vietnam war. We approvingly portray the battlefield results of this policy on TV each evening. Recall the ghastly scenes of the on-the-spot executions, and the expulsion of a network reporter because he filmed a GI setting fire to native homes. Recall again that in most states we retain the death penalty. But more insidious is the kind of permissive violence of which we are scarcely aware. Negroes are aware of it, however, for it strikes against them daily.

4) One of my respondents referred to the problem as being one not of violence, but of "violation." Violence, he said, must be looked at in terms of the violation of the dignity of human beings. In those terms, violence is merely the sporadic counter-response when one's humanity and one's dignity has been violated. A culture in which human relationships are

characterized by a great deal of violation will therefore produce a great deal of violence.

This country . . . has been a personality-violating culture since its birth. It has been unable to solve any of its greatest collective or internal probelms without resort to violence. In addition, new cultural forces associated with the scientific revolution and with bureaucratization carry a special kind of violation. As these technological and organizational varieties of violation have increased, so has the incidence of counterviolation. And this latter more or less impersonal, or "systemic," violation helps account for the more or less impersonal, or "anti-system," violence of the reactions.

5) Respondents in the main agreed to another historical generalization. After the Civil War, the U.S. gave verbal, statutory, and even Constitutional expression to the principle of equal rights for Negroes. But at the same time it instituted an informal — in the South, quite formalized — racist culture in which Jim Crow regulations [laws which restricted Negroes' freedom] and practices of a most degrading (violating) type were enforced generally. We tend to think of Jim Crow as a Southern institution, but it often had its most cruel impact in the North.

The lovely little Northern town — let us call it "Elmstown" — where I grew up had two Negro families. One was headed by the kindly old "handkerchief-head darky" who was barber at the Elks Club, the other by a lady, apparently quite gracious, who served the community otherwise. The reason only two Negro families lived there was that the town had earlier chased the others out, posting signs at each road entering the town: **Nigger, don't let the sun go down on you in Elmstown.** In the larger Northern cities, of course, the pattern of ghettoization — completely unknown at that time in Southern cities — was rigidly enforced.

The result of this uniform human violation was the creation of the myth of Negro inferiority — a myth which was accepted, with very few exceptions, by Negroes themselves. This official violation of Negroes' humanity then was turned inward, leading them to hate themselves and their blackness and their Negroid characteristics. They valued light skins over dark and violated their own natures — as in hair straighteners — in a perpetual effort to suppress their Negroism. Amos 'n' Andy, Stepin Fetchit, Rochester — white man's stereotypes of the good but slavish darky — were accepted by Negroes as their own heroes.

One result of the Negroes' inward turning of violence against themselves was the destruction of any possibility of maintaining an integral family structure. Negro women led all others in deprecating their men, contributing to the so-called emasculation of the Negro male about which we have heard so much. This internalization of violence, when it spilled out, took the form of the Negroes' physical attacks against one another in highly publicized brawls, cuttings, and wifebeatings that authorities reinforced by applying different law enforcement standards for Negroes. Negroes were overpoliced in their relations to property and to whites; they were underpoliced in their relations to each other. It was all right for Negroes to knife other Negroes to death. But it was, in effect, a capital offense to even mildly affront a white. In short, Negroes not only internalized violence, taking it out against each other, but were "paid off" for doing so by the larger society.

The change came after 1954 with *Brown vs. Topeka*. Then, for the first time, Negroes began to turn violence outward against the white society that had violated them — first in the sit-ins and demonstrations, later in the riots. The result was a rebirth, perhaps an inauguration, of Negro self-respect. This assertion of self-respect has been the psychic power of the recent pattern of violence.

6) Sociologist Daniel Bell, in "Crime as an American Way of Life," has pointed out another variant of the tradition of violence. The Anglo-Saxon Protestant, Bell notes, got here first and monopolized all the official avenues to wealth and status. Then came the immigration waves: Irish, Middle European, Jews, etc. Each was faced with a foreclosure of

the normal avenues to participation in the bourgeois bounties of the land. The Irish turned to politics and monopolized the party system, not only using it to gain office, but systematizing graft into a characteristically American kind of capital accumulation. When the Middle Europeans arrived later, not only business but also politics was closed to them. The result, says Bell, was a resort to crime as "an American Way of Life": crime as a way of becoming middle-class Americans.

But what of the Negro? Now we must consider the possibility that violence — direct action in the streets — has become the Negro version of this pattern of Americanization. All other avenues are closed; only direct action, sometimes issuing in violence, is left. This is the historic setting within which the Black Power movement must be understood. That being so, one must also look forward to the possibility that rioting and street demonstrations will become the institution-alized form of Americanization for Negroes.

7) We conclude that there is a large measure of truth to the Black Power charge that America is an imperialist culture. The imperialism with which America approaches the world outside is mirrored by a related form of imperialism that it turns against its own ethnic minorities. Hence, the charge that the Negro (and the Mexican-American, the Spanish-Indian, and others) lives in a colonial status in his own country. The rather transparent validity of this charge is what forges unity between the struggle of the Negro against domestic oppression and the international struggles of the third world against colonialism. Both are essentially anti-imperialist movements and both will have to apply generally similar tactics to achieve their goals. This does not necessarily mean violent tactics, but obviously the situation both at home and abroad is fraught with a very high violence potential. This is also why Mrs. Martin Luther King was right two years ago when she finally convinced her husband that the struggle against racist despotism in America would have to be linked with the struggle against American imperialism abroad.

What is the source of our domestic imperialism? The National Advisory Commission is right as far as it goes. America *is* a racist culture. But the commission doesn't go nearly far enough. Our internal form of despotism begins innocuously, right at birth. The medical evidence is mounting that children who begin life in conditions of emotional and nutritional deprivation develop physical and mental deficiencies that are virtually irreversible, no matter how healthful their conditions may later become. Now, of course, this is a condition that afflicts *all* the poor. But because of the proportional overconcentration of Negroes in the so-called culture of poverty, the effects of deprivation strike selectively against them. So they start life with ineradicable chains dragging down their every step.

Even if this were not so, or even if it were eliminated overnight, another cultural barrier still lies in the Negroes' path, and it will prove to be the most difficult one to eradicate. This has to do with the acculturation process and the way it relates to the educational process. We know that the performance of children in schools is directly correlated with the cultural and economic status of their parents. Children from highly educated, affluent homes will inevitably make better grades, go to better schools, acquire higher degrees, and ultimately find better jobs than those from deprived homes. It is sometimes falsely concluded that this means that education is the bootstrap by which all can pull themselves out of deprivation and ascend the pinnacles of white middle-class society. But that is transparently false, is it not? One has to be middle class to *start* with, in order to be middle class at the end. Education as such has little or nothing to do with it.

The other side of this premise is that deprived boys and girls, starting in school, have no cultural reinforcement at home. They have no stimulus urging them toward cultural heights. They have limited verbal and reading skills to reinforce their schoolroom efforts. As a result they are automatically processed through what we call the "track" system. . .The track system means that even in schools that are technically desegrated, there is an internal segregation based upon test performance. Test performance is sometimes thought to represent innate intellectual ability. In fact, however, intelligence-test results merely reflect the conditions of one's cultural origins.

Under the track system, those from culturally deprived homes are automatically passed through the grades regardless of performance, until legal school-leaving age is reached. At that time they are dumped out on the streets, where they will spend the rest of their lives grubbing for existence through the offal of our cities. The second track is for those with low, but passable, achievement records. They are placed in the manual-arts, nonacademic track and are destined for the menial, semiskilled trades. The highest, of course, are put into the liberal-arts, college preparatory programs, and they inevitably will end up with college degrees and Establishment jobs. The point is that the track system reinforces – and even magnifies – the initial condition with which students begin life. Before the average child is ten years old the school system has already determined, beyond the child's ability to influence it, his entire lifetime career.

There are a few extremely rare cases in which the pattern is overcome, and we paternalistically display these with a great show of pride. This is the cruelest cultural despotism imaginable. It is also remorselessly violent. For who can argue with objective placement tests? What, then is to be done about it? Shouldn't any sensible child – or any sensible high school student, when faced from the beginning of life with a predetermined second-class status, destined to last forever – react with violence to this ultimate violation of his innate talents?

8) An aspect of this same despotism reaches even middle-class children. Our culture has always been goaded on by the whiplash of the dollar. The threat of economic failure (absolutely or relatively) dogs our steps from birth to death. This is a burden that often becomes too much for even the

seemingly well to do. But recently the whiplash of the dollar has become supplemented by that of the school. For each person's status — rich as well as poor — appears to depend upon his grade records. So the grade record becomes the whiplash of the young, terrorizing them from kindergarten on. And where the school stops, the parent takes up. So school (abetted by career-conscious parents) becomes a place of terror whose whiplash is the grade system and which reaches an apex for the hardy in the ultimate indignity of the College Board examinations. So there is little wonder that all students, black and white alike, are today in open rebellion against the school system.

The answer to one of our preliminary questions now begins to reveal itself: The systematic "violation" of our youth brings Negroes, hippies, and university students together into the same framework, struggling together in the same cause.

9)   It was often remarked, two years ago, that Los Angeles was the most unlikely place for a riot to occur. Watts is not a ghetto in the normal sense of the word, for it abounds with single-family homes. I remember ten years ago hearing Eastern Negroes say that Los Angeles was the Negro's "heaven." "Man, *that's* where I want to go when I die." A second comment about Watts was that it was not technically a "race riot"; it was not against whites — at least not personally. So, Watts was the most affluent Negro community in the world, and its riot was directed against that very community. How can we explain this?

There is general agreement that the Watts pattern fits well what is known about *all* the revolutions of history. They do not start among those making up the dregs of society. Moreover, they do not occur when oppression and exploitation are at their worst. So-called revolutions of the belly are statistically rare in history, and when they occur they usually have little effect on the conditions of those in revolt — except death. Rather, revolutions typically occur among those who have experienced a definite, steady rise in their conditions of life, and *then* suffer a setback. Revolutions are made by rising classes rather than by declining classes. And this leads us to the current catch phrase about the "revolutions of rising expectations"; that is, the revolutions being carried out by all peoples in the world who want to enjoy the good things in life made famous by Americans.

There is general agreement that the Negro Revolution is another one of these revolutions of rising expectataions. It is precisely because Negroes desperately want to enjoy the beneficences of the American way of life that they are in revolt. It is *Life* magazine, actively abetted by *Ebony* and multiplied a thousandfold by television programs and commercials, that provides the real stimulus to the Negro revolution. And this is one reason why the revolts take the form of burning and looting. Revolutions destroy the physical symbols of deprivation; in the present case these are tenement houses and the gouging merchants. And then the rebels go on to looting, helping themselves to the gadgets and goodies the mass media have overstimulated them to desire.

10) Finally, there appears to be irrefutable physiological and anthropological evidence that the mere fact of physical overcrowding induces violence. Some anthropologists claim to be able to chart reliable curves of violence-potentials correlated with rates of congestion. Dramatic confirmation comes from experiments with monkeys. They are normally quite peaceful creatures. At the most they engage in their curious ritualized shouting wars in which violence seldom if ever results. In one experiment a collection of monkeys was loaded on a ship for transportation to an uninhabited Caribbean island — as an experimental refuge. During the period of shipboard crowding they developed on their own most of the typical maladies of human beings. They learned how to fight each other, even to death. They acquired coronary problems and they developed a full range of mental diseases. But what is worse, their violent patterns of behavior, once learned on shipboard, were continued even after debarkation on an island where sufficient space and food could have permitted the return to their traditional (presumably instinctual) ways of peace.

So, we have ten general propositions about violence. It is apparent from them that the problem runs quite deep — so deep that not even massive investments in the improvement of the physical conditions of the ghettos will resolve them.

L. Why Did it Happen? The Commission's Answer

> *Report of the National Advisory Commission on Civil Disorders,* Washington, D.C. : Government Printing Office, 1968, pp. 5, 81-83.
>
> 1. Why do policemen serve as "aggression-evoking cues" to many ghetto dwellers?
>
> 2. Which theories seem to be supported by the conclusions of the 1967 Commission?
>
> 3. From what you have read, do the conclusions seem to be accurate and adequate explanations for the recent urban unrest? Why?

The factors within the society at large. . . created a mood of violence among many urban Negroes.

These factors are complex and interacting; they vary significantly in their effect from city to city and from year to year; and the consequences of one disorder, generating new grievances and new demands, become the causes of the next. Thus was created the "thicket of tension, conflicting evidence, and extreme opinions" cited by the President.

Despite these complexities, certain fundamental matters are clear. Of these, the most fundamental is the racial attitude and behavior of white Americans toward black Americans.

Race prejudice has shaped our history decisively; it now threatens to affect our future.

White racism is essentially responsible for the explosive mixture which has been accumulating in our cities since the end of World War II. Among the ingredients of this mixture are:

—Pervasive discrimination and segregation in employment, education, and housing, which have resulted in the continuing exclusion of great numbers of Negroes from the benefits of economic progress.

—Black in-migration and white exodus, which have produced the massive and growing concentrations of impoverished Negroes in our major cities, creating a growing crisis of deteriorating facilities and services and unmet human needs.

—The black ghettos, where segregation and poverty converge on the young to destroy opportunity and enforce failure. Crime, drug addiction, dependency on welfare, and bitterness and resentment against society in general and white society in particular are the result.

At the same time, most whites and some Negroes outside the ghetto have prospered to a degree unparalleled in the history of civilization. Through television and other media, this affluence has been flaunted before the eyes of the Negro poor and the jobless ghetto youth.

Yet these facts alone cannot be said to have caused the disorders. Recently, other powerful ingredients have begun to catalyze [speed-up] the mixture:

—Frustrated hopes are the residue of the unfulfilled expectations aroused by the great judicial and legislative victories of the civil rights movement and the dramatic struggle for equal rights in the South.

—A climate that tends toward approval and encouragement of violence as a form of protest has been created by white terrorism directed against nonviolent protest; by the open defiance of law and Federal authority by state and local officials resisting desegregation; and by some protest groups engaging in civil disobedience who turn their backs on nonviolence, go beyond the constitutionally protected rights of petition and free assembly, and resort to violence to attempt to compel alteration of laws and policies with which they disagree.

—The frustrations of powerlessness have led some Negroes to the conviction that there is no effective alternative to violence as a means of achieving redress of grievances, and of

"moving the system." These frustrations are reflected in alienation and hostility toward the institutions of law and government and the white society which controls them, and in the reach toward racial consciousness and solidarity reflected in the slogan "Black Power."

—A new mood sprung up among Negroes, particularly among the young, in which self-esteem and enhanced racial pride are replacing apathy and submission to "the system."

—The police are not merely a "spark" factor. To some negroes police have come to symbolize white power, white racism, and white repression. And the fact is that many police do reflect and express these white attitudes. The atmosphere of hostility and cynicism is reinforced by the widespread belief among Negroes in the existence of police brutality in a "double standard" of justice and protection — one for Negroes and one for whites.

In almost all the cities surveyed, we found the same major grievance topics among Negro communities — although they varied in importance from city to city. The deepest grievances can be ranked into the following three levels of relative intensity:

First Level of Intensity
1. Police practices.
2. Unemployment and underemployment.
3. Inadequate housing.

Second Level of Intensity
4. Inadequate education.
5. Poor recreation facilities and programs.
6. Ineffectiveness of the political structure and grievance mechanisms.

Third Level of Intensity
7. Disrespectful white attitudes.
8. Discriminatory administration of justice.
9. Inadequacy of Federal programs.
10. Inadequacy of municipal services.
11. Discriminatory consumer and civil practices.
12. Inadequate welfare programs.

An awesome number of conditions generated these twelve factors. The range of inadequacies is listed in specific detail below:

1. *Employment and underemployment.*

   Unemployment and underemployment (general lack of full-time jobs).

   Union discrimination.

   Discrimination in hiring by local and state government.

   Discrimination in placement by state employment service.

   Discrimination in placement by private employment agencies.

2. *Police practices.*

   Physical abuse.

   Verbal abuse.

   Nonexistent or inadequate channels for the redress of grievances against police.

   Discrimination in employment and promotion of Negroes.

   General lack of respect for Negroes, i.e., using derogatory language short of threats.

   Abuse of Negroes in police custody.

   Failure to answer ghetto calls promptly where Negro is victim of unlawful act.

3. *Inadequate housing.*

   Poor housing code enforcement.

   Discrimination in sales and rentals.

   Overcrowding.

4. *Inadequate education.*

   De facto segregation.

   Poor quality of instruction and facilities.

   Inadequacy of curriculum (e.g., no Negro history).

   Inadequate Negro representation on school board.

   Poor vocational education or none at all.

5. *Political structure and grievance mechanism.*

   Lack of adequate Negro representation.

   Lack of response to legitimate grievances of Negroes.

   Grievance mechanism nonexistent or inadequately publicized.

6. *Inadequate programs.*

Poverty programs (OEO) (e.g., insufficient participation of the poor in project planning; lack of continuity in programs; inadequate funding; and unfulfilled promises).

Urban renewal (HUD) (e.g., too little community participation in planning and decisionmaking; programs are not urban renewal but "Negro removal").

Employment training (Labor — HEW) (e.g., persons are trained for jobs that are not available in the community).

7. *Discriminatory administration of justice.*

Discriminatory treatment in the courts.

Lower courts act as arm of police department rather than as an objective arbiter in truly adversary proceedings.

Presumption of guilt when policeman testifies against Negro.

8. *Poor recreation facilities and programs.*

Inadequate facilities (parks, playgrounds, athletic fields, gymnasiums, and pools).

Lack of organized programs.

9. *Racist and other disrespectful white attitudes.*

Racism and lack of respect for dignity of Negroes.

General animosity toward Negroes.

10. *Inadequate and poorly administered welfare programs.*

Unfair qualification regulations (e.g., "man in the house" rule).

Attitude of welfare workers toward recipients (e.g., manifestations of hostility and contempt for persons on welfare).

11. *Inadequate municipal services.*

Inadequate sanitation and garbage removal.

Inadequate health and hospital facilities.

Inadequate street paving and lighting.

12. *Discriminatory consumer and credit practices.*

Inferior quality goods (especially meats and produce).

Overpricing (especially on days welfare checks issued).

Exorbitant interest rates (particularly in connection with furniture and appliance sales).

Fraudulent practices.

COMPARISON OF GRIEVANCE CATEGORIES

	1st place	2d place	3d Place	4th place	Total
	Cities	Cities	Cities	Cities	Cities
Police practices	8	4	0	2	14
Unemployment and underemployment . .	3	7	4	3	17
Inadequate housing	5	2	5	2	14
Inadequate education	2	2	2	3	9
Poor recreation facilities	3	1	4	0	8
Political structure and grievance mechanism	2	1	1	1	5
White attitudes	0	1	1	2	4
Administration of justice	0	0	2	1	3
Federal programs	0	1	0	0	1
Municipal services	0	0	1	0	1
Consumer and credit practices	0	0	0	2	2
Welfare	0	0	0	0	0

The president's commission asked persons in numerous cities to rank grievances in their cities by the twelve categories outlined in the above article. This table shows the results of that ranking. For example, in eight cities "police practices" was rated as the major grievance, while the category was ranked in the top four major grievances in fourteen cities.

Chapter **4**

Riots as Goal-Directed Behavior

When a crowd becomes a mob, restraint is lost. The crowd may have been boisterous and disorderly with only isolated violence. But the arrival on the scene of a hated figure or one who symbolizes the source of real or imagined frustration can transform the crowd into heated frenzy. The crowd suddenly acts together, cohesively, directing its action against the source or symbol of its frustration.

Behavior often depends on momentary suggestion. A momentary impulse can trigger action based upon long-term frustration.

The tendency for the members of a mob to exhibit similar behavior has been referred to by various terms — suggestion, imitation, circular reaction, and social facilitation. We are all familiar with this phenomenon. If, as a person is walking down the street, he sees three persons looking toward the sky, he is almost certain to look upward. In an audience, when one person begins to clap, others follow. The behavior is contagious; one person takes his cue from another. People take the suggestion of, or imitate, others.

The sense of group identification, or sense of group membership which pervades in a crowd, makes possible the kinds of action which could not elsewhere be carried out. The individual loses his identity. His role in a mob provides a protective mask behind which he can join in action he would not perform in a group of known friends and acquaintances. Also, the individual loses a sense of individual responsibility and at the same time gains a sense of power. Losing individual responsibility gives the person freedom to act aggressively without fear of punishment; gaining a sense of power is a source of satisfaction to him. He may do things which were

denied before. He may express feelings which were
unacceptable. For this reason, many riot participants find
mob action a satisfying experience.

In neighborhood crowds and riots, when an individual
participates with his friends and acquaintances, the person
gains freedom and power only as his conduct is approved by
the group. For example, attacking policemen, breaking into
grocery stores, and burning firetrucks are forbidden acts for
which an individual would expect to be punished in ordinary
situations. However, in a ghetto riot, after a police raid on an
illegal tavern or prostitutes' lair, the crowd may approve such
conduct as being "right" or "just" and the policemen's action
"illegal" or "unjust."

Just recall the riots in Washington, D. C., and other cities
following the assassination of Dr. Martin Luther King, Jr. on
April 4, 1968. He was the leader of the Southern Christian
Leadership Conference and a Nobel Peace Prize winner. He
was the great believer in non-violent protest to achieve
equality and opportunity — one may imagine the despair and
frustration felt by black and white Americans. You can recall
the agony of the nation, presented in neighbors' faces and
upon television screens. It is little wonder that riots occurred
in the ghettos.

The riot in Miami during the Republican convention in the
summer of 1968 was followed closely by the nightmare in
Chicago during the Democratic National Convention. TV and
newspaper reports were horrifying. Thousands of
demonstrators converged on the city for a week of wild
melees, a protest for peace. According to reports riots
erupted, this time on the part of police, in the face of
obscene and violent harassment by the protesters. The
emotional inflammation of the situation saw the police yield
to provocation.

The readings in this chapter deal with rioters' behaviors,
their goals, and even their looting. The emphasis upon looting
is necessary for it is this activity which attracts the white
community and brings forth calls for "law and order" and for

the shooting of rioters. Before we heed the calls for shooting kids with stolen TV sets and shoes, we might analyze this behavior and seek some explanations. As you read, try to keep emotional reactions in bounds and think about these general questions:

1. Why do rioters respond aggressively to police? Why do the police respond aggressively?
2. What goals do rioters seem to seek? What do they attack? What opportunities do riots seem to provide?

M. The Riot as Opportunity

Lee Rainwater "Open Letter on White Justice and the Riots," *Trans-action,* September, 1967, pp.22-23, 26-27, 30-32. Copyright 1967 by Washington University, St. Louis, Missouri. Reprinted with persmission by the author and the publisher.

Lee Rainwater is a senior editor of *Trans-action* and professor of sociology and anthropology at Washington University, St. Louis. His current research involves field studies on the problems of race and poverty in St. Louis.

1. How does the author define "riot?"

2. What does the author mean when he distinguishes between a class system and a caste division in America? How does this distinction affect the cause of civil unrest?

3. Why does the author think of riots as opportunities for participants who are engaged in "goal-directed behavior?" What does this interpretation signify for riot prevention?

A great deal of the difficulty in understanding what causes riots and what might be done about them comes from a misunderstanding of exactly what their nature is. A riot seems almost always to begin with an incident in which the police make an effort at enforcing one or another law — whether the culprits involved be a tipsy driver, a traffic law violator, or the operators and patrons of a blind pig [a ghetto tavern selling drinks after the legal closing time]. In other words, riots grow out of effots at social control where society's officials move in on behavior which the informal social controls of the community do not prove sufficient to contain.

As the police go about their business, a curious crowd gathers. The crowd watches what is going on and reflects on it, and some members come to deny the legitimacy of what the police are doing. Rather than responding with satisfaction to the smooth functioning of the social control forces, the crowd members respond with anger and resentment; they identify with the culprits rather than with the law. This identification often takes the form of a belief either that the culprits are innocent, or that they're being treated more roughly than is warranted or just.

The riot develops from this initial incident as the people in the crowd begin to express their anger in response to the situation — they throw rocks at the police, or make attempts to rescue the prisoners. Here they are only acting out the strong and unpleasant emotions stimulated by what they see and the meanings they assign to it. But as this process continues and people talk to each other about what has happened, the matter becomes more ideological — that is, the events are interpreted in an increasingly larger context. The incident becomes an example of society in which whites do as they please, while Negroes are held accountable for every minor infraction, even those infractions involving behavior that is not really voluntary. For example, a man may get drunk because he is depressed and discouraged about his situation, or he may spend his time on the streets and get in trouble there because he has given up looking for a job. The fury of the rioters is probably exacerbated [irritated] by their weariness at trying to manage their lives in such a way that they can avoid the attentive ministrations of the social control agents (and these include truant officers, welfare investigators, and personnel officers, as well as the police).

By now the guilt or innocence of the culprits, and the manner in which the police treat them, are no longer that central. Instead, the focus is on the crowd members' general feelings that they live in a world in which they are constantly held accountable to standards of justice which are not applied to others. They feel that the merchants with whom they deal cheat them, that employers are either indifferent or exploiting toward them, that the police are disrespectful and suspicious of them. Therefore, they feel that the police (as representatives of the society at large) are perpetrating [continuing] the greater evil — an evil by comparison with which the minor peccadillos [petty faults] of the drunken driver, traffic violator, the blind-pig patron are, in human terms, irrelevant.

Further, as incidents like this multiply, and as sophistication about Negro victimization rises in the ghetto community, it becomes increasingly possible to generalize this process without a particular incident. Following the news of the Newark, Detroit, and East Harlem riots in July [1967], a group of Negro teenagers went on a rampage after a rock and roll concert, smashing and looting several of New York's Fifth Avenue stores. They did not need the provocation of an actual encounter with the police to touch off this vivid rejection of legal authority.

A riot is a social event which provides different opportunities to different participants. It is a short-lived "opportunity structure." Of all the aspects of the riot, this is the least well understood. There is no single "rioter," but rather many kinds of activities, each contributing a little bit to make up the total event. We know almost nothing about who takes each of the possible roles in the rioting — looter, sniper, police attacker, sympathetic bystander, ideological interpreter, and so on. It does seem that the most popular category is that of looter. This makes sense; what the rioters are saying, more than anything else, is "we haven't gotten our share." On Detroit's East and West sides [in 1967] the furniture and appliance stores seemed the hardest hit. "Big ticket" items [TV's, radios, furniture] are the proof of the affluent [wealthy] society and the looters knew exactly where to find them. In this respect the riots become a kind of primitive effort at an income redistribution which the society refuses to support in any lawful and regularized way.

The snipers, on the other hand, we can only vaguely understand. Indeed, the evidence seems to suggest that snipers are more often phantom than real; a very few snipers (perhaps none at all) are necessary to legitimate [make "right"] the belief of police and National Guardsmen that they are "at war" and that the danger is so great that they may fire with impunity [without control] into the rioting community. In Detroit, one such phantom sniper was apparently responsible for the National Guard machine-gunning a "white" motel near the General Motors building and inadvertently hitting an out-of-town woman staying there.

Riots are difficult to control precisely because of this voluntary division of labor among the participants. Because their many different sorts of activities require different sorts of responses, the riot becomes a highly complex event that can be brought under control only by a mass show of force (or perhaps by a show of no force at all). This, plus the fact that once the riot gets under way there is almost total denial of legitimacy to the police, means that the area must be *occupied* to be controlled — a process that calls even further into question the legitimacy of the total society and its laws. The riots elicit from the official world exactly the kind of behavior that confirms the ghetto's estimate of white justice. The trigger-happy behavior of the National Guard and the police and the haphazard way in which arrests are or are not made deepens the conviction that being accorded justice depends more on luck than on the rule of law. The rising hysteria of the fatigued and frightened men in uniform seems to release all of their latent hostility to Negroes. In New Jersey, Los Angeles, and numerous smaller cities the civilian officials have hardly behaved better; it is to the credit of Detroit's Mayor Cavanaugh and his cabinet that no hint of such prejudice and bitterness has been apparent there.

Riots, then, provide different kinds of ghetto dwellers with different opportunities to pursue highly varied goals. The larger the riots get, the easier for individuals to become participants, and probably the more varied the goals they pursue.

In this context, it's quite clear from the data on the social characteristics of those arrested and convicted in Watts [1965] that the rioters are probably *not* exclusively "young hoodlums." For example, over half of those arrested in Watts were twenty-five years of age and over and as many as 40 percent were over thirty. Further, about two-thirds of those arrested and convicted were employed. It is certainly true that those arrested were very familiar with the law; less than 30 percent of them had no prior arrest. This, however, is not evidence that they are criminals, but only that they live in the ghetto. (Note, for example, that half of those arrested had never been convicted.) We would need more precise data to know what differences there might be between those who form some kind of active core of the rioters and those who take part more casually, by minor looting and the like. It might well be that the active core is more youthful and more solidly involved in delinquent activity than the others. But the most important fact here is that one could not make a riot of any size with the dominant proportion of the participants composed only of "young hoodlums."

There should be no mistake on this point. A very large proportion of the able-bodied members of any lower class Negro ghetto are potential participants in a riot. And, the riot has an ideological meaning for them; it is not simply a diversion which allows for criminal activity. The man who steals a six-pack of beer or breaks a store window does it not out of "criminal" motivation (it would hardly be worth his while), but because he is expressing some important feelings about his world and trying to put these feelings "on the record." If in the process he can derive some material benefit, like a televison set or a new G.E. range, that is all to the good because it makes his point even clearer. Everyone in America knows that money talks. The greater the damage in terms of the financial cost of the looting and burning, the more effectively the point has been made.

But just as a riot provides a wide range of opportunities, it also involves a wide range of costs — primarily those of being killed, arrested, or burned out. It is probably true that stable working class Negroes (who are often as much prisoners of the ghetto as lower class people) are much less interested in the opportunities of riots and more concerned about the costs. They often share the feeling that legal authority is neither just nor fair, but they also have material possessions and social positions to protect. They don't want their homes burned by rioters or strafed by the National Guard. And they are concerned that their children will become involved in the riot — that they will be treated as, and may come to think of themselves as, the "young hoodlums."

Because this more stable working class in the ghetto usually supplies its "community leaders," there is real danger that any investigating committee will be misled into believing that the riots represent the feelings of only a small minority. These "respectable" spokesmen for the area must not be allowed (no matter how honest their personal views might be) to mislead an investigating group in its analysis of the nature of riot participation.

There is always deep conflict . . . in the ghetto over the issue of police protection versus police harassment. The ghetto is a dangerous place for its inhabitants, and they would like to have firm and competent police surveillance. On the other hand, that very surveillance carries with it the danger of unjust and unseemly behavior by the police. Police rationality dictates that anyone in the ghetto is more suspect of crime than anyone in a white middle class neighborhood. From the police point of view, then, ghetto residents should be more willing to cooperate by answering questions and accepting arrest. The conflict built into this kind of situation can perhaps be somewhat ameliorated [improved] by more integrated police forces, and by vigorous supervision of the police to see that they are not impolite or overly aggressive. but that is no real solution to the problem.

Further, riots may well become more frequent and larger as time goes on due to the diffusion of knowledge, almost technical in nature, about how a riot is carried on. It is not too fanciful to say that anyone who watches television and reads the newspapers learns from the coverage of Watts, Hough [Cleveland], Newark, Harlem, and Detroit how to participate in a riot. Therefore, *without any organization at all* in the sense of a command structure, people in all parts of the nation know what to do and what roles one might take should a riot opportunity present itself. Millions of Americans today could, on request, fashion Molotov cocktails, who a year or two ago would not have known the meaning of the term. Similarly, millions of Americans now know that many rioters are not arrested and that snipers are seldom caught. There is no way of preventing the diffusion of this knowledge; we can only try to prevent the need and willingness to use it.

Finally, the particular quality of the riots reflects the Negro cultural emphasis on expressivity over instrumentality — practical, goal-directed action. A WASP [white Anglo-Saxon protestant] riot under similar conditions would probably be a much more hard-nosed and certainly much more bloody and violent event. The "carnival atmosphere" noted by observers at all major riots is probably a direct reflection of the expressive emphasis in all group activity among Negroes, whether it be church participation, the blues, a rock and roll concert, or street corner banter.

This is perhaps also part of the key to why the riots seem to be relatively unorganized, both locally and nationally. Discussion of an organized national conspiracy is probably a white projection. Whites find it very difficult to understand why Negroes aren't more efficient in their rebellion — why there is no national cadre [leadership], no command structure, no greater efficiency in doing damage. A good part of this may be because this is not the Negroes' preferred way of going about things. Rather, in the midst of an ... [apparent] group solidarity, a kind of free enterprise prevails in which each individual works for himself, perhaps cooperating for short periods of time with others to accomplish some immediate goals, but in the main doing things his own way as an expression of his own feelings. The expressive focus may be very important in formulating an ideology, and thus ultimately have a strong effect on the frequency and nature of rioting. But, that effect is achieved not by *organization,* but rather through *communication* of a developing social doctrine . . . .

When we seek the basic causes of the riots the central question is: Why are there so many Negroes for whom riots provide an opportunity for meaningful self-expression and gain? Further, why are the opportunities sought in such situations so destructive of social order? We know that in other situations which provide technical opportunity, for example, blackouts, nothing of the sort happens, although the authorities always fear that it might.

Much of the popular interpretation of riots has turned on an understanding of the really desperate situation of the worst off in the ghettos, of those who make up the "underclass," which may include anywhere between one-third and one-half of the ghetto population. Again, however, the figures on the Watts arrestees are instructive. Two-thirds of the men arrested and convicted were employed and perhaps as many as one-third of them were earning over $300 a month. Forty percent (or over half of those who had ever been married) were living with their spouses. Thus, when a riot takes place, a significant portion even of those above the poverty line may well be drawn into participation. This should alert us to the fact that rioting is not exclusively a problem of poverty as currently defined.

One may talk about two major kinds of causative factors — one involving *class* (by which is meant simply economic deprivation and all of the cultural and social consequences that flow from it) and the other involving the inferior *caste* position of Negroes to whites. This latter factor is most directly expressed in ghetto hostility toward the police, but it is also involved in the attack the riots come to represent on the total white-dominated society. Even the Negro who is well off in class terms may feel a strong pull toward participation if he has had the experience of being interrogated and perhaps arrested in a ghetto area simply because his face is black. Where men have little to protect and where their experience of hostility and indifference from the white world is even more pervasive, as in the case of the lower class, the resistance to participation will be even less.

The fact that even a significant minority of the participants are members of seemingly stable families earning above poverty level incomes tells us something about what is involved in exclusion from ordinary American society in a city as prosperous as Detroit or Los Angeles. Whatever poverty as minimum subsistence may mean, it is quite clear that people with incomes as high as $5,000 a year are really not able to feel that they participate in the broad spectrum of average American affluence and satisfaction. A community in which the great majority of the families must exist on significantly less than the median [middle] family income for the nation is a community of failures. Inclusion in such a community, compounded as it is by belonging to a historically excluded group and the knowledge that there is connection between racial exclusion and economic exclusion, is undesirable to those who live within its confines as well as to those outside.

Thus, the ghetto community has few informal social controls; people tend to minimize trouble by avoiding each other more than by building up informal social networks which ensure observance of common group standards. Everybody does pretty much what he wants as long as he can stay out of the clutches of the authorities. Thus, the individual has few effective sanctions available at the informal level. Even those who disapprove of rioting are powerless to do much about it by informally punishing those who participate. Any influence they might have is vitiated by the common perception of all that the authorities are just about as unjust as the law-breakers. Ghetto residents will, in desperation, call upon officialdom to punish those of their fellows who are directly making trouble for them, but they do it in much the same way that one might pay the neighborhood bully to discipline an enemy. The bully is called upon because of his power, not because of any legitimate authority.

The riots bring into high relief the ever present schism [split] in the Negro community between those who feel they have nothing to lose, and those who want to protect what they have — while the former riot, the latter deluge the police and mayor's office with telephone calls demanding protection from the rioters, demanding that the riot be put down before their homes are burned, their community destroyed. The physical contrast in Detroit is particularly striking. Not three blocks from the 12th Street riot area are substantial homes on well-maintained tree-lined streets. Their residents, like other stable working and middle class Negro Detroiters, wanted the riots put down with all possible dispatch; the potential cost of getting even with Whitey was too great.

And then there are the Negro businessmen in the ghetto — the "soul brothers." Detroit's Grand River Boulevard, where the riot-damaged buildings string out for miles, has a great many soul brothers (and one soul mother) whose quickly inscribed signs protected them from damage while on either side the looting or burning seemed complete. But, one can't count the "soul brother" signs that are no longer there because the glass was broken; and an occasional sign is still observable when only one broken show window in a soul brother's store was required to accomplish the looting. The signs obviously provided some protection, but exactly how much they lower the risk is a moot point. If the protection is very high, it would suggest that the hostility of the more properous and respectable Negroes is not returned by the rioters; if protection is low the rioters might be saying, as those in Bedford-Stuyvesant [Brooklyn] are reported to have taunted Negro policemen, "Take off your black masks so we can see your white faces."

Summing up: (1) the root cause of the riots lies in a caste system deeply imbedded in our society that has created a situation in which (a) a very large proportion of Negroes are denied the opportunity to achieve an average American standard of living, and (b) even those Negroes who do, by . . . their own efforts, manage to come reasonably close to an average American standard are still subjected to special disabilities and insults because of their confinement to a ghetto community. (2) From the immediate point of view of the rioters, the most pervasive factor which prevents their achieving some sence of decent life is that of living in poverty or near-poverty (as a rough rule form, say, having incomes less than one-half to two-thirds that of the median family income for the nation). This economic exclusion affects almost everything they do – their ability to purchase all those elements that make up the "standard package" that most American families deem their right. And the inability to earn more than this kind of poverty or near-poverty income affects the respect they are able to elicit from their own family members, members of their immediate community, and from the society at large.

It seems likely that the starting mechanisms for a riot are fairly dependent on the existence of pronounced poverty coupled with very high rates of unemployment. This, at least, would seem to be important to the extent that young men (say men under twenty-five) have a disproportionate influence on getting a riot going. This group is excluded not only from the availability of something like an average American life, but is excluded even within its own community. The older men do tend to be employed and to earn incomes reasonably close to the poverty line. It is the younger men in the ghetto who are most completely and dramatically excluded from any participation in the conventional rewards of the society.

If this diagnosis is correct – that the direct cause of participation in the riots (as opposed to the precipitating incidents) is economic marginalty – it should put us on notice that no "community action" programs, whether they involve better police-community relations or rapprochment with the new black militant leaders, will prevent riots. Rather, the necessary condition for any permanent solution to the riot problem will be to provide a reasonable approximation of the "average American standard of living" for every family. This means managing the society so that poverty and near-poverty are eliminated. Only then can those who now participate in and support the riots find themselves in situations where rioting has become a meaningless, useless activity. . . .

N. What Does the Looting Mean?

Russell Dynes and E. L. Quarantelli, "What Looting in Civil Disturbances Really Means," *Trans-action,* May, 1968, pp. 9-14. Reprinted with permission by the authors and the publisher. Copyright © 1968 by Washington University, St. Louis, Missouri.

Russell Dynes and E. L. Quarantelli are professors of sociology at The Ohio State University and are co-directors of the Disaster Research Center. The Center performs research on community functioning in various acute crises.

1. How do the authors define "looting"? What comparisons do they make between looting in disasters and in riots? Why does a difference exist?

2. Why is looting approved by the ghetto community in riots? Why do members of the middle class participate? What levels of looting are defined?

3. According to the authors, what does looting "really mean"? Why are the rioters looting?

In March and April of this year [1968], there were civil disturbances in Memphis, Tenn., Washington, D. C., Chicago, Pittsburgh, and Baltimore. Many films and photographs were taken of people looting other people's property. These looting incidents conformed to the pattern, for according to many reports people may be found looting when a community is having certain kinds of crises. One of these crises is caused by a natural disaster — a flood, hurricane, and so forth. And the other is caused by a civil disturbance, like the ones that have hit American cities every summer since the Watts outbreak of August 1965.

Natural disasters and civil disturbances give people a chance to help themselves to other people's goods. Yet there are important, fascinating differences between what happens in these two crisis situations. For example, looting is far more common in civil disturbances than in disasters. Then too, the *kinds* of goods taken during these two crises are different. And public disdain for the act varies. Sometimes taking other people's property during a community crisis is not even considered looting!

In order to examine the differences between the two crisis situations, let us analyze what happens to private property during natural disasters, and then contrast this with the transfers of property that take place during civil disorders.

The word "looting" has military roots. It implies that invading armies take property by force, generally when the rightful owner cannot protect it. Similarly, in civil disturbances "invading armies" plunder property left unguarded when the owner is forced out by violence or the threat of violence. During disasters, according to common belief, "invading armies" of opportunists take property left unguarded when the owner is forced out by the disaster.

The looting that takes place in these situations is usually interpreted as evidence of human depravity. In periods of natural or civil chaos, goes the explanation, the human animal is stripped of his usual social controls. Without them he is not a noble savage, but an ignoble one. For the general public, reports of looting are easy to incorporate into their images of the "criminal elements" who clean out the corner grocery during a racial disturbance, or the fiends and ghouls who roam disaster-stricken areas.

After the Galveston hurricane of 1900, published accounts told of people being summarily shot when they were caught with pocketsful of severed fingers with rings on them. In 1906, after the San Francisco earthquake and fire, the *Los Angeles Times* reported that "looting by fiends incarnate made a hell broth of the center of the ruined district. Sixteen looters were shot out of hand on April 19, while robbing the dead." In his reconstruction of events after the earthquake, reporter Q. A. Bronson noted "reports . . . of . . . looters wantonly shot in their tracks by Federal troops, miscreants hanged in public squares, and ghouls found cutting off the fingers and ears of corpses for rings and earrings attached."

Today, most radio and television accounts of disasters are less dramatic, but looting is still a major theme. After a tornado hit some suburbs of Chicago in April 1967, a county sheriff reportedly announced that "orders had gone out that beginning at 10 P.M. Friday, any looters . . . were to be shot on sight." After a power failure blacked out the Cincinnati area in May 1967, a wire-service story told of the smashing of store windows and looting in Cincinnati and in neighboring Newport and Covington, Ky.

Public officials, expecting certain kinds of community emergencies to activate human depravity, often request additional law enforcement. They mobilize National Guard units and take extra security measures. These steps are often taken upon the first reports of a civil disturbance or a natural disaster. Frequently, before the situation has even developed, television and radio will report what *is expected to happen* — the fear of looting and the steps being taken to prevent it.

That most people are concerned about looting in civil disorders and disasters is beyond dispute. Reliable evidence, however, points to a surprising fact: While looting clearly does occur in civil disturbances, in disaster situations it is very rare.

Many studies of disasters mention *reports* of looting, but very few cite authenticated cases. One study that did inquire into actual cases of looting was the National Opinion Research Center (N.O.R.C.) study of White County, Ark., after it was ravaged by a tornado in 1952. In the community that suffered the greatest damage, about 1000 of the 1200 residents were left homeless. A random sample of people from this town and adjacent areas were asked whether they had lost any property by looting. Only 9 percent reported that they, or members of their immediate household, had lost property that they even *felt* had been taken by looters. And fully one-third of these people were uncertain whether the loss was really due to looters, or whether the missing items had been blown away or buried in the debris. Finally, most of the articles were of little value.

In contrast, 58 percent of the people questioned said they had heard of *others'* property being stolen. In fact, 9 percent claimed that they had even seen looting in progress or had seen looters being arrested. The N.O.R.C. study team on the scene, however, could verify the theft of only two major items — a cash register and a piano.

Other disaster research confirms the rarity of looting. A study made after the 1953 floods in the Netherlands found that, although there were many reports of looting, law-enforcement agencies could discover not a single verified case. The Dutch researchers attributed many of the reports of looting to memory lapses in the immediate post-flood period, and pointed out that a number of people who reported thefts later found the missing items. Charles Fritz and J. H. Mathewson, in a review of disaster studies published up to 1956, concluded that "the number of verified cases of actual looting in peacetime disasters, in the United States and in foreign countries, is small."

More recent studies point in the same direction. The Disaster Research Center at Ohio State University, in field studies of more than 40 disasters both in the United States and abroad, has found extremely few verfied cases of looting. Actual police records support these findings. For example, in September 1965, the month Hurricane Betsy struck New Orleans, major crimes in the city fell 26.6 percent below the rate for the same month in the previous year. Burglaries reported to the police fell from 617 to 425. Thefts of over $50 dropped from 303 to 264, and those under $50 fell from 516 to 366. . . .

In contrast to what happens in a disaster situation, looting in civil disturbances is widespread, and the looters are usually members of the immediate community. During the past few summers, films and photographs have shown looting actually in progress. The McCone Commission reported that about 600 stores were looted or burned in Watts. In Newark, around 1300 people were arrested, mostly for taking goods. In the July 1967 holocaust in Detroit, unofficial estimates were that about 2700 stores were ransacked.

Disasters and civil disturbances are alike in that the normal order and organization of the community is disrupted. In addition, there is, in both situations, a temporary redefinition of property rights. But the two situations differ in other respects. In a disaster, there is general agreement among community members about community goals, especially about saving lives. As a result, by general agreement, all the resources are put at the disposal of the total community until emergency needs are met. A civil disturbance, on the other hand, represents conflict — not consensus [agreement] — on community goals. The outbreak itself represents disagreement over property rights within the community. Access to existing resources is questionable, and often there is open challenge to prior ownership.

The critical role of attitudes toward property in determining the nature of looting is best seen by contrasting the looting that occurs in civil disturbances with that found in disasters. There are three significant differences. As already noted, widespread looting *does* occur in civil disturbances, while it is infrequent in disasters. Further, the looting in civil disturbances is selective, focusing on particular types of goods or possessions, often symbolic of other values. And, while out-and-out looting is strongly condemned in disaster situations, looters in civil disturbances receive, from certain segments of the local community, strong social support for their actions.

The occurrence of looting in civil disturbances needs no further documentation. And selectivity can be seen in the fact that, in racial outbreaks, looters have concentrated overwhelmingly on certain kinds of stores. In Watts, Newark, and Detroit, the main businesses affected were groceries, supermarkets, and furniture and liquor stores. In contrast, banks, utility stations, industrial plants, and private residences have been generally ignored. Apartments and homes have been damaged, but only because they were in or near burned business establishments. Public installations such as schools and Office of Economic Opportunity centers have also been spared. There has not been indiscriminate looting. Certain kinds of consumer goods have been almost the only targets.

Looters in civil disturbances are also likely to receive support from many people in their community. Spiraling support coincides with shifts in property redefinitions, and these shifts occur in three stages. Initial looting is often a symbolic act of defiance. The second phase, in which more conscious and deliberate plundering develops, is possibly spurred on by the presence of delinquent gangs that loot more from need or for profit than for ideological reasons. Finally, in the third stage, there is widespread seizure of goods. At this point, looting becomes the socially expected thing to do. For example, a sociological survey at U.C.L.A. [University of California at Los Angeles] found that nearly one-fourth of the population participated in the Watts outbreak (although all of these participants probably did not engage in the looting).

If looting means strictly the taking of goods, little of it occurs in the first phase of civil disturbances. Instead, destructive attacks are most frequently directed against symbols of authority in the community. Police cars and fire trucks are pillaged and burned. What is involved here is perhaps illustrated most clearly in other kinds of civil disturbances, such as some of those created by college students. One of the authors once watched a crowd of students determinedly attack, for over an hour, an overhead traffic light. It conveniently symbolized the city administration and police — the actual target of the demonstrators' wrath. In racial civil disturbances, the police and their equipment are also seen as obvious symbols of the larger community toward which the outbreak is directed. How intense this focus can be was shown in the Watts disturbance. About 168 police cars and 100 pieces of fire-fighting equipment were damaged or destroyed.

The full redefinition of certain property rights occurs next. The "carnival spirit" observed in the Newark and Detroit disturbances did not represent anarchy. It represented widespread social support for the new definition of property. In this phase, there is little competition for goods. In fact, in contrast to the stealthy looting that occasionally occurs in disaster situations, looting in civil disturbances is quite open and frequently collective. The looters often work together in pairs, as family units, or in small groups. Bystanders are frequently told about potential loot. And in some instances, as in the Watts outbreak, looters coming out of stores hand strangers goods as "gifts."

Looting in civil disturbances is by insiders — by local community members. These looters apparently come not only from the low socioeconomic levels and from delinquent gangs, but from all segments of the population. During disturbances in Toledo, 91 percent of the 126 adults arrested for taking goods had jobs. A random sample in Detroit found that participants in the outbreak came more or less equally from all income brackets.

In both disasters and civil disturbances, there is a redefinition of property rights within the community. The community authorities, however, respond very differently to two situations. In disasters, responsible officials tolerate, accept, and encourage the transition from private to community property. In civil disturbances, community authorities see looting as essentially criminal behavior — as a legal problem to be handled forcefully by the police. And many segments of the larger community, especially middleclass people, with their almost sacred conception of private property, tend to hold the same view. This view of looting in civil disturbances fits in neatly with the ideas they already have about the criminal propensities of certain ethnic groups, notably Negroes.

At one level, there is no question that looting in civil disturbances is criminal behavior. But the laws that make it so are themselves based on dominant conceptions of property rights. Widespread looting, then, may perhaps be interpreted as a kind of mass protest against our dominant conceptions of property.

Mass protest is not new in history. According to George Rude's analysis, in his book *The Crowd in History,* demonstrating mobs from 1730 to 1848 in England and France were typically composed of local, respectable, employed people rather than the pauperized, the unemployed, or the "rabble" of the slums. The privileged classes naturally regarded these popular agitations as criminal — as fundamentally and unconditionally illegitimate. Rude notes, however, that such protest effectively communicated the desires of a segment of the urban population to the elite. E. J. Hobsbawm, in his analysis of the preindustrial "city mob," takes the same position: "The classical mob did not merely riot as a protest, but because it expected to achieve something by its riot. It assumed that the authorities would be sensitive to its movements, and probably also that they would make some immediate concession . . . This mechanism was perfectly understood by both sides."

In current civil disturbances, a similar mechanism and a similar message may be evolving. An attack against property rights is not necessarily "irrational," "criminal," or "pointless" if it leads to a clearer system of demands and responses, in which the needs and obligations of the contending parties are reasonably clear to themselves and to one another. The scope and intensity of current attacks indicate the presence of large numbers of outsiders living within most American cities. If property is seen as a shared understanding about the allocation of resources, and if a greater consensus can be reached on the proper allocation of these resources, many of these outsiders will become insiders, with an established stake in the communities in which they live.

This, then, is the most fundamental way in which looting in civil disturbances differs from looting after natural disasters: The looting that has occurred in recent racial outbreaks is a bid for the redistribution of property. It is a message that certain deprived sectors of the population want what they consider their fair share — and that they will resort to violence to get it. The fact that looting in riots is more widespread than in disasters, that it concentrates on the prestige items that symbolize the good life, and that it receives the support and approval of many within the deprived sectors who do not participate themselves, merely indicates the true nature and intention of looting under conditions of mass protest.

The basic question now is whether American community leaders can or will recognize that such looting is more than "pointless" or "criminal" behavior. If they do, it may mark the beginning of a new political dialogue, in which the outsiders in our urban communities can express their desires nonviolently to the insiders — insiders who will have finally learned to listen. If not, then in the summers to come, and perhaps in the winters as well, many men and women from the growing urban population may continue to demand a redefinition of property rights through disorder and violence.

Chapter **5**

A Process of Riots

Whenever a riot occurs, there are always factors which have prepared the way. The Federal Bureau of Investigation in its manual for police departments stresses the fact that "frustration breeds aggression on the part of any group." It warns that a frustrated minority group may resort to aggression as well may a frustrated majority. The F.B.I. also outlined a process leading to full-scale rioting.

1. Verbal aggression may have existed for a long time and with increasing intensity. Persons speak out aggressively against the government, a political leader, the business community, or some other source of conflict.
2. Economic frustration and dissatisfaction with status, coupled with a gradually changing social organization, have resulted in increasing irritation.
3. People feeling this irritation band together in various kinds of organizations. Some may be formal groups with leaders and a definite program, while others may be informal, spontaneous groups such as a mob or street crowd. These groups, formed out of frustration and discontent, seem to lend courage and support to the individual member and to tell him that his anger and beliefs are justified. His tendencies toward violence are stimulated.
4. An incident triggers the violence. This precipitating incident, actually a real occurrence or an imagined incident, becomes exaggerated through rumor and blown out of proportion.
5. Isolated cases of violent aggression occur. These serve to increase the existing tension and excitement.

6. Full-scale rioting begins when one or two of these isolated cases take hold and instigate mob action. Mob frenzy takes over. Riotous behavior is promoted by members of the crowd and more people participate. Destruction and other activities are "approved" by this group. Hostility increases.

Alfred McClure Lee, a sociologist who analyzed the 1943 Detroit race riot, suggested a similar pattern in riotous outbursts: (1) an event occurs which dramatizes faults in the society or tensions between groups, which leads to (a) the gathering of a crowd drawing attention to the event and promoting rumors and (b) the milling of a crowd in the streets; (2) the milling of the crowd increases the excitement of the community and the crowd grows in size and intensity; (3) the excitement of the growing crowd excites individuals to express their aggressiveness and encourages others to act violently; (4) these aggressive acts are approved by the mob; (5) action is directed against the objects chosen, almost spontaneously; for example, members of another race or symbols of the source of frustration (policemen, pawnshops, stores, streetlights, etc.).

In this chapter we will review the findings of the Kerner Commission on a riot's process, study data on the 1967 Newark, New Jersey, riot, and examine the summary of the Walker Report on the 1968 Chicago riot. As you read, think about the following general questions:

1. Is there really a pattern in riots? After carefully studying the two patterns presented in this introduction, do you think that they accurately describe what happens as riots break out?

2. If there is a pattern in the riots, what does it suggest for preventing or controlling future riots?

O. The Riot Process

> Report of the National Advisory Commission on Civil Disorders, Washington, D. C.: Government Printing Office, 1968, pp. 67, 3-4.

1. According to the President's commission, was there a definite "process" to the riots of 1967? Did the commission find a pattern such as the two presented in the introduction to this chapter?

2. Describe in your own words the types of conditions the commission found in riots, participants, grievances, and in levels of intensity.

3. Do you think that the occurrence of riots will be more or less probable in the future? Why? Why not?

The Commission has found no "typical" disorder in 1967 in terms of intensity of violence and extensiveness of damage. To determine whether, as is sometimes suggested, there was a typical "riot process," we examined 24 disorders which occurred during 1967 in 20 cities and three university settings. We have concentrated on four aspects of that process:

—The accumulating reservoir of grievances in the Negro community;

—"Precipitating" incidents and their relationship to the reservoir of grievances;

—The development of violence after its initial outbreak;

—The control effort, including official force, negotiation, and persuasion.

We found a common social process operating in all 24 disorders in certain critical respects. These events developed similarly, over a period of time and out of an accumulation of grievances and increasing tension in the Negro community. Almost invariably, they exploded in ways related to the local community and its particular problems and conflicts. But once violence erupted, there began a complex interaction of many elements — rioters, official control forces, counter-rioters — in which the differences between various disorders were more pronounced than the similarities. . . .

The "typical" riot did not take place. The disorders of 1967 were unusual, irregular, complex, and unpredictable social processes. Like most human events, they did not unfold in an orderly sequence. However, an analysis of our survey information leads to some conclusions about the riot process.

In general:

> —The civil disorders of 1967 involved Negroes acting against local symbols of white American society, authority, and property in Negro neighborhoods — rather than against white persons.

> —Of 164 disorders reported during the first nine months of 1967, eight (5 percent) were major in terms of violence and damage; 33 (20 percent) were serious but not major; 123 (75 percent) were minor and undoubtedly would not have received national attention as riots had the Nation not been sensitized by the more serious outbreaks.

> —In the 75 disorders studied by a Senate subcommittee, 83 deaths were reported. Eighty-two percent of the deaths and more than half the injuries occurred in Newark and Detroit. About 10 percent of the dead and 36 percent of the injured were public employees, primarily law officers and firemen. The overwhelming majority of the persons killed or injured in all the disorders were Negro civilians.

> —Initial damage estimates were greatly exaggerated. In Detroit, newspaper damage estimates at first ranged from $200 to $500 million; the highest recent estimate is $45 million. In Newark, early estimates ranged from $15 to $25 million. A month later damage was estimated at $10.2 million, 80 percent in inventory losses.

In the 24 disorders in 23 cities which we surveyed:

—The final incident before the outbreak of disorder, and the initial violence itself, generally took place in the evening or at night at a place in which it was normal for many people to be on the streets.

—Violence usually occurred almost immediately following the occurrence of the final precipitating incident, and then escalated rapidly. With but few exceptions, violence subsided during the day, and flared rapidly again at night. The night-day cycles continued through the early period of the major disorders.

—Disorder generally began with rock and bottle throwing and window breaking. Once store windows were broken, looting usually followed.

—Disorder did not erupt as a result of a single "triggering" or "precipitating" incident. Instead, it was generated out of an increasingly disturbed social atmosphere, in which typically a series of tension-heightening incidents over a period of weeks or months became linked in the minds of many in the Negro community with a reservoir of underlying grievances. At some point in the mounting tension, a further incident — in itself often routine or trivial — became the breaking point and the tension spilled over into violence.

—"Prior" incidents, which increased tensions and ultimately led to violence, were police actions in almost half the cases; police actions were "final" incidents before the outbreak of violence in 12 of the 24 surveyed disorders.

—No particular control tactic was successful in every situation. The varied effectiveness of control techniques emphasized the need for advance training, planning, adequate intelligence systems, and knowledge of the ghetto community.

—Negotiations between Negroes — including young militants as well as older Negro leaders — and white officials concerning "terms of peace" occurred during virtually all the disorders surveyed. In many cases, these negotiations involved discussion of underlying grievances as well as the handling of the disorder by control authorities.

—The typical rioter was a teenager or young adult, a lifelong resident of the city in which he rioted, a high school dropout; he was, nevertheless, somewhat better educated than his nonrioting Negro neighbor, and was usually underemployed or employed in a menial job. He was proud of his race, extremely hostile to both whites and middle-class Negroes and, although informed about politics, highly distrustful of the political system.

A Detroit survey revealed that approximately 11 percent of the total residents of two riot areas admitted participation in the rioting, 20 to 25 percent identified themselves as "bystanders," over 16 percent identified themselves as "counterrioters" who urged rioters to "cool it," and the remaining 48 to 53 percent said they were at home or elsewhere and did not participate. In a survey of Negro males between the ages of 15 and 35 residing in the disturbance area in Newark, about 45 percent identified themselves as rioters, and about 55 percent as "noninvolved."

—Most rioters were young Negro males. Nearly 53 percent of arrestees were between 15 and 24 years of age; nearly 81 percent between 15 and 35.

—In Detroit and Newark about 74 percent of the rioters were brought up in the North. In contrast, of the noninvolved, 36 percent in Detroit and 52 percent in Newark were brought up in the North.

—What the rioters appeared to be seeking was fuller participation in the social order and the material benefits enjoyed by the majority of American citizens. Rather than rejecting the American system, they were anxious to obtain a place for themselves in it.

—Numerous Negro counterrioters walked the streets urging rioters to "cool it." The typical counterrioter was better educated and had higher income than either the rioter or the noninvolved.

—The proportion of Negroes in local government was substantially smaller than the Negro proportion of population. Only three of the 20 cities studied had more than one Negro legislator; none had ever had a Negro mayor or city manager. In only four cities did Negroes hold other important policy-making positions or serve as heads of municipal departments.

—Although almost all cities had some sort of formal grievance mechanism for handling citizen complaints, this typically was regarded by Negroes as ineffective and was generally ignored. . . .

—The results of a three-city survey of various Federal programs — manpower, education, housing, welfare and community action — indicate that, despite substantial expenditures, the number of persons assisted constituted only a fraction of those in need.

The background of disorder is often as complex and difficult to analyze as the disorder itself. But we find that certain general conclusions can be drawn.

—Social and economic conditions in the riot cities constituted a clear pattern of severe disadvantage for Negroes compared with whites, whether the Negroes lived in the area where the riot took place or outside it. Negroes had completed fewer years of education and fewer had attended high school. Negroes were twice as likely to be unemployed and three times as likely to be in unskilled and service jobs. Negroes averaged 70 percent of the income earned by whites and were more than twice as likely to be living in poverty. Although housing cost Negroes relatively more, they had worse housing — three times as likely to be overcrowded and substandard. When compared to white suburbs, the relative disadvantage was even more pronounced.

A study of the aftermath of disorder leads to disturbing conclusions. We find that, despite the institution of some postriot programs:

—Little basic change in the conditions underlying the outbreak of disorder has taken place. Actions to ameliorate Negro grievances have been limited and sporadic; with but few exceptions, they have not significantly reduced tensions.

—In several cities, the principal official response has been to train and equip the police with more sophisticated weapons.

—In several cities, increasing polarization is evident, with continuing breakdown of interracial communication, and growth of white segregationist or black separatist groups.

P. Newark, New Jersey, 1967: An Example

Report of the National Advisory Commission on Civil Disorders, Washington, D. C.: Government Printing Office, 1968, pp. 354, 68-69, 394-395.

1. Drawing upon data from the 1967 Newark, New Jersey, riot, what grievances can you identify from the table comparing statistics for the metropolitan area of Newark, the city of Newark, and Newark's disorder area? Does this help to explain why the riot occurred? Why?

2. How do the "prior incidents" fit into the riot process schemes presented in the introduction to this section?

3. Comparing the two charts, "Levels of Violence" and "Negotiations," how would you describe the course of the riot? Can you see a pattern? Do you think that the riot reduced tensions and, thus, ended? Did the police and troops suppress the rioters? Did rioters feel that they had achieved their goals and injured their oppressors?

Prior Incidents

1965: A Newark policeman shot and killed an 18-year-old Negro boy. After the policeman had stated that he had fallen and his gun had discharged accidentally, he later claimed that the youth had assaulted another officer and was shot as he fled. At a hearing it was decided that the patrolman had not used excessive force. The patrolman remained on duty, and his occasional assignment to Negro areas was a continuing source of irritation in the Negro community.

April 1967: Approximately 15 Negroes were arrested while picketing a grocery store which they claimed sold bad meat and used unfair credit practices.

Late May, early June: Negro leaders had for several months voiced strong opposition to a proposed medical-dental center to be built on 150 acres of land in the predominantly Negro central ward. The dispute centered mainly around the lack of relocation provisions for those who would be displaced by the medical center. The issue became extremely volatile in late May when public "blight hearings" were held regarding the land to be condemned. The hearings became a public forum in which many residents spoke against the proposed center. The city did not change its plan.

Late May, June: The mayor recommended appointment of a white city councilman who had no more than a high school education to the position of secretary to the board of education. Reportedly, there was widespread support from both whites and Negroes for a Negro candidate who held a master's degree and was considered more qualified. The mayor did not change his recommendation. Ultimately, the original secretary retained his position and neither candidate was appointed.

July 8: Several Newark policemen, allegedly including the patrolman involved in the 1965 killing, entered East Orange to assist the East Orange police during an altercation with a group of Negro men.

Final Incident

July 12, approximately 9:30 p.m.: A Negro cab driver was injured during or after a traffic arrest in the heart of the central ward. Word spread quickly, and a crowd gathered in front of the Fourth Precinct stationhouse across the street from a large public housing project.

Initial Violences

Same day, approximately 11:30 p.m.: The crowd continued to grow until it reached 300 to 500 people, One or two Molotov cocktails were thrown at the stationhouse. Shortly after midnight the police dispersed the crowd, and window-breaking and looting began a few minutes later. By about 1 a.m., the peak level of violence for the first night was reached.

NEWARK

Characteristic	SMSA*		City**		Disorder Areas	
	White	Nonwhite	White	Nonwhite	White	Nonwhite
Population:						
Number of people	1,462,248	227,172	265,889	139,331	25,965	78,751
Age distribution:						
Male, under 15	200,041	37,508	32,030	24,422	2,954	13,856
15–24	76,415	13,566	15,577	8,628	1,666	4,869
25–64	366,874	51,620	68,278	30,778	6,907	17,202
65 and over	63,164	4,649	14,373	2,423	1,751	1,381
Female, under 15	193,116	38,263	30,586	24,779	2,953	14,123
15–24	86,067	17,339	16,985	11,105	1,693	6,363
25–64	391,764	58,388	71,127	34,424	6,224	19,394
65 and over	84,807	5,839	16,933	2,772	1,817	1,563
Number of children under 18 living with both parents	424,552	58,735	64,138	37,023	5,042	20,335
Percent of persons age 25 or above having received 8 years or less education	34.2	50.1	49.9	53.1	61.9	56.4
Median school years completed	11.5	9.0	9.0	8.8	8.5	8.6
Households:						
1-person households	54,527	8,892	16,525	6,607	3,474	4,683
2–5 person households	359,343	42,476	66,232	26,196	5,866	14,867
6-or-more-person households	35,772	10,147	5,855	6,357	656	3,558
Economic:						
Median family income	$7,503	$4,807	$5,870	$4,491	$4,567	$4,199
Percent of families with income under $3,000	8.7	23.8	15.2	27.4	25.7	30.3
Percent of males age 14 and over in civilian labor force	80.0	79.9	77.8	80.3	74.8	81.0
Percent of males in civilian labor force who are unemployed	3.2	8.3	5.8	9.7	9.0	11.1

Percent of employed males who are managers, officials, professional, technical, etc.	31.1	6.8	16.7	4.2	10.6	3.9
Percent of employed males who are laborers, service workers, private household workers	10.6	31.6	16.8	32.4	16.6	34.3
Percent of women age 14 and over who are in the labor force	35.0	50.3	38.5	48.0	38.0	48.1
Percent of females in the labor force who are unemployed	5.0	10.6	8.2	14.2	13.4	16.2
Percent of employed females who are managers, officials, professional, technical, etc.	18.9	7.8	13.0	6.5	11.5	5.7
Percent of employed females who are laborers, service workers, private household workers	10.9	44.2	11.3	37.5	17.5	38.1
Percent of women in labor force with own children under 6 years of age	6.6	13.4	7.1	14.3	9.3	14.4
Housing:						
Total occupied units	449,642	61,515	88,612	39,160	9,996	23,108
Percent owner-occupied units	58.2	23.9	26.7	13.2	11.9	8.5
Median value of owner-occupied units	$18,500	$13,000	$13,800	$11,900	$9,500	$12,100
Percent renter-occupied units	41.8	76.1	73.3	86.8	88.1	91.5
Median rent	$87	$78	$77	$77	$68	$74
Percent with 1.01 or more persons per room	5.3	20.4	8.8	22.5	13.3	23.6
Percent built before 1939	66.1	89.3	87.5	91.1	91.8	89.9
Percent sound with all plumbing facilities	90.2	50.4	78.5	42.8	47.5	35.7
Percent of household heads who moved in 1958–60	25.0	37.5	27.0	42.7	32.6	42.0

* The whole metropolitan area including the city and its suburbs.

** The city without the suburbs.

137

Levels of Violence

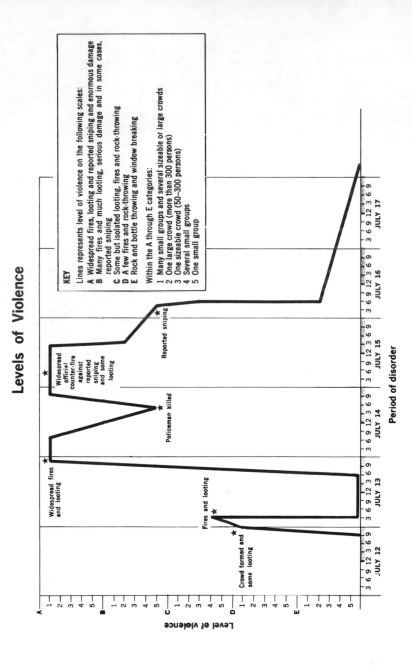

KEY

Lines represents level of violence on the following scales:

A Widespread fires, looting and reported sniping and enormous damage
B Many fires and much looting, serious damage and in some cases, reported sniping
C Some but isolated looting, fires and rock-throwing
D A few fires and rock-throwing
E Rock and bottle throwing and window breaking

Within the A through E categories:

1 Many small groups and several sizeable or large crowds
2 One large crowd (more than 300 persons)
3 One sizeable crowd (50–300 persons)
4 Several small groups
5 One small group

Level of violence

Period of disorder

Widespread fires and looting ★

Policeman killed ★

Widespread official counter-fire against reported sniping and some looting ★

Reported sniping ★

Fires and looting ★

Crowd formed and some looting ★

JULY 12   JULY 13   JULY 14   JULY 15   JULY 16   JULY 17

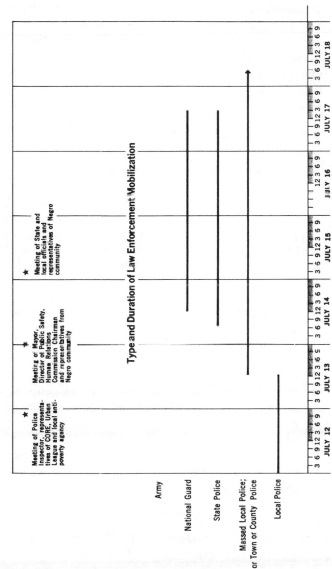

Negotiations

★ Meeting of Police Inspector, representatives of CORE, Urban League and local anti-poverty agency

★ Meeting of Mayor, Director of Public Safety, Human Relations Commission Chairman and representatives from Negro community

★ Meeting of State and local officials and representatives of Negro community

Type and Duration of Law Enforcement Mobilization

Army

National Guard

State Police

Massed Local Police; or Town or County Police

Local Police

3 6 9 12 3 6 9 | 3 6 9 12 3 6 9 | 3 6 9 12 3 6 9 | 3 6 9 12 3 6 9 | 3 6 9 12 3 6 9 | 123 6 9 | 3 6 9 12 3 6 9 | 3 6 9 12 3 6 9

JULY 12 | JULY 13 | JULY 14 | JULY 15 | JULY 16 | JULY 17 | JULY 18

Period of disorder

Q. A Police Riot? A Case Summary of the 1968 Chicago Riot

Riots in Conflict: The Violent Confrontation of Demonstrators and Police in the Parks and Streets of Chicago During the Week of the Democratic National Convention of 1968 (Washington, D. C.: Government Printing Office, 1969) pp. 1-11. A report submitted by the Chicago team, directed by Daniel Walker, to the National Commission on the Causes and Prevention of Violence, Milton Eisenhower, chairman.

Just as a bomb bursts, the Walker report produced a flash when it appeared fifty-three days after the riots. A panel of distinguished citizens and 212 researchers presented the new possibility of police contributions to violence and riotous behavior. This possibility had been considered the excuse of militants and extremists. You should read the Walker Report's summary, quoted here with slight editing, and be alert to the fact that it was considered unfair to the police by Chicago officials and other prominent public figures. Certainly, the final word has not been said!

1. How does the frustration-aggression theory help to explain the police behavior as reported? Are other theories helpful?

2. Did the news media, representing "the public's right to know," pose a serious problem for the police on the scene and by reporting selected, edited aspects of the riot?

3. Do you see any parallels between the "police riot" and the process of riots presented in the introduction to this chapter? What are they, if any?

During the week of the Democratic National Convention, the Chicago police were the targets of mounting provocation by both word and act. It took the form of obscene epithets, and of rocks, sticks, bathroom tiles and even human feces hurled at police by demonstrators. Some of these acts had been planned; others were spontaneous or were themselves provoked by police action. Furthermore, the police had been put on edge by widely published threats of attempts to disrupt both the city and the Convention.

That was the nature of the provocation. The nature of the response was unrestrained and indiscriminate police violence on many occasions, particularly at night.

That violence was made all the more shocking by the fact that it was often inflicted upon persons who had broken no law, disobeyed no order, made no threat. These included peaceful demonstrators, onlookers, and large numbers of residents who were simply passing through, or happened to live in, the areas where confrontations were occurring.

Newsmen and photographers were singled out for assault, and their equipment deliberately damaged. Fundamental police training was ignored; and officers, when on the scene, were often unable to control their men. As one police officer put it: "What happened didn't have anything to do with police work."

The violence reached its culmination on Wednesday night.

A report prepared by an inspector from the Los Angeles Police Department, present as an official observer, while generally praising the police restraint he had observed in the parks during the week, said this about the events that night:

> There is no question but that many officers acted without restraint and exerted force beyond that necessary under the circumstances. The leadership at the point of the conflict did little to prevent such conduct and the direct control of officers by first line supervisors was virtually non-existent.

He is referring to the police-crowd confrontation in front of the Conrad Hilton Hotel. Most Americans know about it, having seen the 17-minute sequence played and replayed on their television screens.

But most Americans do not know that the confrontation was followed by even more brutal incidents in the Loop side streets. Or that it had been preceded by comparable instances of indiscriminate police attacks on the North Side a few nights earlier when demonstrators were cleared from Lincoln Park and pushed into the streets and alleys of Old Town.

How did it start? With the emergence long before convention week of three factors which figured significantly in the outbreak of violence. These were: threats to the city; the city's response; and the conditioning of Chicago police to expect that violence against demonstrators, as against rioters, would be condoned by city officials.

The threats to the City were varied. Provocative and inflammatory statements, made in connection with activities planned for convention week, were published and widely disseminated. There were also intelligence reports from informants.

Some of this information was absurd, like the reported plan to contaminate the city's water supply with LSD. But some were serious; and both were strengthened by the authorities' lack of any mechanism for distinguishing one from the other.

The second factor — the city's response — matched, in numbers and logistics at least, the demonstrators' threats.

The city, fearful that the "leaders" would not be able to control their followers, attempted to discourage an inundation of demonstrators by not granting permits for marches and rallies and by making it quite clear that the "law" would be enforced.

Government — federal, state and local — moved to defend itself from the threats, both imaginary and real. The preparations were detailed and far-ranging: from stationing firemen at each alarm box within a six block radius of the Amphitheatre to staging U.S. Army armored personnel carriers in Soldier Field under Secret Service control. Six thousand Regular Army troops in full field gear, equipped with rifles, flame throwers, and bazookas were airlifted to Chicago on Monday, August 26. About 6,000 Illinois National Guard troops had already been activated to assist the 12,000 member Chicago Police Force.

Of course, the Secret Service could never afford to ignore threats of assassination of Presidential candidates. Neither could the city, against the background of riots in 1967 and 1968, ignore the ever-present threat of ghetto riots, possibly sparked by large numbers of demonstrators, during convention week.

The third factor emerged in the city's position regarding the riots following the death of Dr. Martin Luther King and the April 27th peace march to the Civic Center in Chicago.

The police were generally credited with restraint in handling the first riots – but Mayor Daley rebuked the Superintendent of Police. While it was later modified, his widely disseminated "shoot to kill arsonists and shoot to maim looters" order undoubtedly had an effect.

The effect on police became apparent several weeks later, when they attacked demonstrators, bystanders and media representatives at a Civic Center peace march. There were published criticisms – but the city's response was to ignore the police violence.

That was the background. On August 18, 1968, the advance contingent of demonstrators arrived in Chicago and established their base, as planned, in Lincoln Park on the city's Near North Side. Throughout the week, they were joined by others – some from the Chicago area, some from states as far away as New York and California. On the weekend before the convention began, there were about 2,000 demonstrators in Lincoln Park; the crowd grew to about 10,000 by Wednesday.

There were, of course, the hippies – the long hair and love beads, the calculated unwashedness, the flagrant banners, the open lovemaking and disdain for the constraints of conventional society. In dramatic effect, both visual and vocal, these dominated a crowd whose members actually differed widely in physical appearance, in motivation, in political affiliation, in philosophy. The crowd included Yippies come to "do their thing," youngsters working for a political candidate, professional people with dissenting political views, anarchists and determined revolutionaries, motorcycle gangs, black activists, young thugs, police and secret service undercover agents. There were demonstrators waving the Viet Cong flag and the red flag of revolution and there were the simply curious who came to watch and, in many cases, became willing or unwilling participants.

To characterize the crowd, then, as entirely hippy-Yippie, entirely "New Left," entirely anarchist, or entirely youthful political dissenters is both wrong and dangerous. The stereotyping that did occur helps to explain the emotional reaction of both police and public during and after the violence that occurred.

Despite the presence of some revolutionaries, the vast majority of the demonstrators were intent on expressing by peaceful means their dissent either from society generally or from the administration's policies in Vietnam.

Most of those intending to join the major protest demonstrations scheduled during convention week did not plan to enter the Amphitheatre and disrupt the proceedings of the Democratic convention, did not plan aggressive acts of physical provocation against the authorities, and did not plan to use rallies of demonstrators to stage an assault against any person, institution, or place of business. But while it is clear that most of the protesters in Chicago had no intention of initiating violence, this is not to say that they did not expect it to develop.

It was the clearing of the demonstrators from Lincoln Park that led directly to the violence: symbolically, it expressed the city's opposition to the protesters; literally, it forced the protesters into confrontation with police in Old Town and the adjacent residential neighborhoods.

The Old Town area near Lincoln Park was a scene of police ferocity exceeding that shown on televison on Wednesday night. From Sunday night through Tuesday night, incidents of intense and indiscriminate violence occurred in the streets after police had swept the park clear of demonstrators.

Demonstrators attacked too. And they posed difficult problems for police as they persisted in marching through the streets, blocking traffic and intersections. But it was the police who forced them out of the park and into the neighborhood. And on the part of the police there was enough wild club swinging, enough cries of hatred, enough gratuitous beating to make the conclusion inescapable that individual policemen, and lots of them, committed violent acts far in excess of the requisite force for crowd dispersal or arrest. To read dispassionately the hundreds of statements describing at firsthand the events of Sunday and Monday nights is to become convinced of the presence of what can only be called police riot.

Here is an eyewitness talking about Monday night:

> The demonstrators were forced out onto Clark Street and once again a traffic jam developed. Cars were stopped, the horns began to honk, people couldn't move, people got gassed inside their cars, people got stoned inside their cars, police were the objects of stones, and taunts, mostly taunts. As you must understand, most of the taunting of the police was verbal. There were stones thrown, or course, but for the most part it was verbal. But there were stones being thrown and of course the police were responding with tear gas and clubs and everytime they could get near enough to a demonstrator they hit him.
>
> But again you had this police problem within – this really turned into a police problem. They pushed everybody out of the park, but this night there were a lot more people in the park than there had been during the previous night and Clark Street was just full of people and in addition now was full of gas because the police were using gas on a much larger scale this night. So the police were faced with the task, which took them about an hour or so, of hitting people over the head and gassing them enough to get them out of Clark Street, which they did.

But police action was not confined to the necessary force, even in clearing the park:

> A young man and his girl friend were both grabbed by officers. He screamed, "We're going, we're going," but they threw him into the pond. The officers grabbed the girl, knocked her to the ground, dragged her along the embankment and hit her with their batons on her head, arms, back and legs. The boy tried to scramble up the embankment to her, but police shoved him back in the water at least twice. He finally got to her and tried to pull her in the water, away from the police. He was clubbed on the head five or six times. An officer shouted, "Let's get the . . .!" but the boy pulled her in the water and the police left.

Like the incident described above, much of the violence witnessed in Old Town that night seems malicious and mindless:

> There were pedestrians. People who were not part of the demonstration were coming out of a tavern to see what the demonstration was . . . and the officers indiscriminately started beating everybody on the street who was not a policeman.

Another scene:

> There was a group of about six police officers that moved in and started beating two youths. When one of the officers pulled back his nightstick to swing, one of the youths grabbed it from behind and started beating on the officer. At this point about ten officers left everybody else and ran after this youth, who turned down Wells and ran to the left.
> But the officers went to the right, picked up another youth, assuming he was the one they were chasing, and took him into an empty lot and beat him. And when they got him to the ground, they just kicked him ten times — the wrong youth, the innocent youth who had been standing there.

A federal legal official relates an experience of Tuesday evening:

> I then walked one block north where I met a group of
> 12-15 policemen. I showed them my identification and they
> permitted me to walk with them. The police walked one
> block west. Numerous people were watching us from their
> windows and balconies. The police yelled profanities at
> them, taunting them to come down where the police would
> beat them up. The police stopped a number of people on
> the street demanding identification. They verbally abused
> each pedestrian and pushed one or two without hurting
> them. We walked back to Clark Street and began to walk
> north where the police stopped a number of people who
> appeared to be protesters, and ordered them out of the area
> in a very abusive way. One protester who was walking in the
> opposite direction was kneed in the groin by a policeman
> who was walking towards him. The boy fell to the ground
> and swore at the policeman who picked him up and threw
> him to the ground. We continued to walk toward the
> command post. A derelict who appeared to be very
> intoxicated, walked up to the policeman and mumbled
> something that was incoherent. The policeman pulled from
> his belt a tin container and sprayed its contents into the eyes
> of the derelict, who stumbled around and fell on his face.

It was on these nights that the police violence against media representatives reached its peak. Much of it was plainly deliberate. A newsman was pulled aside on Monday by a detective acquaintance of his who said: "The word is being passed to get newsmen." Individual newsmen were warned, "You take my picture tonight and I'm going to get you." Cries of "get the camera" preceded individual attacks on photographers.

A newspaper photographer describes Old Town on Monday at about 9:00 P.M.:

> When the people arrived at the intersection of Wells and
> Division, they were not standing in the streets. Suddenly a
> column of policemen ran out from the alley. They were

reinforcements. They were under control but there seemed to be no direction. One man was yelling, "Get them up on the sidewalks, turn them around." Very suddenly the police charged the people on the sidewalks and began beating their heads. A line of cameramen was "trapped" along with the crowd along the sidewalks, and the police went down the line chopping away at the cameras.

A network cameraman reports that on the same night:

> I just saw this guy coming at me with his nightstick and I had the camera up. The tip of his stick hit me right in the mouth, then I put my tongue up there and I noticed that my tooth was gone. I turned around then to try to leave and then this cop came up behind me with his stick and he jabbed me in the back.
>
> All of a sudden these cops jumped out of the police cars and started just beating the hell out of people And before anything else happened to me, I saw a man holding a Bell & Howell camera with big wide letters on it, saying "CBS." He apparently had been hit by a cop. And cops were standing around and there was blood streaming down his face. Another policeman was running after me and saying, "Get the . . . out of here." And I heard another guy scream, "Get their . . . cameras." And the next thing I know I was being hit on the head, and I think on the back, and I was just forced down on the ground at the corner of Division and Wells.

If the intent was to discourage coverage, it was successful in at least one case. A photographer from a news magazine says that finally, "I just stopped shooting, because every time you push the flash, they look at you and they are screaming about, 'Get the . . . photographers and get the film.' "

There is some explanation for the media-directed violence. Camera crews on at least two occasions did stage violence and fake injuries. Demonstrators did sometimes step up their activities for the benefit of TV cameras. Newsmen and photographers' blinding lights did get in the way of police clearing streets, sweeping the park and dispersing demonstrators. Newsmen did, on occasion, disobey legitimate police orders to "move" or "clear the streets." News reporting of events did seem to the police to be anti-Chicago and anti-police.

But was the response appropriate to the provocation?

Out of 300 newsmen assigned to cover the parks and streets of Chicago during convention week, more than 60 (about 20%) were involved in incidents resulting in injury to themselves, damage to their equipment, or their arrest. Sixty-three newsmen were physically attacked by police; in 13 of these instances, photographic or recording equipment was intentionally damaged.

The violence did not end with either demonstrators or newsmen on the North Side on Sunday, Monday and Tuesday. It continued in Grant Park on Wednesday. It occurred on Michigan Avenue in front of the Conrad Hilton Hotel, as already described. A high-ranking Chicago police commander admits that on that occasion the police "got out of control." This same commander appears in one of the most vivid scenes of the entire week, trying desperately to keep individual policemen from beating demonstrators as he screams, "For Christ's sake, stop it!"

Thereafter, the violence continued on Michigan Avenue and on the side streets running into Chicago's Loop. A federal official describes how it began:

> I heard a 10-1 call [policeman in trouble] on either my radio or one of the other hand sets carried by men with me and then heard "Car 100 — sweep." With a roar of motors, squads, vans and three-wheelers came from east, west and north into the block north of Jackson. The crowd scattered. A big group ran west on Jackson, with a group of blue shirted policemen in pursuit, beating at them with clubs. Some of the crowd would jump into doorways and the police would rout them out. The action was very tough. In my judgment, unnecessarily so. The police were hitting with a vengeance and quite obviously with relish . . . .

What followed was a club-swinging melee. Police ranged the streets striking anyone they could catch. To be sure, demonstrators threw things at policemen and at police cars; but the weight of violence was overwhelmingly on the side of the police. A few examples will give the flavor of that night in Chicago:

"At the corner of Congress Plaza and Michigan," states a doctor, "was gathered a group of people, numbering between thirty and forty. They were trapped against a railing [along a ramp leading down from Michigan Avenue to an underground parking garage] by several policemen on motorcycles. The police charged the people on motorcycles and struck about a dozen of them, knocking several of them down. About twenty standing there jumped over the railing. On the other side of the railing was a three-to-four-foot drop. None of the people who were stuck by the motorcycles appeared to be seriously injured. However, several of them were limping as if they had been run over on their feet."

A UPI reporter witnessed these attacks, too. He relates in his statement that one officer, "with a smile on his face and a fanatical look in his eyes, was standing on a three-wheel cycle, shouting, 'Wahoo, wahoo,' and trying to run down people on the sidewalk." The reporter says he was chased thirty feet by the cycle.

A priest who was in the crowd says he saw a "boy, about fourteen or fifteen, white, standing on top of an automobile yelling something which was unidentifiable. Suddenly a policeman pulled him down from the car and beat him to the ground by striking him three or four times with a nightstick. Other police joined in . . . and they eventually shoved him to a police van.

"A well-dressed woman saw this incident and spoke angrily to a nearby police captain. As she spoke, another policeman came up from behind her and sprayed something in her face with an aerosol can. He then clubbed her to the ground. He and two other policemen then dragged her along the ground to the same paddy wagon and threw her in."

"I ran west on Jackson," a witness states. "West of Wabash, a line of police stretching across both sidewalks and the street charged after a small group I was in. Many people were clubbed and maced as they ran. Some weren't demonstrators at all, but were just pedestrians who didn't know how to react to the charging officers yelling 'Police!' "

"A wave of police charged down Jackson," another witness relates. "Fleeing demonstrators were beaten indiscriminately and a temporary, makeshift first aid station was set up on the corner of State and Jackson. Two men lay in pools of blood, their heads severely cut by clubs. A minister moved amongst the crowd, quieting them, brushing aside curious onlookers, and finally asked a policeman to call an ambulance, which he agreed to do. . . ."

An Assistant U.S. Attorney later reported that "the demonstrators were running as fast as they could but were unable to get out of the way because of the crowds in front of them. I observed the police striking numerous individuals, perhaps 20 to 30. I saw three fall down and then overrun by the police. I observed two demonstrators who had multiple cuts on their heads. We assisted one who was in shock into a passer-by's car."

Police violence was a fact of convention week. Were the policemen who committed it a minority? It appears certain that they were — but one which has imposed some of the consequences of its actions on the majority, and certainly on their commanders. There has been no public condemnation of these violators of sound police procedures and common decency by either their commanding officers or city officials. Nor (at the time this Report is being completed — almost three months after the convention) has any disciplinary action been taken against most of them. That some policemen lost control of themselves under exceedingly provocative circumstances can perhaps be understood; but not condoned. If no action is taken against them, the effect can only be to discourage the majority of policemen who acted responsibly, and further weaken the bond between police and community.

Although the crowds were finally dispelled on the nights of violence in Chicago, the problems they represent have not been. Surely this is not the last time that a violent dissenting group will clash head-on with those whose duty it is to enforce the law. And the next time the whole world will still be watching.

Chapter **6**

Detroit, 1967: A Case Study

It is now time to pull together what you know about civil disorders and apply this knowledge to an analysis of a case study. The readings in this chapter describe the Detroit riot of 1967, present reactions to it, and offer a glimpse of the future. First, there is a chronological summary written by researchers working for the President's Commission on Civil Disorders. Then, there is a brilliant article by Irving J. Rubin, director of a regional urban planning project in Detroit.

As you read, keep questioning and utilize the theories learned in earlier sections to analyze and explain what happened in Detroit. Perhaps, President Johnson's questions initially addressed to the Commission, will provide adequate guidelines:

1. What happened?
2. Why did it happen? What was the effect?
3. What can be done to prevent it from happening again and again?

R. A Chronological Survey of Events

Report of the National Advisory Commission on Civil Disorders, Washington, D. C.: Government Printing Office, 1968, pp. 47-61, 372-373.

1. What happened? When did it happen? Can you see a "process" or "pattern" in the Detroit events from initial tensions and precipitating incidents to the conclusion?
2. Who were the participants? How would you characterize them? What did the participants hope to achieve?

On Saturday evening, July 22, the Detroit Police Department raided five "blind pigs." The blind pigs had had their origin in prohibition days, and survived as private social clubs. Often, they were after-hours drinking and gambling spots.

The fifth blind pig on the raid list, the United Community and Civic League at the corner of 12th Street and Clairmount, had been raided twice before. Once 10 persons had been picked up; another time, 28. A Detroit vice squad officer had tried but failed to get in shortly after 10 o'clock Saturday night. He succeeded, on his second attempt, at 3:45 Sunday morning.

The Tactical Mobile Unit, the Police Department's crowd control squad, had been dismissed at 3 a.m. Since Sunday morning traditionally is the least troublesome time for police in Detroit . . . only 193 officers were patroling the streets. Of these, 44 were in the 10th precinct where the blind pig was located.

Police expected to find two dozen patrons in the blind pig. That night, however, it was the scene of a party for several servicemen, two of whom were back from Vietnam. Instead of two dozen patrons, police found 82. Some voiced resentment at the police intrusion.

An hour went by before all 82 could be transported from the scene. The weather was humid and warm — the temperature that day was to rise to 86 — and despite the late hour, many people were still on the street. In short order, a crowd of about 200 gathered.

In November of 1965, George Edwards, Judge of the United States Court of Appeals for the Sixth Circuit, and Commissioner of the Detroit Police Department from 1961 to 1963, had written in the *Michigan Law Review:*

> It is clear that in 1965 no one will make excuses for any city's inability to foresee the possibility of racial trouble. . . Although local police forces generally regard themselves as public servants with the responsibility of maintaining law and order, they tend to minimize this

attitude when they are patrolling areas that are heavily populated with Negro citizens. There, they tend to view each person on the streets as a potential criminal or enemy, and all too often that attitude is reciprocated. Indeed, hostility between the Negro communities in our large cities and the police departments, is the major problem in law enforcement in this decade. It has been a major cause of all recent race riots.

At the time of Detroit's 1943 race riot, Judge Edwards told Commission investigators, there was "open warfare between the Detroit Negroes and the Detroit Police Department." As late as 1961, he had thought that "Detroit was the leading candidate in the United States for a race riot."

There was a long history of conflict between the police department and citizens. During the labor battles of the 1930's, union members had come to view the Detroit Police Department as a strike-breaking force. The 1943 riot, in which 34 persons died, was the bloodiest in the United States in a span of two decades.

Judge Edwards and his successor, Commissioner Ray Girardin, attempted to restructure the image of the department. A Citizens Complaint Bureau was set up to facilitate the filing of complaints by citizens against officers. In practice, however, this Bureau appeared to work little better than less enlightened and more cumbersome procedures in other cities.

On 12th Street, with its high incidence of vice and crime, the issue of police brutality was a recurrent theme. A month earlier, the killing of a prostitute had been determined by police investigators to be the work of a pimp [one who finds customers for prostitutes]. According to rumors in the community, the crime had been committed by a vice squad officer.

At about the same time, the killing of Danny Thomas, a 27-year-old Negro Army veteran, by a gang of white youths had inflamed the community. The city's major newspapers played down the story in hope that the murder would not become a cause for increased tensions. The intent backfired. A banner story in the *Michigan Chronicle,* the city's Negro newspaper, began: "As James Meredith marched again Sunday to prove a Negro could walk in Mississippi without fear, a young woman who saw her husband killed by a white gang, shouting: 'Niggers keep out of Rouge Park,' lost her baby.

"Relatives were upset that the full story of the murder was not being told, apparently in an effort to prevent the incident from sparking a riot."

Some Negroes believed that the daily newspapers' treatment of the story was further evidence of the double standard: playing up crimes by Negroes, playing down crimes committed against Negroes.

Although police arrested one suspect for murder, Negroes questioned why the entire gang was not held. What, they asked, would have been the result if a white man had been killed by a gang of Negroes? What if Negroes had made the kind of advances toward a white woman that the white men were rumored to have made toward Mrs. Thomas?

The Thomas family lived only four or five blocks from the raided blind pig.

A few minutes after 5 a.m., just after the last of those arrested had been hauled away, an empty bottle smashed into the rear window of a police car. A litter basket was thrown through the window of a store. Rumors circulated of excess force used by the police during the raid. A youth, whom police nicknamed "Mr. Greensleeves" because of the color of his shirt, was shouting: "We're going to have a riot!" and exhorting the crowd to vandalism.

At 5:20 a.m., Commissioner Girardin was notified. He immediately called Mayor Jerome Cavanagh. Seventeen officers from other areas were ordered into the 10th Precinct. By 6 a.m., police strength had grown to 369 men. Of these, however, only 43 were committed to the immediate riot area. By that time, the number of persons on 12th Street was growing into the thousands and widespread window-smashing and looting had begun.

On either side of 12th Street were neat, middle-class districts. Along 12th Street itself, however, crowded apartment houses created a density of more than 21,000 persons per square mile, almost double the city average.

The movement of people when the slums of "Black Bottom" had been cleared for urban renewal had changed 12th Street from an integrated community into an almost totally black one, in which only a number of merchants remained white. Only 18 percent of the residents were homeowners. Twenty-five percent of the housing was considered so substandard as to require clearance. Another 19 percent had major deficiencies.

The crime rate was almost double that of the city as a whole. A Detroit police officer told Commission investigators that prostitution was so widespread that officers made arrests only when soliciting became blatant. The proportion of broken families was more than twice that in the rest of the city.

By 7:50 a.m., when a 17-man police commando unit attempted to make the first sweep, an estimated 3,000 persons were on 12th Street. They offered no resistance. As the sweep moved down the street, they gave way to one side, and then flowed back behind it.

A shoe store manager said he waited vainly for police for two hours as the store was being looted. At 8:25 a.m., someone in the crowd yelled, "The cops are coming!" The first flames of the riot billowed from the store. Firemen who responded were not harassed. The flames were extinguished.

By midmorning, 1,122 men — approximately a fourth of the police department — had reported for duty. Of these, 540 were in or near the six-block riot area. One hundred eight officers were attempting to establish a cordon [circle of police]. There was, however, no interference with looters, and police were refraining from the use of force.

Commissioner Girardin said: "If we had started shooting in there. . . not one of our policemen would have come out alive. I am convinced it would have turned into a race riot in the conventional sense."

According to witnesses, police at some roadblocks made little effort to stop people from going in and out of the area. Bantering took place between police officers and the populace, some still in pajamas. To some observers, there seemed at this point to be an atmosphere of apathy. On the one hand, the police failed to interfere with the looting. On the other, a number of older, more stable residents, who had seen the street deteriorate from a prosperous commercial thoroughfare to one ridden by vice, remained aloof.

Because officials feared that the 12th Street disturbance might be a diversion, many officers were sent to guard key installations in other sections of the city. Belle Isle, the recreation area in the Detroit River that had been the scene of the 1943 riot, was sealed off.

In an effort to avoid attracting people to the scene, some broadcasters cooperated by not reporting the riot, and an effort was made to downplay the extent of the disorder. The facade of "business as usual" necessitated the detailing of numerous police officers to protect the 50,000 spectators that were expected at that afternoon's New York Yankees-Detroit Tigers baseball game.

Early in the morning, a task force of community workers went into the area to dispel rumors and act as counterrioters. Such a task force had been singularly successful at the time of the incident in the Kercheval district in the summer of 1966, when scores of people had gathered at the site of an arrest. Kercheval, however, has a more stable population, fewer stores, less population density, and the city's most effective police-community relations program.

The 12th Street area, on the other hand, had been determined, in a 1966 survey conducted by Dr. Ernest Harburg of the Psychology Department of the University of Michigan, to be a community of high stress and tension. An overwhelming majority of the residents indicated dissatisfaction with their environment.

Of the interviewed, 93 percent said they wanted to move out of the neighborhood; 73 percent felt that the streets were not safe; 91 percent believed that a person was likely to be robbed or beaten at night; 58 percent knew of a fight within the last 12 months in which a weapon had been employed; 32 percent stated that they themselves owned a weapon; 57 percent were worried about fires.

A significant proportion believed municipal services to be inferior: 36 percent were dissatisfied with the schools; 43 percent with the city's contribution to the neighborhood; 77 percent with the recreational facilities; 78 percent believed police did not respond promptly when they were summoned for help.

U.S. Representative John Conyers, Jr., a Negro, was notified about the disturbance at his home a few blocks from 12th Street, at 8:30 a.m. Together with other community leaders, including Hubert G. Locke, a Negro and assistant to the commissioner of police, he began to drive around the area. In the side streets, he asked people to stay in their homes. On 12th Street, he asked them to disperse. It was, by his own account, a futile task.

Numerous eyewitnesses interviewed by Commission investigators tell of the carefree mood with which people ran in and out of stores, looting and laughing, and joking with the police officers. Stores with "Soul Brother" signs appeared no more immune than others. Looters paid no attention to residents who shouted at them and called their actions senseless. An epidemic of excitement had swept over the persons on the street.

Congressman Conyers noticed a woman with a baby in her arms; she was raging, cursing "whitey" for no apparent reason.

Shortly before noon, Congressman Conyers climbed atop a car in the middle of 12th Street to address the people. As he began to speak, he was confronted by a man in his fifties whom he had once, as a lawyer, represented in court. The man had been active in civil rights. He believed himself to have been persecuted as a result, and it was Conyers' opinion that he may have been wrongfully jailed. Extremely bitter, the man was inciting the crowd and challenging Conyers: "Why are you defending the cops and the establishment? You're just as bad as they are!"

A police officer in the riot area told Commission investigators that neither he nor his fellow officers were instructed as to what they were supposed to be doing. Witnesses tell of officers standing behind sawhorses as an area was being looted — and still standing there much later, when the mob had moved elsewhere. A squad from the commando unit, wearing helmets with face-covering visors and carrying bayonet-tipped carbines, blockaded a street several blocks from the scene of the riot. Their appearance drew residents into the street. Some began to harangue them and to question why they were in an area where there was no trouble. Representative Conyers convinced the police department to remove the commandos.

By that time, a rumor was threading through the crowd that a man had been bayoneted by the police. Influenced by such stories, the crowd became belligerent. At approximately 1 p.m., stonings accelerated. Numerous officers reported injuries from rocks, bottles, and other objects thrown at them. Smoke billowed upward from four fires, the first since the one at the shoe store early in the morning. When firemen answered the alarms, they became the target for rocks and bottles.

At 2 p. m. Mayor Cavanaugh met with community and political leaders at police headquarters. Until then there had been hope that, as the people blew off steam, the riot would dissipate. Now the opinion was nearly unanimous that additional forces would be needed.

A request was made for state police aid. By 3 p.m., 360 officers were assembling at the armory. At that moment looting was spreading from the 12th Street area to other main thoroughfares.

There was no lack of the disaffected to help spread it. Although not yet as hard-pressed as Newark, Detroit was, like Newark, losing population. Its prosperous middle-class whites were moving to the suburbs and being replaced by unskilled

Negro migrants. Between 1960 and 1967, the Negro population rose from just under 30 percent to an estimated 40 percent of the total.

In a decade, the school system had gained 50,000 to 60,000 children. Fifty-one percent of the elementary school classes were overcrowded. Simply to achieve the statewide average, the system needed 1,650 more teachers and 1,000 additional classrooms. The combined cost would be $63 million.

Of 300,000 school children, 171,000, or 57 percent, were Negro. According to the Detroit superintendent of schools, 25 different school districts surrounding the city spent up to $500 more per pupil per year than Detroit. In the inner city schools, more than half the pupils who entered high school became dropouts.

The strong union structure had created excellent conditions for most working men, but had left others, such as civil service and Government workers, comparatively disadvantaged and dissatisfied. In June, the "Blue Flu" had struck the city as police officers, forbidden to strike, had staged a sick-out. In September, the teachers were to go on strike. The starting wages for a plumber's helper were almost equal to the salary of a police officer or teacher.

Some unions, traditionally closed to Negroes, zealously guarded training opportunities. In January of 1967, the school system notified six apprenticeship trades it would not open any new apprenticeship classes unless a large number of Negroes were included. By fall some of the programs were still closed.

High school diplomas from inner-city schools were regarded by personnel directors as less than valid. In July, unemployment was at a 5-year peak. In the 12th Street area, it was estimated to be between 12 and 15 percent for Negro men and 30 percent or higher for those under 25.

The more education a Negro had, the greater the disparity between his income and that of a white with the same level of education. The income of whites and Negroes with a seventh-grade education was about equal. The median income of whites with a high school diploma was $1,600 more per year than that of Negroes. White college graduates made $2,600 more. In fact, so far as income was concerned, it made very little difference to a Negro man whether he had attended school for 8 years or for 12. In the fall of 1967, a study conducted at one inner-city high school, Northwestern, showed that, although 50 percent of the dropouts had found work, 90 percent of the 1967 graduating class was unemployed.

Mayor Cavanaugh had appointed many Negroes to key positions in his administration, but in elective offices the Negro population was still underrepresented. Of nine councilmen, one was a Negro. Of seven school board members, two were Negroes.

Although Federal programs had brought nearly $360 million to the city between 1962 and 1967, the money appeared to have had little impact at the grassroots. Urban renewal, for which $38 million had been allocated, was opposed by many residents of the poverty area.

Because of its financial straits, the city was unable to produce on promises to correct such conditions as poor garbage collection and bad street lighting, which brought constant complaints from Negro residents.

On 12th Street, Carl Perry, the Negro proprietor of a drugstore and photography studio, was dispensing ice cream, sodas, and candy to the youngsters streaming in and out of his store. For safekeeping, he had brought the photography equipment from his studio, in the next block, to the drugstore. The youths milling about repeatedly assured him that, although the market next door had been ransacked, his place of business was in no danger.

In midafternoon, the market was set afire. Soon after, the drug store went up in flames.

State Representative James Del Rio, a Negro, was camping out in front of a building he owned when two small boys, neither more than 10 years old, approached. One prepared to throw a brick through a window. Del Rio stopped him: "That building belongs to me," he said.

"I'm glad you told me, baby, because I was just about to bust you in!" the youngster replied.

Some evidence that criminal elements were organizing spontaneously to take advantage of the riot began to manifest itself. A number of cars were noted to be returning again and again, their occupants methodically looting stores. Months later, goods stolen during the riot were still being peddled.

A spirit of carefree nihilism [destruction], was taking hold. To riot and to destroy appeared more and more to become ends in themselves. Late Sunday afternoon, it appeared to one observer that the young people were "dancing amidst the flames."

A Negro plainclothes officer was standing at an intersection when a man threw a Molotov cocktail into a business establishment at the corner. In the heat of the afternoon, fanned by the 20 to 25 m.p.h. winds of both Sunday and Monday, the fire reached the home next door within minutes. As residents uselessly sprayed the flames with garden hoses, the fire jumped from roof to roof of adjacent two- and three-story buildings. Within the hour, the entire block was in flames. The ninth house in the burning row belonged to the arsonist who had thrown the Molotov cocktail.

In some areas, residents organized rifle squads to protect firefighters. Elsewhere, especially as the wind-whipped flames began to overwhelm the Detroit Fire Department and more and more residences burned, the firemen were subjected to curses and rock-throwing.

Because of a lack of funds, on a per capita basis the department is one of the smallest in the Nation. In comparison to Newark, where approximately 1,000 firemen patrol an area of 16 square miles with a population of 400,000, Detroit's 1,700 firemen must cover a city of 140 square miles with a population of 1.6 million. Because the department had no mutual aid agreement with surrounding communities, it could not quickly call in reinforcements from outlying areas, and it was almost 9 p.m. before the first arrived. At one point, out of a total of 92 pieces of Detroit firefighting equipment and 56 brought in from surrounding communities, only four engine companies were available to guard areas of the city outside of the riot perimeter.

As the afternoon progressed, the fire department's radio carried repeated messages of apprehension and orders of caution:

> There is no police protection here at all; there isn't a policeman in the area...If you have trouble at all, pull out! . . . We're being stoned at the scene. It's going good. We need help! . . . Protect yourselves! Proceed away from the scene. . . . Engine 42 over at Linwood and Gladstone. They are throwing bottles at us so we are getting out of the area. . . All companies without police protection — all companies without police protection — orders are to withdraw, do not try to put out the fires. I repeat — all companies without police protection orders are to withdraw, do not try to put out the fires!

It was 4:30 p.m. when the firemen, some of them exhausted by the heat, abandoned an area of approximately 100 square blocks on either side of 12th Street to await protection from police and National Guardsmen.

During the course of the riot, firemen were to withdraw 283 times.

Fire Chief Charles J. Quinlan estimated that at least two-thirds of the buildings were destroyed by spreading fires rather than fires set at the scene. Of the 683 structures involved, approximately one-third were residential, and in few, if any, of these was the fire set originally.

Governor George Romney flew over the area between 8:30 and 9 p.m. "It look like the city had been bombed on the west side and there was an area two-and-a-half miles with major fires, with entire blocks in flames," he told the Commission.

In the midst of chaos, there were some unexpected individual responses.

Twenty-four-year-old E.G., a Negro born in Savannah, Ga., had come to Detroit in 1965 to attend Wayne State

University. Rebellion had been building in him for a long time because,

> You just had to bow down to the white man... When the insurance man would come by he would always call out to my mother by her first name and we were expected to smile and greet him happily... Man, I know he would never have thought of me or my father going to his home and calling his wife by her first name. Then I once saw a white man slapping a young pregnant Negro woman on the street with such force that she just spun around and fell. I'll never forget that.

When a friend called to tell him about the riot on 12th Street, E.G. went there expecting "a true revolt," but was disappointed as soon as he saw the looting begin: "I wanted to see the people really rise up in revolt. When I saw the first person coming out of the store with things in his arms, I really got sick to my stomach and wanted to go home. Rebellion against the white suppressors is one thing, but one measly pair of shoes or some food completely ruins the whole concept."

E.G. was standing in a crowd, watching firemen work, when Fire Chief Alvin Wall called out for help from the spectators. E.G. responded. His reasoning was: "No matter what color someone is, whether they are green or pink or blue, I'd help them if they were in trouble. That's all there is to it."

He worked with the firemen for 4 days, the only Negro in an all-white crew. Elsewhere, at scattered locations, a half dozen other Negro youths pitched in to help the firemen.

At 4:20 p.m., Mayor Cavanaugh requested that the National Guard be brought into Detroit. Although a major portion of the Guard was in its summer encampment 200 miles away, several hundred troops were conducting their regular week-end drill in the city. That circumstance obviated many problems. The first troops were on the streets by 7 p.m.

At 7:45 p.m., the mayor issued a proclamation instituting a 9 p.m. to 5 a.m. curfew. At 9:07 p.m., the first sniper fire was reported. Following his aerial survey of the city, Governor Romney, at or shortly before midnight, proclaimed that "a state of public emergency exists" in the cities of Detroit, Highland Park and Hamtramck.

At 4:45 p.m., a 68-year-old white shoe repairman, George Messerlian, had seen looters carrying clothes from a cleaning establishment next to his shop. Armed with a saber, he had rushed into the street, flailing away at the looters. One Negro youth was nicked on the shoulder. Another, who had not been on the scene, inquired as to what had happened. After he had been told, he allegedly replied: "I'll get the old man for you!"

Going to Messerlian, who had fallen or been knocked to the ground, the youth began to beat him with a club. Two other Negro youths dragged the attacker away from the old man. It was too late. Messerlian died 4 days later in the hospital.

At 9:15 p.m., a 16-year-old Negro boy, superficially wounded while looting, became the first reported gunshot victim.

At midnight, Sharon George, a 23-year-old white woman, together with her two brothers, was a passenger in a car being driven by her husband. After having dropped off two Negro friends, they were returning home on one of Detroit's main avenues when they were slowed by a milling throng in the street. A shot fired from close range struck the car. The bullet splintered Mrs. George's body. She died less than 2 hours later.

An hour before midnight, a 45-year-old white man, Walter Grzanka, together with three white companions, went into the street. Shortly thereafter, a market was broken into. Inside the show window, a Negro man began filling bags with groceries and handing them to confederates outside the store. Grzanka twice went over to the store, accepted bags, and placed them down beside his companions across the street. On the third occasion he entered the market. When he emerged, the market owner, driving by in his car, shot and killed him.

In Grzanka's pockets, police found seven cigars, four packages of pipe tobacco, and nine pairs of shoelaces.

Before dawn, four other looters were shot, one of them accidentally while struggling with a police officer. A Negro youth and a National Guardsman were injured by gunshots of undetermined origin. A private guard shot himself while pulling his revolver from his pocket. In the basement of the 13th Precinct Police Station, a cue ball, thrown by an unknown assailant, cracked against the head of a sergeant.

At about midnight, three white youths, armed with a shotgun, had gone to the roof of their apartment building, located in an all-white block, in order, they said, to protect the building from fire. At 2:45 a.m., a patrol car, carrying police officers and National Guardsmen, received a report of "snipers on the roof." As the patrol car arrived, the manager of the building went to the roof to tell the youths they had better come down.

The law enforcement personnel surrounded the building, some going to the front, others to the rear. As the manager, together with the three youths, descended the fire escape in the rear, a National Guardsman, believing he heard shots from the front, fired. His shot killed 23-year-old Clifton Pryor.

Early in the morning, a young white fireman and a 49-year-old Negro homeowner were killed by fallen power lines.

By 2 a.m. Monday, Detroit police had been augmented by 800 State Police officers and 1,200 National Guardsmen. An additional 8,000 Guardsmen were on the way. Nevertheless, Governor Romney and Mayor Cavanaugh decided to ask for Federal assistance. At 2:15 a.m., the mayor called Vice President Hubert Humphrey, and was referred to Attorney General Ramsey Clark. A short time thereafter, telephone contact was established between Governor Romney and the attorney general.

There is some difference of opinion about what occurred next. According to the attorney general's office, the governor was advised of the seriousness of the request and told that the applicable Federal statute required that, before Federal troops could be brought into the city, he would have to state that the situation had deteriorated to the point that local and state forces could no longer maintain law and order. According to the governor, he was under the impression that he was being asked to declare a "state of insurrection" existed in the city.

The governor was unwilling to make such a declaration, contending that, if he did, insurance policies would not cover the loss incurred as a result of the riot. He and the mayor decided to re-evaluate the need for Federal troops.

Contact between Detroit and Washington was maintained throughout the early morning hours. At 9 a.m., as the disorder still showed no sign of abating, the governor and the mayor decided to make a renewed request for Federal troops.

Shortly before noon, the President of the United States authorized the sending of a task force of paratroops to Selfridge Air Force Base, near the city. A few minutes past 3 p.m., Lt. Gen. John L. Throckmorton, commander of Task Force Detroit, met Cyrus Vance, former Deputy Secretary of Defense, at the air base. Approximately an hour later, the first Federal troops arrived at the air base.

After meeting with state and municipal officials, Mr. Vance, General Throckmorton, Governor Romney, and Mayor Cavanaugh, made a tour of the city, which lasted until 7:15 p.m. During this tour Mr. Vance and General Throckmorton independently came to the conclusion that — since they had seen no looting or sniping, since the fires appeared to be coming under control, and since a substantial number of National Guardsmen had not yet been committed — injection of Federal troops would be premature.

As the riot alternately waxed and waned, one area of the ghetto remained insulated. On the northeast side, the residents of some 150 square blocks inhabited by 21,000 persons had, in 1966, banded together in the Positive Neighborhood Action Committee (PNAC). With professional help from the Institute of Urban Dynamics, they had organized block clubs and made plans for the improvement of the neighborhood. In order to meet the need for recreational facilities, which the city was not providing, they raised $3,000 to purchase empty lots for playgrounds. Although opposed to urban renewal, they had agreed to co-sponsor with the Archdiocese of Detroit a housing project to be controlled jointly by the archdiocese and PNAC.

When the riot broke out, the residents, through the block clubs, were able to organize quickly. Youngsters, agreeing to stay in the neighborhood, participated in detouring traffic. While many persons reportedly sympathized with the idea of a rebellion against the "system," only two small fires were set — one in an empty building.

During the daylight hours Monday, nine more persons were killed by gunshots elsewhere in the city, and many others were seriously or critically injured. Twenty-three-year-old Nathaniel Edmonds, a Negro, was sitting in his backyard when a young white man stopped his car, got out, and began an argument with him. A few minutes later, declaring he was "going to paint his picture on him with a shotgun," the white man allegedly shotgunned Edmonds to death.

Mrs. Nannie Pack and Mrs. Mattie Thomas were sitting on the porch of Mrs. Pack's house when police began chasing looters from a nearby market. During the chase officers fired three shots from their shotguns. The discharge from one of these accidentally struck the two women. Both were still in the hospital weeks later.

Included among those critically injured when they were accidentally trapped in the line of fire were an 8-year-old Negro girl and a 14-year-old white boy.

As darkness settled Monday, the number of incidents reported to police began to rise again. Although many turned out to be false, several involved injuries to police officers, National Guardsmen, and civilians by gunshots of undetermined origin.

Watching the upward trend of reported incidents, Mr. Vance and General Throckmorton became convinced Federal troops should be used, and President Johnson was so advised. At 11:20 p.m., the President signed a proclamation federalizing the Michigan National Guard and authorizing the use of the paratroopers.

At this time, there were nearly 5,000 Guardsmen in the city, but fatigue, lack of training, and the haste with which they had had to be deployed reduced their effectiveness.

Some of the Guardsmen traveled 200 miles and then were on duty for 30 hours straight. Some had never received riot training and were given on-the-spot instructions on mob control — only to discover that there were no mobs, and that the situation they faced on the darkened streets was one for which they were unprepared.

Commanders committed men as they became available, often in small groups. In the resulting confusion, some units were lost in the city. Two Guardsmen assigned to an intersection on Monday were discovered still there on Friday.

Lessons learned by the California National Guard two years earlier in Watts regarding the danger of overreaction and the necessity of great restraint in using weapons had not, apparently, been passed on to the Michigan National Guard. The young troopers could not be expected to know what a danger they were creating by the lack of fire discipline, not only to the civilian population but to themselves.

A Detroit newspaper reporter who spent a night riding in a command jeep told a Commission investigator of machine guns being fired accidentally, street lights being shot out by rifle fire, and buildings being placed under siege on the sketchiest reports of sniping. Troopers would fire, and immediately from the distance there would be answering fire, sometimes consisting of tracer bullets.

In one instance, the newsman related, a report was received on the jeep radio that an Army bus was pinned down by sniper fire at an intersection. National Guardsmen and police, arriving from various directions, jumped out and began asking each other: "Where's the sniper fire coming from?" As one Guardsman pointed to a building, everyone rushed about, taking cover. A soldier, alighting from a jeep, accidentally pulled the trigger on his rifle. As the shot reverberated through the darkness, an officer yelled: "What's going on?" "I don't know," came the answer. "Sniper, I guess."

Without any clear authorization or direction, someone opened fire upon the suspected building. A tank rolled up and sprayed the building with .50-caliber tracer bullets. Law enforcement officers rushed into the surrounded building and discovered it empty. "They must be firing one shot and running," was the verdict.

The reporter interviewed the men who had gotten off the bus and were crouched around it. When he asked them about the sniping incident, he was told that someone had heard a shot. He asked "Did the bullet hit the bus?" The answer was: " Well, we don't know."

Bracketing the hour of midnight Monday, heavy firing, injuring many persons and killing several, occurred in the southeastern sector, which was to be taken over by the paratroopers at 4 a.m., Tuesday, and which was, at this time, considered to be the most active riot area in the city.

Employed as a private guard, 55-year-old Julius L. Dorsey, a Negro, was standing in front of a market when accosted by two Negro men and a woman. They demanded he permit them to loot the market. He ignored their demands. They began to berate him. He asked a neighbor to call the police. As the argument grew more heated, Dorsey fired three shots from his pistol into the air.

The police radio reported: "Looters, they have rifles." A patrol car driven by a police officer and carrying three National Guardsmen arrived. As the looters fled, the law enforcement personnel opened fire. When the firing ceased, one person lay dead.

He was Julius L. Dorsey.

In two areas — one consisting of a triangle formed by Mack, Gratiot, and E. Grand Boulevard, the other surrounding Southeastern High School — firing began shortly after 10 p.m and continued for several hours.

In the first of the areas, a 22-year-old Negro complained that he had been shot at by snipers. Later, a half dozen civilians and one National Guardsman were wounded by shots of undetermined origin.

Henry Denson, a passenger in a car, was shot and killed when the vehicle's driver, either by accident or intent, failed to heed a warning to halt at a National Guard roadblock.

Similar incidents occurred in the vicinity of Southeastern High School, one of the National Guard staging areas. As early as 10:20 p.m., the area was reported to be under sniper fire. Around midnight there were two incidents, the sequence of which remains in doubt.

Shortly before midnight, Ronald Powell, who lived three blocks east of the high school and whose wife was, momentarily, expecting a baby, asked the four friends with whom he had been spending the evening to take him home. He, together with Edward Blackshear, Charles Glover, and John Leroy climbed into Charles Dunson's station wagon for the short drive. Some of the five may have been drinking but none was intoxicated.

To the north of the high school, they were halted at a National Guard roadblock, and told they would have to detour around the school and a fire station at Mack and St. Jean Streets because of the firing that had been occurring. Following orders, they took a circuitous route and approached Powell's home from the south.

On Lycaste Street, between Charlevoix and Goethe, they saw a jeep sitting at the curb. Believing it to be another roadblock, they slowed down. Simultaneously a shot rang out. A National Guardsman fell, hit in the ankle.

Other National Guardsmen at the scene thought the shot had come from the station wagon. Shot after shot was directed against the vehicle, at least 17 of them finding their mark. All five occupants were injured, John Leroy fatally.

At approximately the same time, firemen, police and National Guardsmen at the corner of Mack and St. Jean Streets, 2½ blocks away, again came under fire from what they believed were rooftop snipers to the southeast, the direction of Charlevoix and Lycaste. The police and guardsmen responded with a hail of fire.

When the shooting ceased, Carl Smith, a young firefighter, lay dead. An autopsy determined that the shot had been fired at street level, and, according to police, probably had come from the southeast.

At 4 a.m., when paratroopers, under the command of Col. A. R. Bolling, arrived at the high school, the area was so dark and still that the colonel thought, at first, that he had come to the wrong place. Investigating, he discovered National Guard troops, claiming they were pinned down by sniper fire, crouched behind the walls of the darkened building.

The colonel immediately ordered all of the lights in the building turned on and his troops to show themselves as conspicuously as possible. In the apartment house across the street, nearly every window had been shot out, and the walls were pockmarked with bullet holes. The colonel went into the building and began talking to the residents, many of whom had spent the night huddled on the floor. He reassured them no more shots would be fired.

According to Lieutenant General Throckmorton and Colonel Bolling, the city, at this time, was saturated with fear. The National Guardsmen were afraid, the residents were afraid, and the police were afraid. Numerous persons, the majority of them Negroes, were being injured by gunshots of undetermined origin. The general and his staff felt that the major task of the troops was to reduce the fear and restore an air of normalcy.

In order to accomplish this, every effort was made to establish contact and rapport between the troops and the residents. Troopers — 20 percent of whom were Negro — began helping to clean up the streets, collect garbage, and trace persons who had disappeared in the confusion. Residents in the neighborhoods responded with soup and sandwiches for the troops. In areas where the National Guard tried to establish rapport with the citizens, there was a similar response.

Within hours after the arrival of the paratroops, the area occupied by them was the quietest in the city, bearing out General Throckmorton's view that the key to quelling a disorder is to saturate an area with "calm, determined, and hardened professional soldiers." Loaded weapons, he believes, are unnecessary. Troopers had strict orders not to fire unless they could see the specific person at whom they were aiming. Mass fire was forbidden.

During five days in the city, 2,700 Army troops expended only 201 rounds of ammunition, almost all during the first few hours, after which even stricter fire discipline was enforced. (In contrast, New Jersey National Guardsmen and state police expended 13,326 rounds of ammunition in three days in Newark.) Hundreds of reports of sniper fire — most of them false — continued to pour into police headquarters; the Army logged only 10. No paratrooper was injured by a gunshot. Only one person was hit by a shot fired by a trooper. He was a young Negro who was killed when he ran into the line of fire as a trooper, aiding police in a raid on an apartment, aimed at a person believed to be a sniper.

General Throckmorton ordered the weapons on all military personnel unloaded, but either the order failed to reach many National Guardsmen, or else it was disobeyed.

Even as the general was requesting the city to relight the streets, Guardsmen continued shooting out the lights, and there were reports of dozens of shots being fired to dispatch one light. At one such location, as Guardsmen were shooting out the street lights, a radio newscaster reported himself to be pinned down by "sniper fire."

On the same day that the general was attempting to restore normalcy by ordering street barricades taken down, Guardsmen on one street were not only, in broad daylight, ordering people off the street, but off their porches and away from the windows. Two persons who failed to respond to the order quickly enough were shot, one of them fatally.

The general himself reported an incident of a Guardsman "firing across the bow" of an automobile that was approaching a roadblock.

As in Los Angeles two years earlier, roadblocks that were ill-lighted and ill-defined — often consisting of no more than a trash barrel or similar object with Guardsmen standing nearby — proved a continuous hazard to motorists. At one such roadblock, National Guard Sgt. Larry Post, standing in the street, was caught in a sudden crossfire as his fellow Guardsmen opened up on a vehicle. He was the only soldier killed in the riot.

With persons of every description arming themselves, and guns being fired accidentally or on the vaguest pretext all over the city, it became more and more impossible to tell who was shooting at whom. Some firemen began carrying guns. One accidentally shot and wounded a fellow fireman. Another injured himself.

The chaos of a riot, and the difficulties faced by police officers, are demonstrated by an incident that occurred at 2 a.m., Tuesday.

A unit of 12 officers received a call to guard firemen from snipers. When they arrived at the corner of Vicksburg and Linwood in the 12th Street area, the intersection was well-lighted by the flames completely enveloping one building. Sniper fire was directed at the officers from an alley to the north, and gun flashes were observed in two buildings.

As the officers advanced on the two buildings, Patrolman Johnie Hamilton fired several rounds from his machinegun. Thereupon, the officers were suddenly subjected to fire from a new direction, the east. Hamilton, struck by four bullets, fell, critically injured, in the intersection. As two officers ran to his aid, they too were hit.

By this time other units of the Detroit Police Department, state police, and National Guard had arrived on the scene, and the area was covered with a hail of gunfire.

In the confusion the snipers who had initiated the shooting escaped.

At 9:15 p.m., Tuesday, July 25, 38-year-old Jack Sydnor, a Negro, came home drunk. Taking out his pistol, he fired one shot into an alley. A few minutes later, the police arrived. As his common-law wife took refuge in a closet, Sydnor waited, gun in hand, while the police forced open the door. Patrolman Roger Poike, the first to enter, was shot by Sydnor. Although critically injured, the officer managed to get off six shots in return. Police within the building and on the street then poured a hail of fire into the apartment. When the shooting ceased, Sydnor's body, riddled by the gunfire, was found lying on the ground outside a window.

Nearby, a state police officer and a Negro youth were struck and seriously injured by stray bullets. As in other cases where the origin of the shots was not immediately determinable, police reported them as "shot by sniper."

Reports of "heavy sniper fire" poured into police headquarters from the two blocks surrounding the apartment house where the battle with Jack Sydnor had taken place. National Guard troops with two tanks were dispatched to help flush out the snipers.

Shots continued to be heard throughout the neighborhood. At approximately midnight — there are discrepancies as to the precise time — a machinegunner on a tank, startled by several shots, asked the assistant gunner where the shots were coming from. The assistant gunner pointed toward a flash in the window of an apartment house from which there had been earlier reports of sniping.

The machinegunner opened fire. As the slugs ripped through the window and walls of the apartment, they nearly severed the arm of 21-year-old Valerie Hood. Her 4-year-old niece, Tonya Blanding, toppled dead, a .50-caliber bullet hole in her chest.

A few seconds earlier, 19-year-old Bill Hood, standing in the window, had lighted a cigarette.

Down the street, a bystander was critically injured by a stray bullet. Simultaneously, the John C. Lodge Freeway, two blocks away, was reported to be under sniper fire. Tanks and National Guard troops were sent to investigate. At the Harlan House Motel, 10 blocks from where Tonya Blanding had died a short time earlier, Mrs. Helen Hall, a 51-year-old white business-woman, opened the drapes of the fourth floor hall window. Calling out to other guests, she exclaimed: "Look at the tanks!"

She died seconds later as bullets began to slam into the building. As the firing ceased, a 19-year-old Marine, carrying a Springfield rifle, burst into the building. When, accidentally, he pushed the rifle barrel through a window, firing commenced anew. A police investigation showed that the Marine, who had just decided to "help out" the law enforcement personnel, was not involved in the death of Mrs. Hall.

R. R., a white 27-year-old coin dealer, was the owner of an expensive three-story house on L Street, an integrated middle-class neighborhood. In May of 1966, he and his wife and child had moved to New York and had rented the house to two young men. After several months, he had begun to have problems with his tenants. On one occasion, he reported to his attorney that he had been threatened by them.

In March of 1967, R. R. instituted eviction proceedings. These were still pending when the riot broke out. Concerned about the house, R. R. decided to fly to Detroit. When he arrived at the house on Wednesday, July 26, he discovered the tenants were not at home.

He then called his attorney, who advised him to take physical possession of the house and, for legal purposes, to take witnesses along.

Together with his 17-year-old brother and another white youth, R. R. went to the house, entered, and began changing the locks on the doors. For protection they brought a .22 caliber rifle, which R. R.'s brother took into the cellar and fired into a pillow in order to test it.

Shortly after 8 p.m., R. R. called his attorney to advise him that the tenants had returned, and he had refused to admit them. Thereupon, R. R. alleged, the tenants had threatened to obtain the help of the National Guard. The attorney relates that he was not particularly concerned. He told R. R. that if the National Guard did appear he should have the officer in charge call him (the attorney).

At approximately the same time, the National Guard claims it received information to the effect that several men had evicted the legal occupants of the house, and intended to start sniping after dark.

A National Guard column was dispatched to the scene. Shortly after 9 p.m., in the half-light of dusk, the column of approximately 30 men surrounded the house. A tank took position on a lawn across the street. The captain commanding the column placed in front of the house an explosive device similar to a firecracker. After setting this off in order to draw the attention of the occupants to the presence of the column, he called for them to come out of the house. No attempt was made to verify the truth or falsehood of the allegations regarding snipers.

When the captain received no reply from the house, he began counting to 10. As he was counting, he said, he heard a shot, the origin of which he could not determine. A few seconds, later he heard another shot and saw a "fire streak" coming from an upstairs window. He thereupon gave the order to fire.

According to the three young men, they were on the second floor of the house and completely bewildered by the barrage of fire that was unleashed against it. As hundreds of bullets crashed through the first- and second-story windows and richocheted off the walls, they dashed to the third floor. Protected by a large chimney, they huddled in a closet until, during a lull in the firing, they were able to wave an item of clothing out of the window as a sign of surrender. They were arrested as snipers.

The firing from rifles and machine guns had been so intense that in a period of a few minutes it inflicted an estimated $10,000 worth of damage. One of a pair of stone columns was shot nearly in half.

Jailed at the 10th precinct station sometime Wednesday night, R. R. and his two companions were taken from their cell to an "alley court," police slang for an unlawful attempt to make prisoners confess. A police officer, who has resigned from the force, allegedly administered such a severe beating to R. R. that the bruises still were visible 2 weeks later.

R. R.'s 17-year-old brother had his skull cracked open, and was thrown back into the cell. He was taken to a hospital only when other arrestees complained that he was bleeding to death.

At the preliminary hearing 12 days later, the prosecution presented only one witness, the National Guard captain who had given the order to fire. The police officer who had signed the original complaint was not asked to take the stand. The charges against all three of the young men were dismissed.

Nevertheless, the morning after the original incident, a major metropolitan newspaper in another section of the country composed the following banner story from wire service reports:

> *Detroit, July 27, (Thursday).* —Two National Guard tanks ripped a sniper's haven with machine guns Wednesday night and flushed out three shaggy-haired white youths. Snipers attacked a guard command post and Detroit's racial riot set a modern record for bloodshed. The death toll soared to 36, topping the Watts bloodbath of 1966 in which 35 died and making Detroit's insurrection the most deadly racial riot in modern U.S. history. . . .
>
> In the attack on the sniper's nest, the Guardsmen poured hundreds of rounds of .50 caliber machine gun fire into the home, which authorities said housed arms and ammunition used by West side sniper squads.
>
> Guardsmen recovered guns and ammunition. A reporter with the troopers said the house, a neat brick home in the neighborhood of $20,000 to $50,000 homes, was torn apart by the machine gun and rifle fire.
>
> Sniper fire crackled from the home as the Guard unit approached. It was one of the first verified reports of sniping by whites. . . .
>
> A pile of loot taken from the riot-ruined stores was recovered from the sniper's haven, located ten blocks from the heart of the 200-square block riot zone.
>
> Guardsmen said the house had been identified as a storehouse of arms and ammunition for snipers. Its arsenal was regarded as an indication that the sniping — or at least some of it — was organized.

As hundreds of arrestees were brought into the 10th precinct station, officers took it upon themselves to carry on investigations and to attempt to extract confessions. Dozens of charges of police brutality emanated from the station as prisoners were brought in uninjured, but later had to be taken to the hospital.

In the absence of the precinct commander, who had transferred his headquarters to the riot command post at a nearby hospital, discipline vanished. Prisoners who requested that they be permitted to notify someone of their arrest were almost invariably told that: "The telephones are out of order." Congressman Conyers and State Representative Del Rio, who went to the station hoping to coordinate with the police the establishing of a community patrol, were so upset by what they saw that they changed their minds and gave up on the project.

A young woman, brought into the station, was told to strip. After she had done so, and while an officer took pictures with a Polaroid camera, another officer came up to her and began fondling her. The negative of one of the pictures, fished out of a wastebasket, subsequently was turned over to the mayor's office.

Citing the sniper danger, officers throughout the department had taken off their bright metal badges. They also had taped over the license plates and the numbers of the police cars. Identification of individual officers became virtually impossible.

On a number of occasions officers fired at fleeing looters, then made little attempt to determine whether their shots had hit anyone. Later some of the persons were discovered dead or injured in the street.

In one such case police and National Guardsmen were interrogating a youth suspected of arson when, according to officers, he attempted to escape. As he vaulted over the hood of an automobile, an officer fired his shotgun. The youth disappeared on the other side of the car. Without making an investigation, the officers and Guardsmen returned to their car and drove off.

When nearby residents called police, another squad car arrived to pick up the body. Despite the fact that an autopsy disclosed the youth had been killed by five shotgun pellets, only a cursory investigation was made, and the death was attributed to "sniper fire." No police officer at the scene during the shooting filed a report.

Not until a Detroit newspaper editor presented to the police the statements of several witnesses claiming that the youth had been shot by police after he had been told to run did the department launch an investigation. Not until 3 weeks after the shooting did an officer come forward to identify himself as the one who had fired the fatal shot.

Citing conflicts in the testimony of the score of witnesses, the Detroit Prosecutor's office declined to press charges.

Prosecution is proceeding in the case of three youths in whose shotgun deaths law enforcement personnel were implicated following a report that snipers were firing from the Algiers Motel. In fact, there is little evidence that anyone fired from inside the building. Two witnesses say that they had seen a man, standing outside of the motel, fire two shots from a rifle. The interrogation of other persons revealed that law enforcement personnel then shot out one or more street lights. Police patrols responded to the shots. An attack was launched on the motel.

The picture is further complicated by the fact that this incident occurred at roughly the same time that the National Guard was directing fire at the apartment house in which Tonya Blanding was killed. The apartment house was only six blocks distant from and in a direct line with the motel.

The killings occurred when officers began on-the-spot questioning of the occupants of the motel in an effort to discover weapons used in the "sniping." Several of those questioned reportedly were beaten. One was a Negro ex-paratrooper who had only recently been honorably discharged, and had gone to Detroit to look for a job.

Although by late Tuesday looting and fire-bombing had virtually ceased, between 7 and 11 p.m. that night there were 444 reports of incidents. Most were reports of sniper fire.

During the daylight hours of July 26, there were 534 such reports. Between 8:30 and 11 p.m., there were 255. As they proliferated, the pressure on law enforcement officers to uncover the snipers became intense. Homes were broken into. Searches were made on the flimsiest of tips. A Detroit newspaper headline aptly proclaimed: "Everyone's Suspect in No Man's Land."

Before the arrest of a young woman IBM operator in the city assessor's office brought attention to the situation on Friday, July 28, any person with a gun in his home was liable to be picked up as a suspect.

Of the 27 persons charged with sniping, 22 had charges against them dismissed at preliminary hearings, and the charges against two others were dismissed later. One pleaded guilty to possession of an unregistered gun and was given a suspended sentence. Trials of two are pending [1968].

In all, more than 7,200 persons were arrested. Almost 3,000 of these were picked up on the second day of the riot, and by midnight Monday 4,000 were incarcerated in makeshift jails. Some were kept as long as 30 hours on buses. Others spent days in an underground garage without toilet facilities. An uncounted number were people who had merely been unfortunate enough to be on the wrong street at the wrong time. Included were members of the press whose attempts to show their credentials had been ignored. Released later, they were chided for not having exhibited their identification at the time of their arrests.

The booking system proved incapable of adequately handling the large number of arrestees. People became lost for days in the maze of different detention facilities. Until the later stages, bail was set deliberately high often at $10,000 or more. When it became apparent that this policy was unrealistic and unworkable, the prosecutor's office began releasing on low bail or on their own recognizance hundreds of those who had been picked up. Nevertheless, this fact was not publicized for fear of antagonizing those who had demanded a high-bail policy.

Of the 43 persons who were killed during the riot, 33 were Negro and 10 were white. Seventeen were looters, of whom two were white. Fifteen citizens (of whom four were white), one white National Guardsman, one white fireman, and one Negro private guard died as the result of gunshot wounds. Most of these deaths appear to have been accidental, but criminal homicide is suspected in some.

Two persons, including one fireman, died as a result of fallen powerlines. Two were burned to death. One was a drunken gunman; one an arson suspect. One white man was killed by a rioter. One police officer was felled by a shotgun blast when a gun, in the hands of another officer, accidentally discharged during a scuffle with a looter.

Action by police officers accounted for 20 and, very likely, 21 of the deaths; action by the National Guard for seven, and, very likely, nine; action by the Army for one. Two deaths were the result of action by store-owners. Four persons died accidentally. Rioters were responsible for two, and perhaps three of the deaths; a private guard for one. A white man is suspected of murdering a Negro youth. A perpetrator of one of the killings in the Algiers Motel remains unknown.

Damage estimates, originally set as high as $500 million, were quickly scaled down. The city assessor's office placed the loss — excluding business stock, private furnishings, and the buildings of churches and charitable institutions — at approximately $22 million. Insurance payments, according to the State Insurance Bureau, will come to about $32 million, representing an estimated 65 to 75 percent of the total loss.

By Thursday, July 27, most riot activity had ended. The paratroopers were removed from the city on Saturday. On Tuesday, August 1, the curfew was lifted and the National Guard moved out.

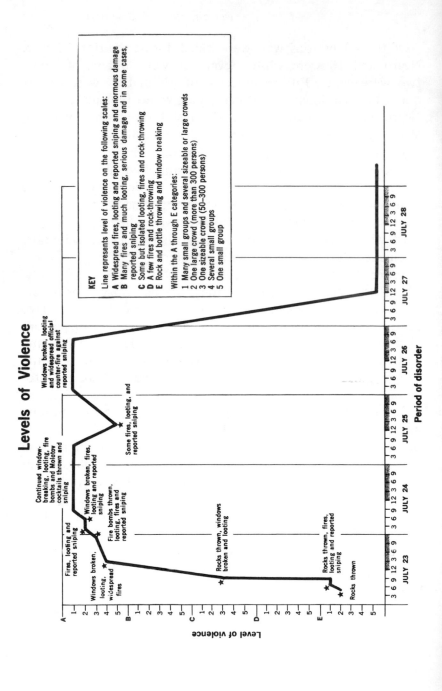

Levels of Violence

KEY

Line represents level of violence on the following scales:

A Widespread fires, looting and reported sniping and enormous damage
B Many fires and much looting, serious damage and in some cases, reported sniping
C Some but isolated looting, fires and rock-throwing
D A few fires and rock-throwing
E Rock and bottle throwing and window breaking

Within the A through E categories:

1 Many small groups and several sizeable or large crowds
2 One large crowd (more than 300 persons)
3 One sizeable crowd (50–300 persons)
4 Several small groups
5 One small group

Period of disorder

Level of violence

Fires, looting and reported sniping

Continued window-breaking, looting, fire bombs and Molotov cocktails thrown and sniping

Windows broken, looting and reported sniping

Windows broken, fires, looting and reported sniping

Windows broken, looting and widespread official counter-fire against reported sniping

Windows broken, looting, widespread fires

Fire bombs thrown, looting, fires and reported sniping

Some fires, looting, and reported sniping

Rocks thrown, windows broken and looting

Rocks thrown, fires, looting and reported sniping

Rocks thrown

JULY 23   JULY 24   JULY 25   JULY 26   JULY 27   JULY 28

184

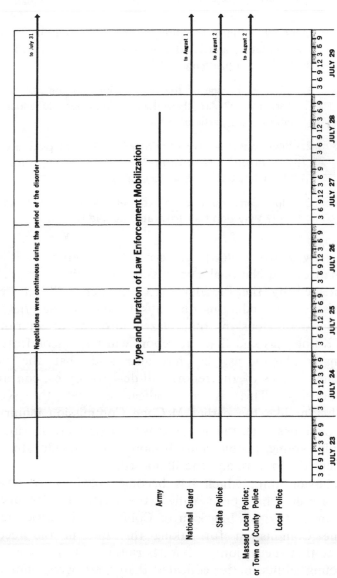

Negotiations

Negotiations were continuous during the period of the disorder | to July 31

Type and Duration of Law Enforcement Mobilization

Army

National Guard | to August 1

State Police | to August 2

Massed Local Police; or Town or County Police | to August 2

Local Police

	JULY 23	JULY 24	JULY 25	JULY 26	JULY 27	JULY 28	JULY 29
3 6 9 12 3 6 9	3 6 9 12 3 6 9	3 6 9 12 3 6 9	3 6 9 12 3 6 9	3 6 9 12 3 6 9	3 6 9 12 3 6 9	3 6 9 12 3 6 9

Period of disorder

S. Participation in Detroit's Riot

Irving J. Rubin, "Analyzing Detroit's Riot: The Causes and Response," *The Reporter,* February 22, 1968, pp. 34-35. Reprinted with permission of the author and the publisher. Copyright © 1968 by the Reporter Magazine Company.

Irving J. Rubin is director of the Detroit Regional Transportation and Land Use Study, where he is involved in regional urban planning.

1. What is the age of the rioters? What is the sex of most participants? Are these factors important to understand why people participated in riots?

2. What was the "typical rioter" like? What picture comes to mind? Hoodlums? Kids? What important characteristics can you ascertain?

3. How can you explain why all ghetto dwellers do not riot? Why don't all frustrated people riot?

In a few weeks [1968], Governor Otto Kerner of Illinois, chairman of the National Commission on Civil Disorders that was created by the President last summer, will release his groups's recommendations on ways to redress the grievances and relieve the tensions that blazed into the urban riots of 1967. Kerner has said that the report will be "uncomfortable" for many Americans; he has also said that the major recommendations of the report will deal with jobs, education, and housing. This is an indication that the Kerner commission, like the earlier McCone Commission inquiry on Watts, assumes that the Negroes who participate in riots are primarily young people and dropouts, the uneducated and unskilled, the jobless, and the ill-housed.

This assumption, which has become conventional wisdom about rioters, has been called the "riff-raff" theory by Professor Robert M. Fogelson of Columbia. He criticized the McCone Commission for taking this line in the face of evidence that the majority of Watts rioters were not teen-agers but young adults, better educated than their peers, employed, and resident in Los Angeles for at least five years. The participants in the Detroit riots of 1967 did not conform to the riffraff stereotype either. By a fortunate circumstance, detailed data on the inhabitants of the Detroit riot areas are available. They were collected as part of a survey of the metropolitan region made by the University of Michigan Center for Urban Studies for the Detroit Regional Transportation and Land Use Study, of which I am the director. And they have been supplemented by statistics on persons arrested during the riots, gathered by the Urban Law Center of the University of Detroit and other responsible sources. The profile of the Detroit rioter that emerges from these data supports the evidence of Watts and other cities and indicates to me that solutions based primarily on improving schools, housing, and employment opportunities for urban Negroes are not responsive to the deeper needs behind the violence. They are the *comfortable* solutions, the things that our society knows how to do best, when it chooses, but they are not what the riots are all about. What is disturbing to me about the data we have collected — which has been available to both national and local bodies investigating the riots — is the absence of evidence that the message of the findings has got through.

There are 600,000 Negroes in Detroit and some twenty-six per cent of their households have incomes below the poverty level [below $3,000 per year income]. The majority of these poor live in the deep core of the city, which was not the scene of the riots. These are obviously the people who most need direct aid to improve their lot, but the best evidence suggests that relatively few of them took part in the violence. Who then were the rioters?

In the main riot areas, according to our survey, the median annual income of Negro households is $6,200. This is slightly higher than the figure for all Negro households in Detroit, $5,600, and not far below the median [middle] white household income of $6,800. (About a third of all Detroit Negroes, including those who are better off than most, do not live in either the poverty or the riot areas).

A comparison of characteristics bearing on the family stability of Negroes living within the riot area with all Negroes in Detroit shows relatively little difference in most respects. The percentage of households with male heads (76.7) and of household heads who are married and living with spouse (67.1) is about the same. The proportion who own or are buying their homes is forty per cent in the riot area and forty-five per cent for Negroes in the city as whole. (Sixty-nine per cent of whites in Detroit own or are buying their homes.) Forty-two per cent of Negroes in the riot area and forty-three per cent in the entire city have lived at their present address five years or more. Educational attainment of Negro household heads — forty-five per cent were high-school graduates or better — is higher in the riot area than throughout the city. Seventy per cent of Negro households in the riot area have autos available, compared to sixty-five per cent for all Negro households in Detroit.

Negroes living within the riot area are substantially better off in every respect than Negroes who live inside the deep core. They also are somewhat better off than the whites who live in the riot neighborhoods.

Although it seemed reasonable to assume that the characteristics of the rioters were similar to those of the riot-area residents, the picture that emerged was so at variance with the conventional assumptions that additional, more direct data on those arrested seemed to be necessary. These gradually became available from several sources, and they tended to confirm the general picture.

Detroit Police Department arrest records show that only ten per cent of the Negroes arrested were juveniles; eighteen per cent were between seventeen and nineteen years old, twenty-four per cent between twenty and twenty-four, seventeen per cent between twenty-five and twenty-nine, and thirty-one per cent over thirty. The Urban Law Center's survey of 1,200 non-juvenile male arrestees shows that eighty-three per cent were employed, forty per cent of them by the three major auto companies and an equal percentage by other large (and mostly unionized) employers. No income data were gathered, but annual wages of $6,000 and more can be assumed. Forty-five per cent of the male arrestees were married, and eighty per cent of them lived with their spouses. Two-thirds had no previous criminal convictions, and an additional twenty per cent had one previous conviction. Only about half as large a proportion owned or were buying their own homes as for all Negroes in Detroit – the only characteristic in which the arrestees differed significantly from the "average young Negro male."

Programs in the areas of jobs, housing, and education are, of course, vitally needed in Detroit, as elsewhere. Yet these are in danger because many politicians anticipate popular opposition to, or are themselves against, anything that might appear to "reward" the rioters. This is ironic, since such programs would actually reward the non-rioters. The overwhelming majority of the rioters had good jobs, few would be eligible for low-cost housing, and only a small proportion were of school age.

It becomes increasingly clear that the strident declarations of Negro militants and the more reasonable stated interpretations of increasing numbers of Negro moderates are accurate: the riots were an outburst of frustration over unmet demands for dignity and for economic and political power. They were a tragic, violent, but understandable declaration of manhood and an insistence that Negroes be able to participate in and to control their own destinies and community affairs.

As de Tocqueville put it long ago, "Only consummate statecraft can enable a king to save his throne when after a long spell of oppressive rule he sets to improving the lot of his subjects. Patiently endured so long as it seemed beyond redress, a grievance comes to appear intolerable once the possibility of removing it crosses men's minds. For the mere fact that certain abuses have been remedied draws attention to the others and they now appear more galling; people may suffer less, but their sensibility is exacerbated."

Last summer brought just this kind of lower-middle-class rebellion. Such rebellions can be put down temporarily with more police and guns and fire engines and tear gas, but to eliminate the tension, frustration, and hostility that underlie the violence, the nations must demonstrate to the Negro who has met his basic material needs that equality of opportunity is a fact and that we will deliver on our promises. . . .

Chapter **7**

America Facing Its Future

In this final chapter we must concentrate upon solutions to the nation's civil unrest. If neat, final solutions are beyond our grasp, we must at the very least wrestle with the problem, speculate upon individual behavior, formulate public policies, and evaluate them in light of what we know about civil disorder. We must pull together knowledge from the previous chapters — the concepts, theories of explanation, and generalizations about riots and participants — to form viable policies.

Assuming that our goal is to achieve a decent and orderly democratic society, we must devise ways to get people to alter their behavior, so that they will pursue goals and air grievances in legal ways. Or we must change the society and its institutions to permit people to achieve goals in legal socially acceptable ways. As former President Johnson noted: "We seek more than the uneasy calm of martial law. We seek peace based upon one man's respect for another man — and upon mutual respect for law. We seek a public order that is built on steady progress in meeting the needs of all of our people.

An angry, emotional reaction to looting and burning is not much of an answer. It is unlikely that such feeling will generate positive policies, but rather, is more likely to bring paratroopers, riot tanks, shooting, and bayonets into the streets. Certainly we today should know what Napoleon's advisor told him long ago — "You can do everything with bayonets, except sit on them." We can subdue rioters with violence; however, what do we do next? Can we rule with bayonets? Must American cities become garrisons?

Some authorities tell us that the most effective way to prevent riots is to eliminate the conditions which cause them, conditions which produce resentment, resistance, and retaliation. But if violence is an innate or an instinctive response of man, what can we do to prevent riots? Suppress men with fear of a countervailing force such as police and troops? Or if violent behavior is learned in our society, what can we do to prevent the outbreak of riots? Change the pattern of rearing children? Ban guns and certain TV shows? What can we do if it is not the actual conditions in the cities which cause riots, but the attitudes between the races and toward the poor which cause people to turn to violence? What can we do if improving conditions in the cities raises peoples' aspirations, and in turn, increases their frustration?

As you read this final chapter, think about these general questions which are oriented toward developing public policies and changes in behavior:

1. If a man or a group employs violence to attain a goal, is it morally justifiable to use violence to suppress them?

2. How can conflicts between individuals or groups be resolved without violence and rioting? Repression by police and troops? Concessions? Diversions, such as sports festivals, job programs, and educational projects? Other means?

3. If you agree with the recommendations of the President's National Advisory Commission on Civil Disorders, how can these recommendations be implemented by public policy and individual behavior? If you disagree, what specific policies would you recommend? How would you implement them?

T. Generalizations, 1967

Report of the National Advisory Commission on Civil Disorders, Washington, D. C.: Government Printing Office, 1968, pp. 64-65.

1. Do these generalizations developed by the President's Commission on the 1967 riots, tend to coincide with those which you developed as you read this book? What are the differences?

2. Do these generalizations help us to predict when and where riots will occur in the future? How precise might these predictions be?

3. Do these generalizations suggest solutions to the problem of urban riots? For example?

Based upon information derived from our surveys, we offer the following generalizations:

1. No civil disorder was "typical" in all respects. Viewed in a national framework, the disorders of 1967 varied greatly in terms of violence and damage. . .
2. While the civil disorders of 1967 were racial in character, they were not *inter*racial. The 1967 disorders, as well as earlier disorders of the recent period, involved action within Negro neighborhoods against symbols of white American society — authority and property — rather than against white persons.
3. Despite extremist rhetoric [speech], there was no attempt to subvert the social order of the United States. Instead, most of those who attacked white authority and property seemed to be demanding fuller participation in the social order and the material benefits enjoyed by the vast majority of American citizens.
4. Disorder did not typically erupt without pre-existing causes as a result of a single "triggering" or "precipitating" incident. Instead, it developed out of an increasingly disturbed social atmosphere, in which typically a series of tension-heightening incidents over a period of weeks or months became linked in the minds of many in the Negro community with a shared reservoir of underlying grievances.

5. There was, typically, a complex relationship between the series of incidents and the underlying grievances. For example, grievances about allegedly abusive police practices, unemployment and underemployment, housing, and other conditions in the ghetto, were often aggravated in the minds of many Negroes by incidents involving the police, or the inaction of municipal authorities on Negro complaints about police action, unemployment, inadequate housing or other conditions. When grievance-related incidents recurred and rising tensions were not satisfactorily resolved, a cumulative process took place in which prior incidents were readily recalled and grievances reinforced. At some point in the mounting tension, a further incident — in itself often routine or even trivial — became the breaking point, and the tension spilled over into violence.

6. Many grievances in the Negro community result from the discrimination, prejudice and powerlessness which Negroes often experience. They also result from the severely disadvantaged social and economic conditions of many Negroes as compared with those of whites in the same city and, more particularly, in the predominantly white suburbs.

7. Characteristically, the typical rioter was not a hoodlum, habitual criminal or riffraff; nor was he a recent migrant, a member of an uneducated underclass or a person lacking broad social and political concerns. Instead, he was a teenager or young adult, a lifelong resident of the city in which he rioted, a high school dropout — but somewhat better educated than his Negro neighbor — and almost invariably under-employed or employed in a menial job. He was proud of his race, extremely hostile to both whites and middle-class Negroes and, though informed about politics, highly distrustful of the political system and of political leaders.

8. Numerous Negro counterrioters walked the streets urging rioters to "cool it." The typical counterrioter resembled in many respects the majority of Negroes, who neither rioted nor took action against the rioters, that is, the noninvolved. But certain differences are crucial: the counterrioter was better educated and had higher income than either the rioter or the noninvolved.

9. Negotiations between Negroes and white officials occurred during virtually all the disorders surveyed. The negotiations often involved young, militant Negroes as well as older, established leaders. Despite a setting of chaos and disorder, negotiations in many cases involved discussion of underlying grievances as well as the handling of the disorder by control authorities.

10. The chain we have identified— discrimination, prejudice, disadvantaged conditions, intense and pervasive grievances, a series of tension-heightening incidents, all culminating in the eruption of disorder at the hands of youthful, politically-aware activists — must be understood as describing the central trend in the disorders, not as an explanation of all aspects of the riots or of all rioters. Some rioters, for example, may have shared neither the conditions nor the grievances of their Negro neighbors, some may have coolly and deliberately exploited the chaos created by others; some may have been drawn into the melee merely because they identified with, or wished to emulate, others. Nor do we intend to suggest that the majority of the rioters, who shared the adverse conditions and grievances, necessarily articulated in their own minds the connection between that background and their actions.

11. The background of disorder in the riot cities was typically characterized by severely disadvantaged conditions for Negroes, especially as compared with those for whites; a local government often unresponsive to these conditions; Federal programs which had not yet

reached a significantly large proportion of those in need; and the resulting reservoir of pervasive and deep grievance and frustration in the ghetto.

12. In the immediate aftermath of disorder, the status quo of daily life before the disorder generally was quickly restored. Yet, despite some notable public and private efforts, little basic change took place in the conditions underlying the disorder. In some cases, the result was increased distrust between blacks and whites, diminished interracial communication, and growth of Negro and white extremist groups.

U. Beyond the Riots: A Suggested Plan

Elmo Roper, "Beyond the Riots," *The Saturday Review* October 7, 1967, pp. 24-25. Reprinted with permission of the author and publisher. Copyright © 1967 Saturday Review, Inc.

1. Do you agree with the author's identification of specific misconceptions? If people have held these misconceptions as truth, how might this have affected their formulation of public policies?

2. What is the author's plan to achieve social harmony "beyond the riots?" Do you think that it might work? Why?

The reaction of certain people to the recent riots in Negro ghettoes is quite clear: Get tough and don't let it happen again. The reaction of others is less clear. Many liberals seem to be experiencing a mixture of bewilderment, hurt feelings, distaste, and a sentiment of "What's the point of all our attempts to help, when hoodlums and extremists have taken over the Negro movement?" The result is too often avoidance and withdrawal from the civil rights scene. I would like to talk about the reasons for this withdrawal and the misconceptions I believe it is based on.

The first misconception is that the violence that has occurred across the nation can be described as race riots. A race riot is a violent confrontation between two races, whose motivating power is racial enmity [hatred]. While it can't be denied that racial hatred has been evident in the recent outbursts — both by whites and Negroes — this has by no means been the only or even the dominant motivating force behind the riots. In fact, the major victims of the riots have been Negroes — middle — and upper-class Negroes whose residences have been burned, Negro shopkeepers whose shops have been looted, Negroes who happened to be around when the shooting started and got killed as a result. Actually, what we have been witnessing might be more accurately described as riots of the "have-nots" against the "haves." The "have-not" rioters are predominantly but by no means exclusively Negro, as was made clear in Detroit, when white snipers were a visible part of the action. So it is grossly unfair to react to the riots as if they were examples of general Negro violence against whites.

In fact, most of the disturbances did not begin as violence against *people* at all. They began as looting expeditions where the focus was on the taking of *things* which have been out of economic reach of the "have-nots" involved. They often moved on to destruction of these same things that others possessed and they did not. Moreover, the violence was committed by only a small minority — probably by less than 5 per cent — of the Negro community, most of whom are decent, law-abiding people with as great a horror of ghetto violence as anybody else. So it is not "Negroes" who rioted but a particular kind of Negro, who, in a recent study Roper Research Associates completed in six Northern cities, was described by other Negroes in distinctly unflattering terms. Asked to select from a list the types of people most likely to get actively involved in riots, the most frequently mentioned types were the unemployed (57 per cent), hoodlums (53 per cent), kids looking for excitement (44 per cent), and people who want an excuse to steal and loot (42 per cent). Such descriptions as civil rights leaders (13 per cent), idealists (7 per cent), and ordinary people (8 per cent) were seldom selected. The majority of Negroes interviewed also expressed the view that only a small minority of Negroes are in sympathy with riots. This is not to deny that bitterness and frustration are widespread among Negroes today, who are angry both at the conditions in which they live and the speed with which those conditions are being changed. But this has not led *most* Negroes to look for the solution in destructive violence. Yet most of the press has been quick to call lawlessness and looting by the name of race riots.

The second misconception is that articulate racist extremists like Stokely Carmichael and H. Rap Brown are leaders who validly express the mood of Negroes today. The importance of these leaders is very largely an illusion created by a naïve press, for the ability to shock and to generate publicity is quite a different thing from the ability to attract a following. Followings they may have, but they are among a minority of Negroes and the numbers are shrinking. These people are the Black Bilboes of our day. The same six-city survey showed that in none of the cities was an organization like SNCC approved by a majority of Negroes. However, organizations like the Urban League, the NAACP, and the Southern Christian Leadership Conference had large followings indeed. Despite the contemptuous attitude of Negro extremists, it is the older, more moderate organizations which remain the real channels of Negro thought and feeling. The difference is that these organizations do not make flashy, fiery talk; they concentrate their energies on getting things done to change the Negro's position in America. They *have* gotten things done, and the fact that their Negro memberships are increasing is evidence that Negroes know it. The black racists have not taken over the movement; they have only taken over the headlines.

The third misconception is in the expectations of certain white liberals about what is possible in race relations today. I think it is naïve for educated, upper- and middle-class whites, whose own social lives are lived in an almost exclusively white world, to expect that the breakthrough on racial integration would come among uneducated, lower-economic-level whites and Negroes. In their quest for better jobs and housing, Negroes seem to be threatening the position of economically and socially insecure whites, who are often first- or second-generation European immigrants who have themselves fought rather recently for their place in America. It is unrealistic to expect these intellectually unsophisticated and economically competitive whites and Negroes to embrace each other and understand the other's point of view. These people are almost certain to be the last, rather than the first, to integrate.

Who, then, should be the first? Who can, by example, lead the way to an acceptance of the fact that intellectual kinship is far more important than skin color? I think the obvious candidate is the upper- and middle-class white person, who has the intellectual background as well as the economic security to permit him to look at larger horizons. Until educated upper- and middle-class whites reach out to educated upper- and middle-class Negroes on an individual basis, we are not going to have integration. Instead of adding to the isolation of Negro moderates, who today are feeling the scorn of Negro militants as well as the more polite withdrawal of whites, I believe this is exactly the moment when white Americans of goodwill should go out of their way to make concrete their support of genuine racial integration. There are a number of ways this can be done.

For example, white doctors and lawyers should make efforts to get Negro doctors and lawyers to join and become active in medical and bar associations and become active in committees where it will be obvious that they are there as respected members of the bar or the medical profession, not as Negroes. The same thing can be done by trade associations; after all, a Negro jeweler and a white jeweler do have that in common. There are literally dozens of areas where responsible and intelligent whites and responsible and intelligent Negroes could be seen working together because of some mutuality of interest. The next step is to make these contacts more frequent and more personal.

That the racial heat is on is no excuse for faltering in the long-range, step-by-step effort to bring the races together; it is reason to redouble these efforts. There must be a model of racial friendliness and goodwill to counter the image of racial contempt and antagonism so visible today. I have no illusions that small, individual efforts to bridge the gulf between the races present a magical solution to the problems of racial disharmony. But it seems clear to me that if educated, high-minded people who believe in the concept of racial brotherhood cannot make a reality of closeness between the races, no one can. If we cannot develop genuine and meaningful relationships between whites and Negroes whose education and backgrounds make it easiest and most natural, we have no right to expect those with narrower vistas to do so.

People of lesser education and lesser economic security must be able to see in their daily lives a growing pattern of kinship between the better educated and economically better situated whites and Negroes — or the road to racial peace is going to be a long, long road.

V. A Moral Equivalent for Riots

Harvey Wheeler, A Moral Equivalent for Riots," *The Saturday Review,* May 11, 1968, pp. 19-22, 51. Reprinted with permission by the author and publisher. Copyright © 1968 Saturday Review, Inc.

1. This is the second half of Mr. Wheeler's article; the first half which describes theories was presented as Reading K. Can you describe Mr. Wheeler's proposals in your own words?

2. On what points does Mr. Wheeler concur with Mr.
   Roper? Would Mr. Wheeler's suggestions make good
   public policies which would ameliorate the conditions
   causing riots? Think carefully about your explanations
   for riots.

So, we have ten general propositions about violence. It is
apparent from them that the problem runs quite deep – so
deep that not even massive investments in the improvement of
the physical conditions of the ghettos will resolve them. A
few propositions, however, can be derived from what we have
uncovered:

Self-strengthening. One of the most important functions of
the riots has been to permit Negroes to turn to violence
outward. Violence allowed them to sublimate the
self-destructive internalized aggression patterns of the
post-Civil War era. It has provided a way for them to build
their own self-respect. It has also given them avenues to
power – "riot Power" as an American way of life. Seen from
below, riots are a "good" kind of violence. . . .

So, to paraphrase William James, what the Negro – and the
society in general – needs is the moral equivalent of riots:
officially provided self-strengthening institutions. *Not*
institutions *given* the Negro, ready-built by whites– especially
not by white liberals, who commiserate today over being
excluded from the "Movement." The white liberal today is
one of the Negro's most serious obstacles to
self-strengthening. For in wanting to help, and to participate,
and remain a part of the Movement, the white liberal stands
directly in the way of the indigenous self-strengthening the
Negro must build for himself – just as he built his riots for
himself. The liberal becomes, unwittingly, the most
patronizing and the most dangerous Uncle Tom creator
confronting the Negro today.

What can be done? Because the solutions must be as
profound as the causes, we must have the faith to be
innovative in spite of seeming danger:

1. We must facilitate the establishment of Negro *community corporations.* We must foster the creation and maturation of Black Power by enabling it: by providing the funds whereby Negroes may organize their communities for themselves. . . .

2. Just as the developing world insists upon achieving development on its own, expelling its former white masters and organizing and administering its affairs for itself, so also with our Negro communities. We can provide them with funds for sending representatives abroad to the most successful parts of the developing world where they can learn directly about the problems of cultural development. This means funding study programs for Negroes in Tanzania, Ghana, Israel, and even Cuba. The lessons learned can be applied not only to the problems of urban organization, but also, perhaps using the Israel kibbutz [cooperative communities] model, to the problems of agricultural development throughout the South. There is no reason why the Government cannot finance cadres of Negroes to learn kibbutz management in Israel, and then finance the acquisition of large tracts of Southern farm land where such cadres [leaders] can develop creative, productive, and healthful farming communities. Integration, of a new sort, will come one day, but only after the self-strengthening process has been fulfilled.

3. Finally, programs for the autonomous development of Negro culture must be subsidized. . . . The Negro, like the French Canadian, is fully justified in insisting on having his own autonomy [independence]. This can find political representation in a new kind of nonterritorial federalism in which the institutions expressing Negro autonomy may be politically represented, as in a third legislative chamber: a black Congress.

Rioting as an American way of life. Direct action – the sort that now issues in violence too often – must be given fuller

Constitutional protection. This is not because we fear that each summer will bring a new wave of rioting. On the contrary, riots appear to be like lightning — they are devastating but they don't strike twice in the same place. The self-respect they engender mitigates against their repetition. Moreover, a riot produces a strange. . . love. The same ghetto which before the riot seemed to be a prison of alienation is made into one's own by the act of rioting against it. And once Negroes feel they own their ghettos they'll never burn them down. But this being so, the need for a moral alternative becomes even more necessary for the post-riot future.

We must have a new Constitutional right to civil disobedience. It will involve reinterpretation of the First Amendment. It will require expanding the freedom of speech clause and the clause protecting the right to petition for redress of grievances. Qualifications and safeguards are needed, but we know how to apply them. We have already the clear-and-present danger test. Long ago, union picketing was established as a right under the free speech clause of the First Amendment. Such actions as the Memphis garbage workers' protest, and even the [Benjamin] Spock draft resistance protest, may lead the way to the moral equivalent for riots.

Cultural deprivation. This is the most serious concern — the element at the root of the built-in despotism that hounds the poor into a lifetime of ingrown poverty and deprivation. We must facilitate the acquisition of a specially designed and consciously engendered supplementary culture. It must be provided to all who need it virtually from birth, so that the cultural deprivation of the ghetto can be overstepped and each child can be provided with a sufficiently supportive environment to enable him to spring to the highest possible cultural and intellectual attainments. This will require drastic programs:

1. *Cottage schools.* Blackboard jungles must be torn down and cottage boarding schools established in their place.

Class sizes must be held down to something around twenty. Moreover, it must be possible for each child to look forward to progression through his entire primary and secondary school career in the same class. This means that it must be possible for the culturally deprived to live in these schools — in a good boarding school — and also to commute to his own school from across town, or even across the nation, staying with his own class through graduation. If this sounds expensive, well, it is. It is like guaranteeing an. . . [excellent] education to every child. And this is exactly what we must do.

2. *Multimedia homes.* This may provide the ultimate solution for the cultural deprivation of us all. Consider the technological possibilities we now possess. We have television, audiotapes, records, newspapers, magazines, encyclopedias, movie films — and computers to run them all. We have the possibility of integrating all these into a home-sized multimedia installation. This means that we can all "subscribe" to a total information, cultural, educational, and amusement "program," the way we now subscribe to separate newspapers and journals. Moreover, these programs can be specially designed for individual family needs, so that we can start with the most depressed family imaginable and design progressive, long-term multi-media cultural programs in much the way insurance consultants now design lifetime protection policies for their clients. Through such means it is technologically possible to bring even the most deprived person through all the stages of cultural development within a single lifetime.

The city. We know that a megalopolis [huge city] is not only obsolete; it is the breeding ground of cultural and physical disease. We also know that it is now technologically feasible to have any kind of city we wish. Today in the Midwest there is an exciting new plan for the construction of an autonomous urban community of not more than 250,000 people. The computer and other new technological advances now make such cultural and economic autonomy possible. They also make it possible for us to engage in what Robert Hutchins calls the "learning society," with the quest for creature comforts giving way to the quest for culture comforts. We shall have to build these new cities sooner or later. We might as well start now.

Dr. Hutchins likes to tell about the time Marshal Lyautey, who was the French Governor General of Morocco, asked his gardener about a beautiful tree he had seen, wishing to have more of them for his own garden. "But General," said the gardener, "that tree takes 200 years to reach maturity." "In that case," said Marshal Lyautey, "we have no time to lose. Plant them this afternoon."

We have less time to lose — and quicker and more beautiful results to expect. We must start planting seeds of our new and more humane culture today.

W. Recommendations from an Earlier Riot: Chicago, 1919

"Recommendations of the Commission, Chicago, 1919," *The Negro in Chicago: A Study in Race Relations and a Race Riot,* Chicago: University of Chicago Press, 1922, pp. 640-651. Reprinted with permission by the publisher. Copyright © 1922 by The University of Chicago.

1. Following the 1919 riot in Chicago, a commission investigated the causes of the riot. What do the recommendations imply about the causation of riots? Is this implication accurate by what you know?

2. Do the recommendations for social and governmental action seem relevant to today's unrest? How? Would these recommendations be helpful in formulating policies today?

Many of our citizens who were appalled by the rioting and murders of 1919, feeling the need of a solution of the problem dealt with in this investigation, have hoped that this Commission might suggest some ready remedy, some quick means of assuring harmony between the races.

Careful consideration of the facts set forth in this report shows that no such suggestion is possible. No one, white or Negro, is wholly free from an inheritance of prejudice in feeling and in thinking as to these questions. Mutual understanding and sympathy between the races will be followed by harmony and co-operation. But these can come completely only after the disappearance of prejudice. Thus the remedy is necessarily slow; and it is all the more important that the civic conscience of the community should be aroused, and that progress should begin in a direction steadily away from the disgrace of 1919. . . .

To the Police, Militia, State's Attorney, and Courts:

1. We recommend that the police and militia work out, at the earliest possible date, a detailed plan for joint action in the control of race riots.

2. In accordance with such a plan, and in the event of race rioting, we specifically recommend: (a) that the militia, white and Negro, be promptly mobilized at the beginning of the outbreak; (b) that police and deputy sheriffs and militia, white and Negro, be so distributed as adequately to protect both races in white and Negro neighborhoods and to avoid the gross inequalities of protection which, in the riot of 1919, permitted widespread depredations, including murder, against Negroes in white neighborhoods, and attacks in Negro neighborhoods by invading white hoodlums; (c) that the police and militia be stationed with special reference to main street-car lines and transfer points used by Negroes in getting to and from work; (d) that substantial assurance be given of adequate and equal protection by all agencies of law enforcement, thus

removing the incentive to arm in self-defense; (e) that in the appointment of special peace officers there shall be no discrimination against Negroes; (f) that all rioters, white and Negro, be arrested without race discrimination; (g) that all reports and complaints of neglect of duty or participation in rioting by police, deputy sheriffs, or militia be promptly investigated and the offenders promptly punished; (h) that all persons arrested in connection with rioting be systematically booked on distinct charges showing such connection, in order to avoid the confusion and evasions of justice following the riot of 1919.

3. We recommend that, without regard to color, all persons arrested in connection with rioting be promptly tried and the guilty speedily punished.

4. We recommend prompt and vigorous action by the police, state's attorney, and courts to suppress the bombings of Negro and white houses, these acts being criminal and likely to provoke race rioting.

5. The testimony of court officials before the Commission and its investigations indicate that Negroes are more commonly arrested, subjected to police identification, and convicted than white offenders, that on similar evidence they are generally held and convicted on more serious charges, and that they are given longer sentences. We point out that these practices and tendencies are not only unfair to Negroes, but weaken the machinery of justice and, when taken with the greater inability of Negroes to pay fines in addition to or in lieu of terms in jail, produce misleading statistics of Negro crime. We recognize that these practices and tendencies are in a large degree the unconscious results of traditional race prejudice. We recommend to the police, state's attorney, judges, and juries that they consider these conditions in the effort to deal fairly (and without discrimination) with all persons charged with crime.

6. We recommend that, in order to encourage respect for

law by both Negroes and whites, the courts discountenance the facetiousness which is too common in dealing with cases in which Negroes are involved. . . .

8. We recommend better co-operation between the city and park police in and near parks, bathing-beaches, and other public recreation places, especially where there has been or is likely to be race friction; and in the speedy punishment of persons guilty of stoning houses, molesting individuals, or committing other depredations calculated to arouse race antagonism.

9. We recommend that the police pay particular and continuous attention to the so-called "athletic clubs" on the South Side, which we have found to be a fruitful source of race conflict, and that when race conflict arises or is imminent the members and meeting places of such clubs be searched for arms and that, if deemed necessary, such clubs be closed. . . .

To the City Council and Administrative Boards, the Park Boards and the Municipal Bureau of Parks, Playgrounds, and Bathing-Beaches:

11. We recommend that the most stringent means possible be applied to control the importation, sale, and possession of firearms and other deadly weapons.

12. In order to facilitate police supervision of so-called "athletic clubs," we recommend that all such clubs be required to file with the city clerk statements of their purposes and, at stated intervals, lists of their members and officers, with their addresses.

13. We recommend that the authorities exercise their powers to condemn and raze all houses unfit for human habitation, many of which the Commission has found to exist in the Negro residence areas on the South and West sides.

14. We recommend better enforcement of health and sanitary laws and regulations in the care, repair, and upkeep of streets and alleys and the collection and

disposal of rubbish and garbage in areas of Negro residence, where the Commission has found these matters to be shamefully neglected. . . .

To the Board of Education:

16. We recommend that in the areas where the main part of the Negro population lives, and where elementary-school accommodations are notably deficient, buildings, equipment, and teaching forces be provided which shall be at least equal to the average standard for the city, in order that the present conditions of overcrowding, arrangement of pupils in shifts, and the assignment of too large classes to teachers may be remedied.

17. We recommend the establishment of night schools and community centers in sections of the city not now adequately provided with such facilities.

18. Having found that many Negro children who quit school at an early age, as in the case of similar white children, appear later as criminals and delinquents, we urge strict enforcement of regulations as to working permits for such children, and we especially recommend that truant officers give attention to school attendance by the children of Negro families migrating here from the South.

19. Since the attitude of principals and teachers vitally influences the relations of white and Negro children in the public schools, we recommend that special care be exercised in appointing principals and teachers who have a sympathetic and intelligent interest in promoting good race relations in the schools.

20. We recommend that public-school principals and teachers encourage participation by children of both races in student activities as a means of promoting mutual understanding and good race relations in such schools and in the community.

To Social and Civic Organizations, Labor Unions, and Churches:

21. Being convinced by our inquiry that much of the antagonism evinced in the areas of marked hostility toward Negroes is founded upon tradition which is itself without foundation in fact or justice, we recommend to schools, social centers and agencies, churches, labor unions, and other organizations in these areas, and to public-spirited citizens, white and Negro, that they endeavor to dispel the false notions of each race about the other and promote mutual tolerance and friendliness between them.

22. We recommend that both white and Negro churches seek and use means to improve race relations, and that these means include the finding of frequent occasion for having their congregations addressed by representatives of both races on the subject of race sympathy and tolerance. . . .

To the Public:

27. We are convinced by our inquiry: (a) that measures involving or approaching deportation or segregation are illegal, impracticable, and would not solve, but would accentuate, the race problem and postpone its just and orderly solution by the process of adjustment; (b) that the moral responsibility of race rioting does not rest upon hoodlums alone, but also upon all citizens, white or black, who sanction force or violence in interracial relations or who do not condemn and combat the spirit of racial hatred thus expressed; (c) that race friction and antagonism are largely due to the fact that each race too readily misunderstands and misinterprets the other's conduct and aspirations.

   We therefore urge upon all citizens, white and Negro, active opporition to the employment of force or violence in interracial relations and to the spirit of antagonism and hatred. We recommend dispassionate, intelligent, and sympathetic consideration by each race of the other's needs and aims; we also recommend the dissemination of proved or trustworthy information about all phases of race relations as a useful means for effecting peaceful racial adjustment.

28. Since rumor, usually groundless, is a prolific source of racial bitterness and strife, we warn both whites and Negroes against the acceptance or circulation by either of reports about the other whose truth has not been fully established. We urge all citizens, white and Negro, vigorously to oppose all propaganda of malicious or selfish origin which would tend to excite race prejudice.

29. We commend race contacts in cultural and co-operative efforts as tending strongly to mutual understanding and the promotion of good race relations.

30. We condemn the provocation or fostering of race antagonism by associations or organizations ostensibly founded or conducted for purposes of patriotism or local improvements or the like. . . .

To the White Members of the Public:

32. We call to public attention the fact that intensity of racial feeling is not necessarily due to the presence of Negroes in a neighborhood, either in the majority or minority, and that such feeling is not the rule but the exception. . . .

33. Our inquiry has shown that insufficiency in amount and quality of housing is an all-important factor in Chicago's race problem; there must be more and better housing to accommodate the great increase in Negro population which was at the rate of 148 per cent from 1910 to 1920. This situation will be made worse by methods tending toward forcible segregation or exclusion of Negroes, such as the circulation of threatening statements and propaganda by organizations or persons to prevent Negroes from living in certain areas, and the

lawless and perilous bombing of houses occupied by Negroes or by whites suspected of encouraging Negro residence in the district.

We therefore recommend that all white citizens energetically discourage these futile, pernicious, and lawless practices, and either co-operate in or start movements to solve the housing problem by constructive and not destructive methods.

34. Testimony before the Commission and investigations made by it show two important facts (a) that depreciation of residence property generally charged exclusively to the presence of Negroes in a neighborhood is often largely due to other factors; (b) that many Negroes of this city meet their obligations in such a manner as to make their home-building and home-owning investments seem a more desirable risk than has been generally supposed. We therefore recommend that these facts be taken into consideration in connection with loans on Negro property.

35. We condemn and urge the discontinuance of the practice of property owners who arbitrarily advance rents merely because Negroes become tenants.

36. We recommend that white persons seek information from responsible and representative Negroes as the basis of their judgments about Negro traits, characteristics, and tendencies, and thereby conteract the common disposition, arising from erroneous tradition and literature, to regard all Negroes as belonging to one homogeneous group and as being inferior in mentality and morality, given to emotionalism, and having an innate tendency toward crime, especially sex crime.

To the Negro Members of the Public:

37. We recommend to Negroes the promulgation of sound racial doctrines among the uneducated members of their group, and the discouragement of propaganda and agitators seeking to inflame racial animosity and incite Negroes to violence.

38. We urge Negroes to contribute more freely of their money and personal effort to the social agencies developed by public-spirited members of their group; also to contribute to the general social agencies of the community.

39. We recommend that the Negro community, through the extension or establishment of the necessary social agencies, undertake to supply means and encouragement for leisure activities, and undertake work among Negro boys and girls along the lines of prevention of vice and crime; also that it provide institutional care of dependent Negro children. . . .

41. We commend the important work done by the Chicago Urban League, the Negro churches, and other organizations in facilitating the adjustment of migrant Negroes from the South to the conditions of living in Chicago and urge its extension. We also commend the work already done by Negroes through community associations in bettering the appearance and sanitary condition of housing and recommend its further extension.

42. While we recognize the propriety and social values of race pride among Negroes, we warn them that thinking and talking too much in terms of race alone are calculated to promote separation of race interests and thereby to interfere with racial adjustment.

To Employers and Labor Organizations:

43. We have found that in struggles between capital and labor Negro workers are in a position dangerous to themselves and to peaceful relations between the races, whether the issues involve their use by employers to undermine wage standards or break strikes, or efforts by organized labor to keep them out of certain trades while refusing to admit them to membership in the unions in such trades. We feel that unnecessary racial bitterness is provoked by such treatment of Negro workers, that racial prejudice is played upon by both parties, and that

through such practices injury comes, not alone to Negroes, but to employers and labor organizations as well.

We therefore recommend to employers that they deal with Negroes as workmen on the same plane as white workers; and to labor unions that they admit Negroes to full membership whenever they apply for it and possess the qualifications required of white workers.

44. We commend to the attention of employers who fear clashes or loss of white workers by taking on Negro workers the fact that in 89 per cent of the industries investigated by this Commission, Negroes were found working in close association with white employees, and that friction between these elements had rarely been manifested.

45. In view of the limited field of employment within which Negroes are restricted we recommend that employers in all lines enlarge that field and permit Negroes an equal chance with whites to enter all positions for which they are qualified by efficiency and merit. In this connection especial attention is called to the fact that opportunity is generally denied to Negroes for gaining experience in business methods through service in responsible positions in business houses. Such opportunities, if made available for them, would not only be of benefit to Negroes in the development of sounder business methods among them and the building up of their resources, but would also be a gain to the business establishments and the community at large.

46. We have found that Negroes are denied equal opportunity with whites for advancement and promotion where they are employed. As a measure of justice we urge that Negroes be employed, advanced, and promoted according to their capacities and proved merit. We call to the attention of those concerned the high qualifications of many Negro workers in sleeping-car and dining-car service, and recommend that

when they deserve it and the opportunity offers, they be made eligible for promotion to positions as conductors and stewards.

47. We point out that as an injustice and a cause of racial antagonism the practice of some employers who having hired Negroes as strike breakers discharge them when the strike is settled to make places for former white employes. . . .

To Negro Workers:

51. We recommend that qualified Negro workers desiring membership in labor organizations join unions which admit both races equally, instead of organizing separate Negro labor unions. . . .

To the Press:

58. In view of the recognized responsibility of the press in its general influence upon public opinion concerning Negroes — especially important as related to the suppression of race rioting — we recommend: (a) that the newspapers generally, including the foreign-language press, apply the same standards of accuracy, fairness, and sense of proportion, with avoidance of exaggeration, in publishing news about Negroes as about whites; in this connection special attention is called to the fact that emphasis, greatly out of proportion to that given their creditable acts, is frequently place on the crimes and misdeeds of Negroes, who unlike other groups, are identified with each incident and thus constantly associated with discreditable conduct; (b) that the manner of news treatment be no different in the case of Negroes than in that of whites, to the end that there shall always be the unwritten assumption that the same responsibility for equal consideration of the rights of the one by the other rests on whites and Negroes alike, in respect of the matter involved in the publication;

(c) that, in consideration of the great ease with which the public is influenced against the whole Negro group by sensational articles and headlines, the press should exercise great caution in dealing with unverified reports of crimes of Negroes against white women, and should avoid the designation of trivial fights as race riots; (d) that in recognition of the dangers of racial antagonism on the part of the ignorant, the unthinking and the prejudiced of both races, publication be made, as òpportunities offer, of such matters as shall in their character tend to dispel prejudice and promote mutual respect and good will.

We specially recommend more frequent publications concerning: (1) creditable achievements of consequence by Negroes; (2) their efforts toward a higher cultural and social life; and (3) their improvement of the physical conditions of their own communities; (4) the common obligation of all citizens of all races to recognize in their interrelations the supreme duty of strict obedience to the law, in spirit as well as in deed; (5) verification, so far as practicable, of all news concerning Negroes and their activities by reference to recognized Negro agencies or responsible representative Negroes.

We further recommend the capitalization of the word "Negro" in racial designation, and avoidance of the word "nigger," as contemptuous and needlessly provocative.

59. To the Negro press we recommend greater care and accuracy in reporting incidents involving whites and Negroes, the abandonment of sensational headlines and articles on racial questions, and more attention to educating Negro readers as to the available means and opportunities of adjusting themselves and their fellows into more harmonious relations with their white neighbors and fellow-citizens, and as to the lines of individual conduct and collective effort which will tend

to minimize interracial friction, promote their own social and economic development, and hasten interracial adjustment.

Chicago, December 6, 1921

X. What Can Be Done... Now?

Report of the National Advisory Commission on Civil Disorders, Washington, D.C.: Government Printing Office, 1968, pp. 8–13.

1. The President's Commission of 1967 has made some specific recommendations to federal, state, and local governments and to private citizens. What do these recommendations imply about the cause of riots? Is the implication accurate?

2. How do these recommendations of 1967 compare to the recommendations of 1919? What are the similarities?

3. If you agree with the 1967's commission's recommendations, how would you proceed to implement these recommendations? Do you agree with the implementations suggested by the commission? Why? If you do not agree with the commission's recommendations, what objections do you have? What alternative recommendations would you make?

The Community Response

Our investigation of the 1967 riot cities establishes that virtually every major episode of violence was foreshadowed by an accumulation of unresolved grievances and by widespread dissatisfaction among Negroes with the unwillingness or inability of local government to respond.

Overcoming these conditions is essential for community

support of law enforcement and civil order. City governments need new and more vital channels of communication to the residents of the ghetto; they need to improve their capacity to respond effectively to community needs before they become community grievances; and they need to provide opportunity for meaningful involvement of ghetto residents in shaping policies and programs which affect the community.

The Commission recommends that local governments:

> —Develop Neighborhood Action Task Forces as joint community-government efforts through which more effective communication can be achieved, and the delivery of city services to ghetto residents improved.

> —Establish comprehensive grievance-response mechanisms in order to bring all public agencies under public scrutiny.

> —Bring the institutions of local government closer to the people they serve by establishing neighborhood outlets [offices] for local, state, and Federal administrative and public service agencies.

> —Expand opportunities for ghetto residents to participate in the formulation of public policy and the implementation of programs affecting them through improved political representation, creation of institutional channels for community action, expansion of legal services, and legislative hearings on ghetto problems.

In this effort, city governments will require State and Federal support.

The Commission recommends:

> —State and Federal financial assistance for mayors and city councils to support the research, consultants, staff, and other resources needed to respond effectively to Federal program initiatives.

> —State cooperation in providing municipalities with the jurisdictional tools needed to deal with their problems; a fuller measure of financial aid to urban areas; and the focusing of the interests of suburban communities on the physical, social, and cultural environment of the central city.

Police and the Community

The abrasive relationship between the police and minority communities has been a major—and explosive—source of grievance, tension, and disorder. The blame must be shared by the total society.

The police are faced with demands for increased protection and service in the ghetto. Yet the aggressive patrol practices thought necessary to meet these demands themselves create tension and hostility. The resulting grievances have been further aggravated by the lack of effective mechanisms for handling complaints against the police. Special programs for bettering police-community relations have been instituted, but these alone are not enough. Police administrators, with the guidance of public officials, and the support of the entire community, must take vigorous action to improve law enforcement and to decrease the potential for disorder.

The Commission recommends that city government and police authorities:

—Review police operations in the ghetto to ensure proper conduct by police officers, and eliminate abrasive practices.

—Provide more adequate police protection to ghetto residents to eliminate their high sense of insecurity and the belief in the existence of a dual standard of law enforcement.

—Establish fair and effective mechanisms for the redress of grievances against the police and other municipal employees.

—Develop and adopt policy guidelines to assist officers in making critical decisions in areas where police conduct can create tension.

—Develop and use innovative programs to insure widespread community support for law enforcement.

—Recruit more Negroes into the regular police force, and review promotion policies to insure fair promotion for Negro officers.

—Establish a "Community Service Officer" program to attract ghetto youths between the ages of 17 and 21 to police work. These junior officers would perform duties in ghetto neighborhoods, but would not have full police authority. The Federal Government should provide support equal to 90 percent of the costs of employing CSO's on the basis of one for every 10 regular officers.

Control of Disorder

Preserving civil peace is the first responsibility of government. Unless the rule of law prevails, our society will lack not only order but also the environment essential to social and economic progress.

The maintenance of civil order cannot be left to the police alone. The police need guidance, as well as support, from mayors and other public officials. It is the responsibility of public officials to determine proper police policies, support adequate police standards for personnel and performance, and participate in planning for the control of disorders.

To maintain control of incidents which could lead to disorders, the Commission recommends that local officials:

—Assign seasoned, well-trained policemen and supervisory officers to patrol ghetto areas, and to respond to disturbances.

—Develop plans which will quickly muster maximum police manpower and highly qualified senior commanders at the outbreak of disorders.

—Provide special training in the prevention of disorders, and prepare police for riot control and for operation in units, with adequate command and control and field communication for proper discipline and effectiveness.

—Develop guidelines governing the use of control equipment and provide alternatives to the use of lethal weapons. Federal support for support for research in this area is needed.

—Establish an intelligence system to provide police and other public officials with reliable information that may help to prevent the outbreak of a disorder and to institute effective control measures in the event a riot erupts.

—Develop continuing contacts with ghetto residents to make use of the forces for order which exist within the community.

—Establish machinery for neutralizing rumors, and enabling Negro leaders and residents to obtain the facts. Create special rumor details to collect, evaluate, and dispel rumors that may lead to a civil disorder.

The Commission believes there is a grave danger that some communities may resort to the indiscriminate and excessive use of force. The harmful effects of over-reaction are incalculable. The Commission condemns moves to equip police departments with mass destruction weapons, such as automatic rifles, machine guns, and tanks. Weapons which are designed to destroy, not to control, have no place in densely populated urban communities.

The Commission recommends that the Federal Government share in the financing of programs for improvement of police forces, both in their normal law enforcement activities as well as in their response to civil disorders.

To assist government authorities in planning their response to civil disorder, this report contains a Supplement on Control of Disorder. It deals with specific problems encountered during riot control operations, and includes:

—Assessment of the present capabilities of police, National Guard and Army forces to control major riots, and recommendations for improvement.

—Recommended means by which the control operations of those forces may be coordinated with the response of other agencies, such as fire departments, and with the community at large.

—Recommendations for review and revision of Federal, state and local laws needed to provide the framework for control efforts and for the callup and interrelated action of public safety forces.

The Administration of Justice Under Emergency Conditions

In many of the cities which experienced disorders last summer, there were recurring breakdowns in the mechanisms for processing, prosecuting, and protecting arrested persons. These resulted mainly from long-standing structural deficiencies in criminal court systems, and from the failure of communities to anticipate and plan for the emergency demands of civil disorders.

In part, because of this, there were few successful prosecutions for serious crimes committed during the riots. In those cities where mass arrests occurred, many arrestees were deprived of basic legal rights.

The Commission recommends that the cities and states:

—Undertake reform of the lower courts so as to improve the quality of justice rendered under normal conditions.

—Plan comprehensive measures by which the criminal justice system may be supplemented during civil disorders so that its deliberative functions are protected, and the quality of justice is maintained.

Such emergency plans require broad community participation and dedicated leadership by the bench and bar. They should include:

—Laws sufficient to deter and punish riot conduct.

—Additional judges, bail and probation officers, and clerical staff.

—Arrangements for volunteer lawyers to help prosecutors and to represent riot defendants at every stage of proceedings.

—Policies to insure proper and individual bail, arraignment, pretrial, trial, and sentencing proceedings.

—Adequate emergency processing and detention facilities. . . .

The News Media and the Disorders

In his charge to the Commission, the President asked: "What effect do the mass media have on the riots?"

The Commission determined that the answer to the President's question did not lie solely in the performance of the press and broadcasters in reporting the riots. Our analysis had to consider also the overall treatment by the media of the Negro ghettos, community relations, racial attitudes, and poverty — day by day and month by month, year in and year out.

A wide range of interviews with Government officials, law enforcement authorities, media personnel and other citizens, including ghetto residents, as well as a quantitative analysis of riot coverage and a special conference with industry representatives, leads us to conclude that:

> Despite instances of sensationalism, inaccuracy and distortion, newspapers, radio and television tried on the whole to give a balanced, factual account of the 1967 disorders.

> —Elements of the news media failed to portray accurately the scale and character of the violence that occurred last summer. The overall effect was, we believe, an exaggeration of both mood and event.

> —Important segments of the media failed to report adequately on the causes and consequences of civil disorders and on the underlying problems of race relations. They have not communicated to the majority of their audience — which is white — a sense of the degradation, misery, and hopelessness of life in the ghetto.

These failings must be corrected, and the improvement must come from within the industry. Freedom of the press is not the issue. Any effort to impose governmental restrictions would be inconsistent with fundamental constitutional precepts.

We have seen evidence that the news media are becoming aware of and concerned about their performance in this field. As that concern grows, coverage will improve. But much more must be done, and it must be done soon.

The Commission recommends that the media:

—Expand coverage of the Negro community and of race problems through permanent assignment of reporters familiar with urban and racial affairs, and through establishment of more and better links with the Negro community.

—Integrate Negroes and Negro activities into all aspects of coverage and content, including newspaper articles and television programing. The news media must publish newspapers and produce programs that recognize the existence and activities of Negroes as a group within the community and as a part of the larger community.

—Recruit more Negroes into journalism and broadcasting and promote those who are qualified to positions of significant responsibility. Recruitment should begin in high schools and continue through college; where necessary, aid for training should be provided.

—Improve coordination with police in reporting riot news through advance planning, and cooperate with the police in the designation of police information officers, establishment of information centers, and development of mutually acceptable guidelines for riot reporting and the conduct of media personnel.

—Accelerate efforts to insure accurate and responsible reporting of riot and racial news, through adoption by all news-gathering organizations of stringent internal staff guidelines.

—Cooperate in the establishment of a privately organized and funded Institute of Urban Communications to train and educate journalists in urban affairs, recruit and train more Negro journalists, develop methods for improving police-press relations, review coverage of riots and racial issues, and support continuing research in the urban field.

The Future of the Cities

By 1985, the Negro population in central cities is expected to increase by 68 percent to approximately 20.3 million. Coupled with the continued exodus of white families to the suburbs, this growth will produce majority Negro populations in many of the Nation's largest cities.

The future of these cities, and of their burgeoning Negro populations, is grim. Most new employment opportunities are being created in suburbs and outlying areas. This trend will continue unless important changes in public policy are made.

In prospect, therefore, is further deterioration of already inadequate municipal tax bases in the face of increasing demands for public services, and continuing unemployment and poverty among the urban Negro population.

Three choices are open to the Nation:

—We can maintain present policies, continuing both the proportion of the Nation's resources now allocated to programs for the unemployed and the disadvantaged, and the inadequate and failing effort to achieve an integrated society.

—We can adopt a policy of "enrichment" aimed at improving dramatically the quality of ghetto life while abandoning integration as a goal.

—We can pursue integration by combining ghetto "enrichment" with policies which will encourage Negro movement out of central city areas.

The first choice, continuance of present policies, has ominous consequences for our society. The share of the Nation's resources now allocated to programs for the disadvantaged is insufficient to arrest the deterioration of life in central-city ghettos. Under such conditions, a rising proportion of Negroes may come to see in the deprivation and segregation they experience, a justification for violent protest, or for extending support to now isolated extremists who advocate civil disruption. Large-scale and continuing violence could result, followed by white retaliation, and, ultimately, the separation of the two communities in a garrison state.

Even if violence does not occur, the consequences are unacceptable. Development of a racially integrated society, extraordinarily difficult today, will be virtually impossible when the present black central-city population of 12.1 million has grown to almost 21 million.

To continue present policies is to make permanent the division of our country into two societies: one, largely Negro and poor, located in the central cities, the other, predominantly white and affluent, located in the suburbs and in outlying areas.

The second choice, ghetto enrichment coupled with abandonment of integration, is also unacceptable. It is another way of choosing a permanently divided country. Moreover, equality cannot be achieved under conditions of nearly complete separation. In a country where the economy, and particularly the resources of employment, are predominantly white, a policy of separation can only relegate Negroes to a permanently inferior economic status.

We believe that the only possible choice for America is the third — a policy which combines ghetto enrichment with programs designed to encourage integration of substantial numbers of Negroes into the society outside the ghetto.

Enrichment must be an important adjunct to integration, for no matter how ambitious or energetic the program, few Negroes now living in central cities can be quickly integrated. In the meantime, large-scale improvement in the quality of ghetto life is essential.

But this can be no more than an interim strategy. Programs must be developed which will permit substantial Negro movement out of the ghettos. The primary goal must be a single society, in which every citizen will be free to live and work according to his capabilities and desires, not his color.

Recommendations for National Action

Introduction

No American — white or black — can escape the consequences of the continuing social and economic decay of our major cities.

Only a commitment to national action on an unprecedented scale can shape a future compatible with the historic ideals of American society.

The great productivity of our economy, and a Federal revenue system which is highly responsive to economic growth, can provide the resources.

The major need is to generate new will — the will to tax ourselves to the extent necessary to meet the vital needs of the Nation.

We have set forth goals and proposed strategies to reach those goals. We discuss and recommend programs not to commit each of us to specific parts of such programs, but to illustrate the type and dimension of action needed.

The major goal is the creation of a true union — a single society and a single American identity. Toward that goal, we propose the following objectives for national action:

> —Opening up opportunities to those who are restricted by racial segregation and discrimination, and eliminating all barriers to their choice of jobs, education, and housing.

> —Removing the frustration of powerlessness among the disadvantaged by providing the means for them to deal with the problems that affect their own lives and by increasing the capacity of our public and private institutions to respond to these problems.

> —Increasing communication across racial lines to destroy stereotypes, halt polarization, end distrust and hostility, and create common ground for efforts toward public order and social justice.

We propose these aims to fulfill our pledge of equality and to meet the fundamental needs of a democratic and civilized society — domestic peace and social justice.

Employment

Pervasive unemployment and underemployment are the most persistent and serious grievances in minority areas. They are inextricably linked to the problem of civil disorder.

Despite growing Federal expenditures for manpower development and training programs, and sustained general economic prosperity and increasing demands for skilled workers, about 2 million — white and nonwhite — are permanently unemployed. About 10 million are underemployed, of whom 6.5 million work full time for wages below the poverty line.

The 500,000 "hard-core" unemployed in the central cities who lack a basic education and are unable to hold a steady job are made up in large part of Negro males between the ages of 18 and 25. In the riot cities which we surveyed, Negroes were three times as likely as whites to hold unskilled jobs, which are often part time, seasonal, low paying and "dead end."

Negro males between the ages of 15 and 25 predominated among the rioters. More than 20 percent of the rioters were unemployed, and many who were employed held intermittent, low status, unskilled jobs which they regarded as below their education and ability.

The Commission recommends that the Federal Government:

> —Undertake joint efforts with cities and states to consolidate existing manpower programs to avoid fragmentation and duplication.

> —Take immediate action to create 2 million new jobs over the next 3 years — 1 million in the public sector and 1 million in the private sector — to absorb the hard-core unemployed and materially reduce the level of underemployment for all workers, black and white. We propose 250,000 public sector and 300,000 private sector jobs in the first year.

—Provide on-the-job training by both public and private employers with reimbursement to private employers for the extra costs of training the hard-core unemployed, by contract or by tax credits.

—Provide tax and other incentives to investment in rural as well as urban poverty areas in order to offer to the rural poor an alternative to migration to urban centers.

—Take new and vigorous action to remove artificial barriers to employment and promotion, including not only racial discrimination but, in certain cases, arrest records or lack of a high school diploma. Strengthen those agencies such as the Equal Employment Opportunity Commission, charged with eliminating discriminatory practices, and provide full support for . . . the 1964 Civil Rights Act allowing Federal grant-in-aid funds to be withheld from activities which discriminate on grounds of color or race.

The Commission commends the recent public commitment of the National Council of the Building and Construction Trades Unions, AFL—CIO, to encourage and recruit Negro membership in apprenticeship programs. This commitment should be intensified and implemented.

Education

Education in a democratic society must equip children to develop their potential and to participate fully in American life. For the community at large, the schools have discharged this responsibility well. But for many minorities, and particularly for the children of the ghetto, the schools have failed to provide the educational experience which could overcome the effects of discrimination and deprivation.

This failure is one of the persistent sources of grievance and resentment within the Negro community. The hostility of Negro parents and students toward the school system is generating increasing conflict and causing disruption within many city school districts. But the most dramatic evidence of the relationship between educational practices and civil disorders lies in the high incidence of riot participation by ghetto youth who have not completed high school.

The bleak record of public education for ghetto children is growing worse. In the critical skills — verbal and reading ability — Negro students are falling further behind whites with each year of school completed. The high unemployment and underemployment rate for Negro youth is evidence, in part, of the growing educational crisis.

We support integration as the priority education strategy; it is essential to the future of American society. In this last summer's disorders we have seen the consequences of racial isolation at all levels, and of attitudes toward race, on both sides, produced by three centuries of myth, ignorance, and bias. It is indispensable that opportunities for interaction between the races be expanded.

We recognize that the growing dominance of pupils from disadvantaged minorities in city school populations will not soon be reversed. No matter how great the effort toward desegregation, many children of the ghetto will not, within their school careers, attend integrated schools.

If existing disadvantages are not to be perpetuated, we must drastically improve the quality of ghetto education. Equality of results with all-white schools must be the goal.

To implement these strategies, the Commission recommends:

> —Sharply increased efforts to eliminate de facto segregation in our schools through substantial federal aid to school systems seeking to desegregate either within the system or in cooperation with neighboring school systems:

> —Elimination of racial discrimination in Northern as well as Southern schools by vigorous application . . . of the Civil Rights Act of 1964.

> —Extension of quality early childhood education to every disadvantaged child in the country.

> —Efforts to improve dramatically schools serving disadvantaged children through substantial federal funding of year-round quality compensatory education programs, improved teaching, and expanded experimentation and research.

—Elimination of illiteracy through greater Federal support for adult basic education.

—Enlarged opportunities for parent and community participation in the public schools.

—Re-oriented vocational education emphasizing work-experience training and the involvement of business and industry.

—Expanded opportunities for higher education through increased federal assistance to disadvantaged students.

—Revision of state aid formulas to assure more per student aid to districts having a high proportion of disadvantaged school age children.

The Welfare System

Our present system of public welfare is designed to save money instead of people, and tragically ends up doing neither. This system has two critical deficiencies:

First, it excludes large numbers of persons who are in great need, and who, if provided a decent level of support, might be able to become more productive and self-sufficient. No Federal funds are available for millions of unemployed and underemployed men and women who are needy but neither aged, handicapped nor the parents of minor children.

Second, for those included, the system provides assistance well below the minimum necessary for a decent level of existence, and imposes restrictions that encourage continued dependency on welfare and undermine self-respect.

A welter of statutory requirements and administrative practices and regulations operate to remind recipients that they are considered untrustworthy, promiscuous, and lazy. Residence requirements prevent assistance to people in need who are newly arrived in the state. Searches of recipients' homes violate privacy. Inadequate social services compound the problems.

The Commission recommends that the Federal Government, acting with state and local governments where necessary, reform the existing welfare system to:

Establish, for recipients in existing welfare categories, uniform national standards of assistance at least as high as the annual "poverty level" of income, now set by the Social Security Administration at $3,335 per year for an urban family of four.

—Require that all states receiving Federal welfare contributions participate in the Aid to Families with Dependent Children-Unemployed Parents Program (AFDC—UP) that permits assistance to families with both father and mother in the home, thus aiding the family while it is still intact.

—Bear a substantially greater portion of all welfare costs — at least 90 percent of total payments.

—Increase incentives for seeking employment and job training, but remove restrictions recently enacted by the Congress that would compel mothers of young children to work.

—Provide more adequate social services through neighborhood centers and family-planning programs.

—Remove the freeze placed by the 1967 welfare amendments on the percentage of children in a State that can be covered by Federal assistance.

—Eliminate residence requirements.

As a long-range goal, the Commission recommends that the Federal Government seek to develop a national system of income supplementation based strictly on need with two broad and basic purposes:

—To provide, for those who can work or who do work, any necessary supplements in such a way as to develop incentives for fuller employment.

—To provide, for those who cannot work and for mothers who decide to remain with their children, a minimum standard of decent living, and to aid in saving children from the prison of poverty that has held their parents.

A broad system of supplementation would involve substantially greater Federal expenditures than anything now contemplated. The cost will range widely depending on the standard of need accepted as the "basic allowance" to individuals and families, and on the rate at which additional income above this level is taxed. Yet if the deepening cycle of poverty and dependence on welfare can be broken, if the children of the poor can be given the opportunity to scale the wall that now separates them from the rest of society, the return on this investment will be great indeed.

Housing

After more than three decades of fragmented and grossly underfunded Federal housing programs, nearly 6 million substandard housing units remain occupied in the United States.

The housing problem is particularly acute in the minority ghettos. Nearly two-thirds of all nonwhite families living in the central cities today live in neighborhoods marked by substandard housing and general urban blight. Two major factors are responsible:

First: Many ghetto residents simply cannot pay the rent necessary to support decent housing. In Detroit, for example, over 40 percent of the nonwhite-occupied units in 1960 required rent of over 35 percent of the tenants' income.

Second: Discrimination prevents access to many nonslum areas, particularly the suburbs, where good housing exists. In addition, by creating a "back pressure" in the racial ghettos, it makes it possible for landlords to break up apartments for denser occupancy, and keeps prices and rents of deteriorated ghetto housing higher than they would be in a truly free market.

To date, Federal programs have been able to do comparatively little to provide housing for the disadvantaged. In the 31-year history of subsidized Federal housing, only about 800,000 units have been constructed, with recent production averaging about 50,000 units a year. By comparison, over a period only 3 years longer, FHA [Federal Housing Administration] insurance guarantees have made possible the construction of over 10 million middle and upper income units.

Two points are fundamental to the Commission's recommendations:

First: Federal housing programs must be given a new thrust aimed at overcoming the prevailing patterns of racial segregation. If this is not done, those programs will continue to concentrate the most impoverished and dependent segments of the population into the central-city ghettos where there is already a critical gap between the needs of the population and the public resources to deal with them.

Second: The private sector must be brought into the production and financing of low and moderate-rental housing to supply the capabilities and capital necessary to meet the housing needs of the Nation.

The Commission recommends that the Federal Government:

> —Enact a comprehensive and enforceable Federal open-housing law to cover the sale or rental of all housing, including single-family homes.

> —Reorient Federal housing programs to place more low- and moderate-income housing outside of ghetto areas.

> —Bring within the reach of low- and moderate-income families within the next 5 years 6 million new and existing units of decent housing, beginning with 600,000 units in the next year.

To reach this goal we recommend:

> —Expansion and modification of the rent supplement program to permit use of supplements for existing housing, thus greatly increasing the reach of the program.

> —Expansion and modification of the below-market interest rate program to enlarge the interest subsidy to all sponsors,

provide interest-free loans to nonprofit sponsors to cover pre-construction costs, and permit sale of projects to nonprofit corporations, co-operatives, or condominiums.

—Creation of an ownership supplement program similar to present rent supplements, to make home ownership possible for low-income families.

—Federal writedown of interest rates on loans to private builders constructing moderate-rent housing.

—Expansion of the public housing program, with emphasis on small units on scattered sites, and leasing and "turnkey" programs.

—Expansion of the Model Cities program.

—Expansion and re-orientation of the urban renewal program to give priority to projects directly assisting low-income households to obtain adequate housing.

Conclusion

One of the first witnesses to be invited to appear before this Commission was Dr. Kenneth B. Clark, a distinguished and perceptive scholar. Referring to the reports of earlier riot commissions, he said:

> I read that report . . . of the 1919 riot in Chicago, and it is as if I were reading the report of the investigating committee on the Harlem riot of '35, the report of the investigating committee on the Harlem riot of '43, the report of the McCone Commission on the Watts riot.
> I must again in candor say to you members of this Commission — it is a kind of Alice in Wonderland — with the same moving picture reshown over and over again, the same analysis, the same recommendations, and the same inaction.

These words come to our minds as we conclude this report. We have provided an honest beginning. We have learned much. But we have uncovered no startling truths, no unique insights, no simple solutions. The destruction and the bitterness of racial disorder, the harsh polemics of black revolt and white repression have been seen and heard before in this country.

It is time now to end the destruction and the violence, not only in the streets of the ghetto but in the lives of people.

Bibliography

Throughout this volume we have been analyzing urban riots and civil unrest through the writings of scholars and reporters. This selection of readings scratched the surface of the huge body of literature on the subject. The following bibliography has been added to guide further reading and student research. Each item has been selected for its intrinsic interest and/or its scholarly analysis. The editors hope that students will want to read further and will find the items below of special value.

Baldwin, James, *The Fire Next Time*. New York: Dell Publishing Company, 1964. This short volume is now a classic for any bibliography on contemporary Negro affairs or recent civil unrest in the nation's ghettos. It provides a poignant view of the life of a Negro boy growing up in America as well as Baldwin's social observations.

Bennet, Lerone, Jr., *Confrontation: Black and White*. Baltimore: Penguin Books, Inc., 1965. A longer book than *The Negro Mood*, this volume stresses the historical context of the Negroes' plight.

—— *The Negro Mood*. New York: Ballantine Books, Inc., 1964. An older volume by the senior editor of *Ebony* magazine, it is an interesting analysis at a modest price.

Berkowitz, Leonard, *Aggression: A Social Psychological Analysis*. New York: McGraw-Hill Book Company, 1962. A scholarly volume, this is difficult reading but makes a superb reference book for bright students.

Carmichael, Stokely, and Charles V. Hamilton, *Black Power: The Politics of Liberation in America*. New York: Random House Vintage Books, 1967. As the title suggests and as the authors' names now connote, this volume presents a militant point of view on the current crisis.

Cohen, Jerry and William S. Murphy, *Burn, Baby, Burn: The Los Angeles Race Riot, August, 1965.* New York: E. P. Dutton & Company, Inc., 1966. The Watts riot, the first major disorder of the 1960's, is described in vivid prose by the authors.

Conot, Robert, *Rivers of Blood, Years of Darkness.* New York: Bantam Books, Inc., 1967. This is a narrative account of the 1965 Watts (Los Angeles) riot, including an analysis of causes and the riot process.

Cuban, Larry, *The Negro in America.* Glenview, Ill. Scott, Foresman & Company, 1964. A brief but comprehensive treatment of the Negroes' lot in American history and contemporary affairs.

Franklin, John Hope and Isidore Starr, eds., *The Negro in Twentieth Century America.* New York: Random House Vintage Books, 1967. The editors have put together an excellent large collection of articles on many facets of the topic. It is a valuable reference with selections by persons with widely different points of view.

Hayden, Tom, *Rebellion in Newark.* New York: Random House Vintage Books, 1967. This is an analysis of the Newark (1967) riot by a leader of the New Left. It tells more about Hayden as a New Left leader than about the riot, but it is valuable as it presents reactions by ghetto dwellers during and following the riot.

Heaps, Willard, *Riots, USA.* New York: The Seabury Press, Inc., 1966. A volume for secondary school students, the author has written brief sketches of riots in America from colonial days to the current period of unrest. It makes interesting, if often emotional, reading.

Hersey, John, *The Algiers Motel Incident.* New York: Bantam Books, Inc., 1968. The results of Hersey's personal investigation of an "incident" during the 1967 Detroit riot when three Negroes were killed at the Algiers Motel. The details and personal judgments make for provocative reading to be set against forthcoming court decisions.

Hoffer, Eric, *The True Believer.* New York: New American Library, Inc., Mentor Books, 1951. An unconventional scholar, the author presents a fast-moving analysis of the types of personalities that are drawn to radical movements of all kinds.

Killian, Lewis M., *The Impossible Revolution: Black Power and The American Dream.* New York: Random House, Inc., 1968. Simply written, this scholarly, short book predicts violence by the Negro community, totally destructive to its general welfare and eventually the cause of the loss of civil liberties for all of America.

Logan, Rayford W., *The Negro in the United States.* Princeton, N. J.: D. Van Nostrand, Co., Inc., Anvil, 1957. In one hundred pages, the author outlines the role of the Negro throughout American history, and then, in the final pages, presents an array of key documents affecting and reflecting the Negroes' lot.

Lomax, Louis E., *The Negro Revolt.* New York: New American Library, Inc., 1962. A well-written tract which analyzes the Negroes' position in contemporary America and a strategy of mass action to ameliorate that position.

Mailer, Norman, *Miami and the Siege of Chicago.* New York: The New American Library, Inc., Signet Special, 1968. Mailer presents his views and analysis of the 1968 Republican and Democratic National Conventions in his usual candid style. The language is not for readers with faint hearts.

Report of the National Advisory Commission on Civil Disorders. Washington: Government Printing Office, 1968, *or* New York: Bantam Books, Inc., 1968. This is the report of the President's Commission appointed in July, 1967, to study civil unrest in the nation's cities during the summer of that year. It tells what happened, why it happened, and what can be done.

Rights in Conflict: The Violent Confrontation of Demonstrators and Police in the Parks and Streets of Chicago During the Week of the Democratic National Convention of 1968. Washington: Government Printing Office, 1969, *or* New York: Bantam Books, Inc., 1968. This is the controversial report on the "Police Riots" of Chicago, known as the Walker Report.

Rudwick, Elliot M., *Race Riot at East St. Louis, July 2, 1917.* Carbondale, Ill.: Southern Illinois University Press, 1964. One of the best scholarly accounts of a race riot, the book offers an analysis and an historical account which is interestingly written in exciting prose.

Shapiro, Fred C. and James W. Sullivan, *Race Riots: New York 1964.* New York: Thomas Y. Crowell Company, 1964. The authors analyze the causes and consequences of racial conflict in the nation's largest city.

Shogan, Robert and Thomas Craig, *The Detroit Race Riot: A Study in Violence.* Philadelphia: Chilton Book Company, 1964. This volume by former newspaper reporters offers the reader a concise description of the 1943 Detroit race riot. It makes an interesting contrast to the case study in this book.

Turner, Darwin T. and J. M. Bright, *Images of the Negro in America.* Boston: D. C. Heath & Company, 1965. A collection of (historical) readings, the volume gives students an excellent opportunity to review the basis for the stock stereotypes and attitudes of his own day.

Waskow, Arthur, Jr., *From Race Riot to Sit-in: 1919 and the 1960's.* Garden City, New York: Doubleday & Company, Inc., 1965. This volume present the connection between conflict and violence with an historical comparison of the 1919 race riots and the Negro-ghetto resident unrest of the 1960's.

Wish, Harvey, ed., *The Negro Since Emancipation.* Englewood Cliffs, N. J.: Prentice-Hall, Inc., 1964. The editor collected an array of solid statements on the course of Negro history since the Civil War — drawing upon accounts of events such as lynchings and writings by various men, Booker T. Washington, Marcus Garvey, and Elijah Muhammed, among others.

Wright, Nathan, Jr., *Black Power and Urban Unrest.* New York: Hawthorn Books, Inc., 1967. The author, a Negro clergyman, presents a brief analysis of the link between conditions, Black Power, and urban violence and unrest. The analysis is not theoretical, but based upon personal experience in the streets and meeting places where men labor to improve conditions.

——*Ready to Riot.* New York: Holt, Rinehart & Winston, Inc., 1968. In this volume, the author depicts urban conditions which predispose many ghetto dwellers to riot.